LET'S GO

PAGES PACKED WITH ESSENTIAL INFORMATION

"Value-packed, unbeatable, accurate, and comprehensive."

—The Los Angeles Times

"The guides are aimed not only at young budget travelers but at the independent traveler; a sort of streetwise cookbook for traveling alone."

—The New York Times

"Unbeatable; good sight-seeing advice; up-to-date info on restaurants, hotels, and inns; a commitment to money-saving travel; and a wry style that brightens nearly every page."

—The Washington Post

THE BEST TRAVEL BARGAINS IN YOUR BUDGET

"All the dirt, dirt cheap."

—People

"Let's Go follows the creed that you don't have to toss your life's savings to the wind to travel—unless you want to."

—The Salt Lake Tribune

REAL ADVICE FOR REAL EXPERIENCES

"The writers seem to have experienced every rooster-packed bus and lunar-surfaced mattress about which they write."

—The New York Times

"[Let's Go's] devoted updaters really walk the walk (and thumb the ride, and trek the trail). Learn how to fish, haggle, find work—anywhere."

—Food & Wine

"A world-wise traveling companion—always ready with friendly advice and helpful hints, all sprinkled with a bit of wit."

—The Philadelphia Inquirer

A GUIDE WITH A SPIRIT AND A SOCIAL CONSCIENCE

"Lighthearted and sophisticated, informative and fun to read. [Let's Go] helps the novice traveler navigate like a knowledgeable old hand."

—Atlanta Journal-Constitution

"The serious mission at the book's core reveals itself in exhortations to respect the culture and the environment—and, if possible, to visit as a volunteer, a student, or a teacher rather than a tourist."

—San Francisco Chronicle

LET'S GO PUBLICATIONS

TRAVEL GUIDES

Australia
Austria & Switzerland
Brazil
Britain
California
Central America
Chile
China
Costa Rica
Costa Rica, Nicaragua & Panama
Eastern Europe
Ecuador
Egypt
Europe
France
Germany
Greece
Guatemala & Belize
Hawaii
India & Nepal
Ireland
Israel
Italy
Japan
Mexico
New Zealand
Peru
Puerto Rico
Southeast Asia
Spain & Portugal with Morocco
Thailand
USA
Vietnam
Western Europe
Yucatan Peninsula

ROADTRIP GUIDE

Roadtripping USA

ADVENTURE GUIDES

Alaska
Pacific Northwest
Southwest USA

CITY GUIDES

Amsterdam
Barcelona
Berlin, Prague & Budapest
Boston
Buenos Aires
Florence
London
London, Oxford, Cambridge & Edinburgh
New York City
Paris
Rome
San Francisco
Washington, DC

POCKET CITY GUIDES

Amsterdam
Berlin
Boston
Chicago
London
New York City
Paris
San Francisco
Venice
Washington, DC

LET'S GO

ROME

RESEARCHERS
EMILY CHERTOFF JUSTIN MONTICELLO

IYA MEGRE MANAGING EDITOR
BEATRICE FRANKLIN RESEARCH MANAGER

EDITORS
COURTNEY A. FISKE   RUSSELL FORD RENNIE
CHARLIE E. RIGGS   SARA PLANA
OLGA I. ZHULINA

HOW TO USE THIS BOOK

PRICE DIVERSITY AND RANKINGS. Our researchers list establishments within each neighborhood in order of value from best to worst. Our absolute favorites are denoted by the Let's Go thumbs-up (🔀). Since the best value does not always mean the cheapest price, we have incorporated a system of price ranges for Food and Accommodations listings, denoted by a price icon (❶-❺); see p. VIII for a price range breakdown.

COVERING THE BASICS. The first chapter, **Discover Rome (p. 1)**, contains highlights of the city, complete with descriptions of Rome's neighborhoods and Suggested Itineraries to take you from one to seven days on the road. **Essentials** (p. 11) has all the info you'll need to navigate everything from Roman transportation to bureaucracy. **Life and Times** (p. 47) should help you with your way around even more complex constructs—Roman history, culture, and customs. This is where you can learn the difference between a Latin and an Etruscan, and just how many emperors there actually were. Our **Beyond Tourism** (p. 79) chapter holds tons of options for travelers looking to volunteer, study, and work in Rome. **Practical Information** (p. 91) contains a list of local services, from libraries to fitness clubs, while the **Appendix** (p. 297) has a phrasebook and maps for each neighborhood.

WHEN TO USE IT

TWO MONTHS BEFORE. Our book is filled with practical information to help you before you go. **Essentials** (p. 11) has advice about passports, visas, plane tickets, insurance, and more. The **Accommodations** (p. 97) section can help you with booking a room from home.

ONE MONTH BEFORE. Take care of travel insurance, and write down a list of emergency numbers and hotlines to take with you. Make a list of packing essentials, and shop for anything you need. Make reservations, if necessary.

TWO WEEKS BEFORE. Start thinking about the things you don't want to miss during your stay. **Discover Rome** (p. 1) is a good place to start, with Suggested Itineraries and Let's Go Picks. Page through the **Sights** (p. 131) and **Museums** (p. 193) chapters and see what catches your eye. Don't forget to consider some **Daytrips** (p. 245); you may want to see more than just the one city.

ON THE ROAD. **Food** (p. 113) and **Nightlife** (p. 229) list plenty of options to feed your belly and your liver. If you want to indulge even more, page to **Shopping** (p. 213). The **Sights** (p. 131), **Museums** (p. 193), and **Life and Times** (p. 47) chapters are full of information and historical anecdotes about the art and architecture you will see at nearly every minute of every day. Speaking of which, we know that we're a pretty entertaining read, but don't forget to take your nose out of the book and look around every now and then.

A NOTE TO OUR READERS. The information for this book was gathered by Let's Go researchers from May through August of 2009. Each listing is based on one researcher's opinion, formed during his or her visit at a particular time. Those traveling at other times may have different experiences since prices, dates, hours, and conditions are always subject to change. You are urged to check the facts presented in this book beforehand to avoid inconvenience and surprises.

CONTENTS

RESEARCHERS

Emily Chertoff   *Vatican City, Piazza di Spagna, Centro Storico, Villa Borghese, Lazio daytrips*

When we saw Emily's pre-departure *Roman Holiday*-esque haircut, we knew she would fit right into the Eternal City. She battled British soccer fans and unreliable Lazian buses to bring the most chic, unique establishments to our pages; she even went where no Researcher had gone before to do as the Romans really do. And, of course, she managed it all while sharing her witty and articulate take on the scenes around her in her marginalia, keeping us laughing all summer long.

Justin Monticello   *Ancient City, Termini, Southern Rome, Trastevere, Campania daytrips*

After a harrowing first day on the road, Justin's travel karma skyrocketed and he proved to be an indefatigable researcher. Between finding each hilarious anecdote and legend about Ancient Rome and wrangling a discount for LG readers at nearly every establishment he visited—you're welcome—he still somehow found time to do nightlife research until all hours of the morning and satisfy his culinary cravings with the best pizza in the world. We suspect magic. Or a lot of espresso. Magic espresso?

STAFF WRITERS

Charlotte Alter	Kyle Bean	Elias Berger
Julia Cain	Brianne Farrar	Alexandra Perloff-Giles
Harker Rhodes	Ansley Rubinstein	Madeleine Schwartz
Maria Vassileva	Sara Joe Wolansky	

CONTRIBUTING WRITERS

Kathleen Coleman teaches Latin and Roman history at Harvard University. She incorporates the collections of the Harvard Art Museums into her teaching whenever possible. Her ambition is to visit every Roman province before she gets too decrepit to travel any more.

Clem Wood has spent summers in both Florence and Rome. He graduated from Harvard in the spring of 2008 with an A.B. in Classics and plans to return to Italy for further adventures and studies in the near future.

ACKNOWLEDGMENTS

BEATRICE THANKS: Emily and Justin, for going above and beyond the call of duty every day and for finding out more about my hometown than I ever could. Plus for being the most witty and irreverent; I am truly going to miss reading your marginalia. The RMs for solidarity and everything else. Iya, for dorking it up with me and holding my hand through two books and a season of heart-wrenching SYTYCD obsession. The rest of LGHQ for guidance, fun, impeccable music taste, and ▓Discuss. My roommates for making a couch a home. Team ML for keeping up a virtual Vergnugenzelt throughout the summer. *Bella Roma*, for being a city really worth writing about. Gli amici Romani, for showing me what was worth including. And my family, for letting me go yet again and teaching me about Italy in the first place. *Tanti grazie a tutti.*

EDITORS THANK: The Ed Team would first and foremost like to thank our lord (Jay-C) and savior (Starbucks, Terry's Chocolate Orange). We also owe gratitude to Barack Obama (peace be upon Him), the Oxford comma, the water cooler, bagel/payday Fridays, the HSA "SummerFun" team for being so inclusive, Rotio (wherefore art thou Rotio?), the real Robinson Crusoe, the Cambridge weather and defective umbrellas, BoltBus, Henry Louis Gates, Jr. (sorry 'bout the phone call), the office blog, gratuitous nudity, the 20-20-20 rule and bananas (no more eye twitches), the Portuguese flag, trips to the beach (ha!), sunbathing recently-married Mormon final club alums, non-existent free food in the square, dog-star puns, and last but not least, America. The local time in Tehran is 1:21am.

But seriously, to the MEs and RMs, our researchers (and all their wisdom on tablecloths and hipsters), LGHQ, HSA, our significant others (future, Canadian, and otherwise), and families (thanks Mom).

Managing Editor
Iya Megre
Research Manager
Beatrice Franklin
Editors
Courtney A. Fiske, Sara Plana, Russell Ford Rennie, Charlie E. Riggs, Olga I. Zhulina
Typesetter
C. Alexander Tremblay

Publishing Director
Laura M. Gordon
Editorial Director
Dwight Livingstone Curtis
Publicity and Marketing Director
Vanessa J. Dube
Production and Design Director
Rebecca Lieberman
Cartography Director
Anthony Rotio
Website Director
Lukáš Tóth
Managing Editors
Ashley Laporte, Iya Megre, Mary Potter, Nathaniel Rakich
Technology Project Manager
C. Alexander Tremblay
Director of IT
David Fulton-Howard
Financial Associates
Catherine Humphreville, Jun Li

President
Daniel Lee
General Manager
Jim McKellar

② PRICE RANGES ③ ④
ROME
① ⑤

Our researchers list establishments in order of value from best to worst, honoring our favorites with the Let's Go thumbs-up (🔥). Because the best *value* is not always the cheapest *price*, we have incorporated a system of price ranges based on a rough expectation of what you will spend. For **accommodations,** we base our range on the cheapest price for which a single traveler can stay for one night. For **restaurants,** we estimate the average amount one traveler will spend in one sitting. The table below tells you what you'll *typically* find in Rome at the corresponding price range, but keep in mind that no system can allow for the quirks of individual establishments.

ACCOMMODATIONS	RANGE	WHAT YOU'RE *LIKELY* TO FIND
❶	under €20	HI hostels and basic dorm rooms. Expect bunk beds and a communal bath; you may have to provide or rent towels and sheets. Probably in a neighborhood outside the center.
❷	€20-35	Upper-end hostels or lower-end *pensiones*. You may have a private bathroom, or there may be a sink in your room and a communal shower in the hall. Meals may be available cheaply to hostel guests.
❸	€36-50	A small room with a private bath, probably in a budget hotel or *pensione*. Should have decent amenities, like a phone and TV. Breakfast may be included for your toast-hoarding convenience.
❹	€51-65	Similar to ❸, but should have more amenities or be in a more highly touristed or conveniently located area. Breakfast is often included in the price of your room.
❺	over €65	Large hotels, upscale chains, or very close to the Centro Storico. If it's a ❺ and it doesn't have the perks or service you're looking for, you've probably paid too much.

FOOD	RANGE	WHAT YOU'RE *LIKELY* TO FIND
❶	under €6	Probably a slice of pizza or a sandwich from a bar. Rarely a sit-down meal, unless you're sitting at the bar feasting on free food with your *aperitivo*—always a good call.
❷	€6-12	*Primo* and a drink, or possibly a lunch menu. May be sit-down or take-out, sometimes with a server.
❸	€13-19	Typically a sit-down meal. *Secondo*, dessert, and a drink, or a set dinner menu—and that extra euro for tip.
❹	€20-25	Entrees are more expensive than ❸, but you're paying for quality service, ambience, and decor. Few restaurants in this range have a dress code, but you'll want to clean yourself up after a day of travel.
❺	over €25	Your meal might cost more than your hostel, but here's hoping it's something fabulous, famous, or involving a lot of good wine.

ABOUT LET'S GO

THE STUDENT TRAVEL GUIDE

Let's Go publishes the world's favorite student travel guides, written entirely by Harvard students. Armed with pens, notebooks, and a few changes of clothes stuffed into their backpacks, our student researchers go across continents, through time zones, and above expectations to seek out invaluable travel experiences for our readers. Because we are a completely student-run company, we have a unique perspective on how students travel, where they want to go, and what they're looking to do when they get there. If your dream is to grab a machete and forge through the jungles of Costa Rica, we can take you there. If you'd rather bask in the Riviera sun at a beachside cafe, we'll set you a table. In short, we write for readers who know that there's more to travel than tour buses. To keep up, visit our website, www.letsgo.com, where you can sign up to blog, post photos from your trips, and connect with the Let's Go community.

TRAVELING BEYOND TOURISM

We're on a mission to provide our readers with sharp, fresh coverage packed with socially responsible opportunities to go beyond tourism. Each guide's Beyond Tourism chapter shares ideas about responsible travel, study abroad, and how to give back to the places you visit while on the road. To help you gain a deeper connection with the places you travel, our fearless researchers scour the globe to give you the heads-up on both world-renowned and off-the-beaten-track opportunities. We've also opened our pages to respected writers and scholars to hear their takes on the countries and regions we cover, and asked travelers who have worked, studied, or volunteered abroad to contribute first-person accounts of their experiences.

FIFTY YEARS OF WISDOM

Let's Go has been on the road for 50 years and counting. We've grown a lot since publishing our first 20-page pamphlet to Europe in 1960, but five decades and 54 titles later our witty, candid guides are still researched and written entirely by students on shoestring budgets who know that train strikes, stolen luggage, food poisoning, and marriage proposals are all part of a day's work. This year, for our 50th anniversary, we're publishing 26 titles—including 6 brand new guides—brimming with editorial honesty, a commitment to students, and our irreverent style. Here's to the next 50!

THE LET'S GO COMMUNITY

More than just a travel guide company, Let's Go is a community that reaches from our headquarters in Cambridge, MA all across the globe. Our small staff of dedicated student editors, writers, and tech nerds comes together because of our shared passion for travel and our desire to help other travelers get the most out of their experience. We love it when our readers become part of the Let's Go community as well—when you travel, drop us a postcard (67 Mt. Auburn St., Cambridge, MA 02138, USA), send us an e-mail (feedback@letsgo.com), or sign up on our website (www.letsgo.com) to tell us about your adventures and discoveries.

For more information, updated travel coverage, and news from our researcher team, visit us online at www.letsgo.com.

DISCOVER ROME

In the books you'll read, the pictures you'll see, and the pithy sayings you'll hear, Rome is the idealized city, an eternal metropolis that seamlessly transitions from history to the present in a matter of city blocks. It has been canonized for its invaluable cultural treasures, from ancient temples to Michelangelo's *Pietà*. Rome is the capital of kingdoms and republics, its genesis the empire that defined the Western world in antiquity. Its system of government is still imitated today, its architecture has laid the course for modern building techniques, and its most recent contribution to world culture, its cinema, is revered. These claims are not exaggerations; the city will live up to its reputation. Expect no excuse for how overwhelming it can be.

This city of 2.7 million people isn't a dreamy idyll, though—or at least, it's more than one. Not as pretty as Paris, not as efficient as Berlin, Rome is a thrumming modern metropolis, a commercial and cultural hub. It is also a city of contradictions. The quiet and respectable neighborhoods around the Vatican rub up against buzzy Trastevere. A 10min. walk takes you from the designer stores around the Spanish Steps to the bargain basements near Termini station. Everywhere you turn, the Holy See has renovated a crumbling pagan building and repurposed it as a Catholic church. Nightclubs and chic hotels pop up in the ruins of the Ancient City. If all this pull between the past and the future gets overwhelming, just take a break and settle right back into the present.

Visitors to Rome often try to do too much—they rush through every cathedral and by every painting. Sometimes, it's worth kicking back with a *caffè* and watching the city march past. In these moments of reflection, you'll see the city's separate identities—romantic shrine, modern metropolis, living archaeological site, and place to build a home—all twirled together like pasta around a fork. Enjoy your newfound understanding of this singular city. You'll realize how much you're going to miss it, and you'll know you can always come back. This stuff has been around a while; it's not going anywhere.

FACTS AND FIGURES

POPULATION: 2,722,907.

URBAN AREA: 496.2 sq. miles.

AGE: 2,762 (we believe the Romulus and Remus story).

SACKINGS WITHSTOOD: 9—by the Goths, the Arabs, the French, and everyone in between.

SISTER CITIES: One, Paris—because "Only Paris is worthy of Rome, and only Rome is worthy of Paris."

NUMBER OF CHURCHES: We stopped counting at 900.

NUMBER OF CHURCHES IN ROME BUT NOT ACTUALLY IN ROME: 3—the extraterritorial Vatican basilicas.

NUMBER OF MOVIES MADE AT CINE-CITTA: Over 3,000.

NUMBER OF TOURISTS ANNUALLY: 19,000,000.

CHANCES THAT THE PERSON NEXT TO YOU IS ROMAN: About 1 in 9.

WHEN TO GO

The Roman **spring** is nothing short of heaven. The weather is pleasantly balmy (hovering around 50-70°F), although often rainy, and the tourists haven't caught on. By June, both the temperature and the tourist industry have picked up considerably. Roman **summer** is sweltering (75-95°F) and congested, but you can catch major exhibitions, exciting festivals, and concerts under the stars. When the city gets too oppressive, you can cool off in the Mediterranean or in cold volcanic lakes. From late July to August, the Romans leave town; you may not find as many *trattorie* or nightclubs open, but the crowds will subside a bit. The trend continues into the fall, when the temperatures drop (45-60° F) and the prices do, too. **Winter** brings cold (35-55° F), rain, and some of the lowest prices of the year; it also brings the holidays, which are a major to-do in the city of St. Peter.

NEIGHBORHOODS

The **Tiber River** runs north-south and cuts Rome in two, with most of the city center on the eastern side, except for the Vatican City and Trastevere on the west. Rome's ancient streets are notoriously difficult to navigate; a good map is a must. Still, for the most part, the river, Termini, P. del Popolo, and the Vittoriano Monument are helpful landmarks that can serve as points of reference.

ANCIENT CITY

The Ancient City begins directly south of P. Venezia, the center of the city and home to the huge Vittorio Emanuele II Monument. Directly behind the monument, the **Capitoline Hill**, capped by Michelangelo's **Piazza del Campidoglio,** is accessible by **Via del Teatro di Marcello,** which runs southwest toward the **Velabrum** and the **Tiber.** On the other side of the monument, **Via dei Fori Imperiali** runs all the way to the **Colosseum.** Off V. dei Fori Imperiali are the **Imperial Fora** and the **Roman Forum** itself. Behind the Forum looms the **Palatine Hill** and, beyond that, the **Circus Maximus.**

The Ancient City is renowned primarily for its sights, but there are enough cafes and restaurants to feed even the most ravenous tourist hordes. The nightlife around **Via Labicana** is also worth visiting. Accommodations in the region, thanks to the numerous sights, are likely to be expensive.

CENTRO STORICO

The medieval neighborhood of Rome spreads north and west from P. Venezia, bordered by **Via del Corso** on the east and the **Tiber** to the west. **Corso Vittorio Emanuele II** runs northwest from P. Venezia toward the Vatican; much of the Centro south of this thoroughfare is taken up by the **Jewish Ghetto.** Off C. Vittorio is **Largo Argentina,** the Centro's other transportation hub. From here the convenient **tram #8** travels to **Viale di Trastevere.**

Good values can be found among Centro establishments, though most are exorbitant. **Campo de' Fiori** and **Piazza Navona** are nightlife hubs, while the Ghetto and the area around **Via del Governo Vecchio** teem with cool boutiques and worthwhile restaurants.

PIAZZA DI SPAGNA AND THE CORSO

East of the Corso, stretching from P. Venezia up to Villa Borghese, is the area around the **Spanish Steps.** The famous steps themselves, which climb from

Piazza di Spagna up to **Piazza Trinità dei Monti,** are four blocks from the Corso along Rome's most exclusive shopping area, **Via Condotti.** On the western side of the Corso lie the famous **Mausoleum of Augustus** and the **Ara Pacis.** South of the Spanish Steps is the horrifically crowded **Trevi Fountain;** east is the spacious **Quirinale,** home of the Italian President. **Via del Tritone** runs east from the Corso to **Piazza Barberini,** and continues on toward Termini as **Via Barberini.**

This neighborhood is the most consistently expensive region of Rome. Shopping streets, luxurious hotels, and swanky restaurants offer plenty of opportunities to dispose of some of your euro. However, the high prices shouldn't keep you away—the area embodies quintessential Italian glamour.

VILLA BORGHESE

Northeast of P. del Popolo and the Spanish Steps is the **Villa Borghese**, a vast park that is home to the zoo and several museums. Its verdant paths provide ample opportunity for strolling or rides on the bicycles available for rent. Beyond the park are the neighborhoods of **Parioli** and **Flaminio,** which offer a number of enjoyable restaurants.

BORGO, PRATI & VATICAN CITY

Across the Tiber, northwest from the Centro Storico, is the Vatican City. Crossing the Ponte Vittorio Emanuele II from Corso Vittorio Emanuele II takes you directly to **Via della Conciliazione,** the avenue that leads west to **Piazza San Pietro** and its **Basilica,** with the **Vatican Museums** right next door. At the eastern end of V. del Conciliazione, **Castel Sant'Angelo,** the Pope's historic residence, overlooks the Tiber. Between Castel Sant'Angelo and the Vatican is the quiet **Borgo** neighborhood. To the north is the less quiet **Prati,** home to scattered hotels, restaurants, and pubs. **Via Cola di Rienzo,** a major shopping street, runs through Prati from **Piazza del Risorgimento,** next to the Vatican, across **Ponte Regina Margherita** to **Piazza del Popolo.**

The neighborhoods in this area are more residential, with a lower concentration of establishments than others in Rome. Still, there are a few outstanding hostels, restaurants, and cafes—in addition to every possible kind of Papal-themed item (Pope pops, anyone?) in the neighboring stores.

TRASTEVERE

Trastevere, easily Rome's most picturesque neighborhood—and certainly its most entertaining to navigate—is south of the Vatican and west, across the Tiber from the Centro Storico. **Viale Trastevere,** the neighborhood's main drag, runs across **Ponte Garibaldi** all the way to **Largo Argentina** from the **Stazione di Trastevere.** Most of Trastevere's points of interest (delicious, inexpensive *trattorie* and bustling pubs) lie near this street and not far from the river, especially around the **Piazza di Santa Maria** in Trastevere and **Piazza Trilussa.** The area around the latter offers a nightlife scene less club-focused than Testaccio's. Between Trastevere and the Vatican is the mostly residential **Janiculum Hill,** or the Gianicolo, which is the tallest hill in the city (though not one of the original seven) and offers spectacular views.

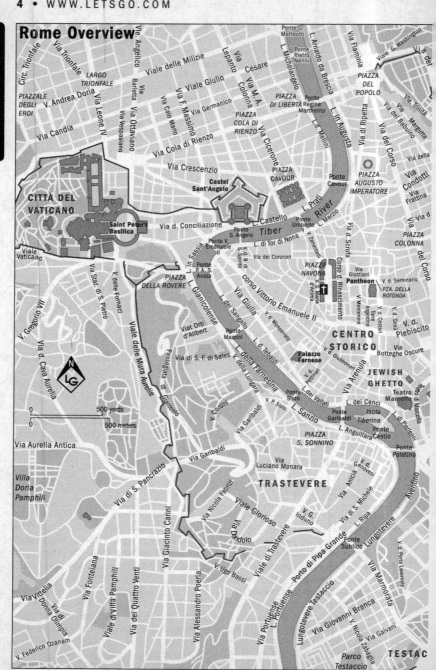

Rome Overview

DISCOVER

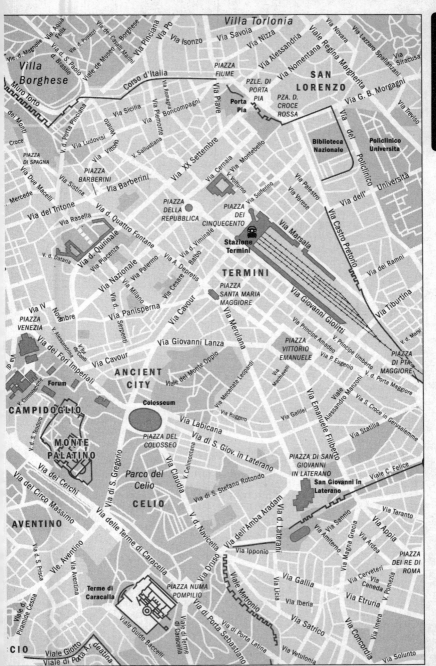

◪LET'S GO PICKS

MOST AUTHENTIC PLACE TO WEAR A TOGA (OUTSIDE OF A FRAT HOUSE): In an ancient Roman house below the **Chiesa dei Santi Giovanni e Paolo** (p. 179).

MOST ROSES TO STOP AND SMELL: The **Roseto Comunale** (p. 181), on the Aventine Hill.

BEST REMINDER THAT YOU EXIST TO SERVE THE STATE: Mussolini's **obelisk** (p. 184) at the center of P. Guglielmo Marconi in EUR.

BEST PLACE TO RELIEVE YOURSELF OF SIN: **San Clemente** (p. 178), which features a 12th-century church on top of a 4th-century church on top of a 2nd-century shrine on top of an ancient sewer.

BEST PLACE TO RELIEVE YOURSELF: The toilet at **Jonathan's Angels** (p. 232).

BEST PLACE FOR A COMMUNIST PARTY: Rialto Santambrogio (p. 231), a multipurpose nightclub, event, and political space.

WORST PLACE TO TALK SMACK ABOUT SWITZERLAND: The Vatican (p. 162). The Swiss Guards may look silly, but any one of them could kill you with his pinky finger in a tenth of a second.

BEST PLACE TO CONTEMPLATE YOUR MORTALITY WHILE GETTING DRUNK: The bars in **Campo dei Fiori** (p. 229), which look out onto the statue of the martyr Giordano Bruno.

BEST ADVERTISEMENT FOR SUN-SCREEN: The beach at **Ostia** (p. 249).

BEST SUNBATHING: The **Piscine Naturali** (p. 250) on Ponza.

MOST PAPAL BULL: The junky souvenir shops on **Corso di Rinascimento** in the Vatican. John Paul II-themed flashlights, anyone?

BEST ITALIAN BEER BAR NONE: Peroni. Or Nastro Azzurro? Peroni. No, Nastro Azzurro. No, Peroni. Just a minute.

TERMINI & SAN LORENZO

Located east of the center of town, this is the area most people see first when arriving in Rome. Get used to it, because it's also where most budget travelers stay. The neighborhood immediately northeast of **Stazione Termini** is jam-packed with hotels, hostels, restaurants, and internet cafes. East of the station is the **Città Universitaria,** home to Rome's **La Sapienza University.** South of that is **San Lorenzo,** the student neighborhood, which is home to plenty of cheap, delicious restaurants as well as a healthy dose of left-wing student spirit. **Via XX Settembre** (or **Via Nomentana**) cuts through the quieter area northwest of the station; in front of the station, **Via Nazionale** runs from **Piazza della Repubblica** west to the older center of town, and **Via Cavour** runs southeast from the station to the **Colosseum.**

AVENTINE & TESTACCIO

Across the river from Trastevere and south of the Jewish Ghetto and the Ancient City are the posh Aventine Hill and the working-class Testaccio district. The former is full of interesting and less-traveled sights, including some early churches and the non-Catholic **cemetery;** the latter is home to some marvelous local restaurants and many of Rome's most popular nightclubs. The **Caelian Hill,** northeast of the Aventine, is crowned by the **Church of San Giovanni in Laterano,** Rome's cathedral.

FARTHER SOUTH

South of the Aventine is **Ostiense,** a residential neighborhood with little to draw travelers; **Marconi,** which provides food to fuel late night clubbers; and **Esposizione Universale Roma (EUR),** Mussolini's prototype neighborhood of wide boulevards, nationalistic slogans, and museums. To the south and east is the **Appian Way,** which features catacombs and ruins.

SUGGESTED ITINERARIES

ONE DAY

Any attempt to squeeze the best of the Eternal City into a day will require a gladiator's fortitude and Ben-Hur's chariot. In the morning, take our half-day walking tour through the medieval **Centro Storico** (p. 194), but begin at the **Spanish Steps** so that you end at **Piazza Navona**. Break for an espresso along the way and have lunch at one of the restaurants on nearby V. del Governo Vecchio. Hop a bus from there to **Piazza Venezia** (p. 154)—with its venerable wedding cake/typewriter—and take our other half-day walking tour of the **Best of Rome** (p. 148), ending at **Saint Peter's Basilica** in **Vatican City**. Finish up with dinner at a *pizzeria* in **Trastevere** (p. 121), then head back across the Tiber to **Campo dei Fiori** (p. 229) and environs for some nighttime fun.

THREE DAYS

DAY ONE: GETTING ORIENTED. Begin with a modified **Best of Rome** walking tour (p. 148), hitting the Colosseum, Roman Forum, Bocca della Verità, Campidoglio/Santa Maria in Aracoeli, and Teatro di Marcello. Cross the river through the **Isola Tiberina** (p. 165) and visit **Santa Maria** (p. 167) in Trastevere. From there, hike up the **Gianicolo Hill** (p. 168)—even taller than the original seven—and see the **Chiesa di San Pietro in Montorio** (p. 168). Take in the panorama from the piazza in front of the Acqua Paola. Once you've had your fill of the view (if such a thing is possible), a stroll back down the hill can end at any of the delicious *trattorie* in Trastevere (p. 121).

DAY TWO: VATICAN CITY. Wake up early (p. 74), go to the **Vatican Museums** (p. 198), get in line, and avoid the temptation to race through the galleries to get to the **Sistine Chapel.** Enjoy the countless works of art that line the walls and rooms of the museums; the Chapel may be crowded, but you'll still be able to see the ceiling. Be sure to spend some time at **Saint Peter's Basilica** (p. 163) and make the climb to the top of the dome. Before heading off to dinner, explore Hadrian's mausoleum, better known as **Castel Sant'Angelo** (p. 165). After eating in the **Borgo/Prati** (p. 113) neighborhood, take in some cullture and catch some jazz at **Alexanderplatz** (p. 223) jazz club.

DAY THREE: VILLA BORGHESE TO THE SPANISH STEPS. Make an early reservation—this must be done in advance—at the **Galleria Borghese** (p. 203) for the best 2hr. of concentrated art you've ever experienced in your life. Afterward, wander through the gardens of the **Villa Borghese** (p. 169) and then exit through the Porta Pinciana onto the **Via Veneto** (p. 170). A stroll down this leafy street will take you past some of Rome's old-glamour hotels, and bring you to the doorstep of the **Capuchin Crypt** (p. 170), a reminder of the transience of material joys. After you've been sufficiently humbled and grossed out, visit **Piazza Barberini** (p. 170) and the vast **Piazza del Quirinale** (p. 174), home of the President of the Italian Republic. The remainder of the day can be spent enjoying the sights around the Corso, from the **Fontana di Trevi** (p. 160) to the **Ara Pacis** (p. 162) and back to the **Piazza di Spagna** (p. 160) and **Piazza del Popolo** (p. 161). Food and shopping options in the area will fill your belly and empty your wallet.

FIVE DAYS

DAY FOUR: A MODERN PILGRIMAGE THROUGH ROME'S BEST CHURCHES. Begin the long day of religious art and architecture at the grand basilica of **San Giovanni in Laterano** (p. 177). Hit **San Clemente** (p. 178) for a taste of three churches in one, **Santa Maria Maggiore** (p. 171) for the site of a meteorological miracle,

LEAVE THE GUN, TAKE THE GELATO

Who, aside from the dangerous dregs of society and the lactose intolerant (poor souls), doesn't like ice cream? The creamy texture, the delicious flavor... Now imagine something even creamier and lower in fat, with vivid flavors ranging from fruity to nutty to chocolatey! What's that, you say? Gelato, which makes ice cream look downright vanilla.

Literally "frozen," gelato is a super-dense combination of cream, sugar, and flavoring and the highlight of any mid-afternoon break. Or pre-lunch snack. Or post-dinner walk. Or all of them. Flavor is the watchword at most gelaterie. Almost all of them offer a wide variety, made from the freshest ingredients. Not just chocolate, vanilla, and strawberry—these shops offer tiramisu, champagne, blood orange, and even rose.

If you're looking for the ultimate in gelato, you can tell the quality by the color. The best shops have banana that's tan and pistachio that's the palest mint. If you see bright yellow or green, it'll still be delicious, but it probably won't be the one you rave about when you come home. Once you find your favorite gelateria, you'll find yourself coming back as often as possible—whether it's to try every flavor or simply to eat the same one again and again (think of us if you get the hazelnut).

and **San Pietro in Vincoli** (p. 147) for Michelangelo's *Moses*. Refuel, wait out the afternoon break when many churches are closed, and then push on to the churches in the Centro Storico: **Il Gesù** (p. 155), **Sant'Ignazio** (p. 155), **San Luigi dei Francesi** (p. 156), and the **Chiesa Nuova** (p. 157). These Baroque masterpieces contain innumerable stunning works, including ones by Caravaggio and Peter Paul Rubens. Stop by the **Pantheon** (p. 156) along the way and appreciate the astounding diversity of Rome's religious structures.

DAY FIVE: SOUTHERN ROME. Start out with a return to antiquity, visiting the **Circus Maximus** (p. 153) and the **Baths of Caracalla** (p. 153). Continue on to the early churches of **San Saba** and **Santa Sabina** (p. 181) on the Aventine Hill; a stop at **Giacomini's** (p. 127) on Vle. Aventino is recommended to grab a *panino* and then picnic in the **Giardino degli Aranci** (p. 181) next to Santa Sabina. Afterward, walk through the residential Aventine neighborhood to the **Protestant Cemetery** (p. 183), resting place of Keats, Gramsci, and other notable non-Catholics. Then either walk or take the Metro to Ⓜ️Garbatella to the **Museo Centrale Montemartini** (p. 210), where Classical sculptures adorn an old power plant. Finally, take the Metro again to the **Basilica di San Paolo Fuori le Mura** (p. 183). Return to **Testaccio** for dinner (p. 126) and dancing (p. 239).

SEVEN DAYS

DAY SIX: SOUTHERN-ER ROME. Take a bus to the **Appian Way** (p. 185) and explore its catacombs and other sights. In the afternoon, a visit to **Mussolini's EUR** (p. 184) will provide you with enough wide boulevards and gleaming square buildings to last a lifetime; a gelato from **Giolitti** (p. 117), an outpost of the famous store near the Pantheon, enjoyed by the **laghetto** (p. 184) will make you less skeptical about Italian achievements.

DAY SEVEN: OSTIA. If your thirst for ancient history still hasn't been quenched, visit the ruins at **Ostia Antica** (p. 247). On the other hand, if you're still craving more modern Italian culture, head to the beach at **Ostia** (p. 249) for sunbathing and people-watching—the prevalence of high heels paired with bikinis will astound you. During summertime, there is no shortage of evening dance parties in the clubs along the *lungomare*.

HOTEL NAVONA

Via dei Sediari,
8 00186 Roma
Tel. +39 06 6864203
www.hotelnavona.com

Hotel Navona is situated in the historical center of Rome, only a few steps away from the splendid Piazza Navona, an ancient palace of the 1400s where you can see Roman ruins.

Our convenient location also allows you to reach the beautiful squares and famous monuments of Rome in just a few minutes. The Pantheon, the Trevi Fountain, Piazza di Spagna, St. Peter's and the Colosseum are all easily accessible and just a stone's throw from Hotel Navona.

Elegantly restructured with care given to every detail, Hotel Navona offers spacious rooms designed with ancient caisson ceilings and delicate frescoes and equipped with every modern amenity—satellite TV, air conditioning, safes, hair dryers and telephones.

Singles: 90-120 €
Doubles: 120-150 €
Triples: 170-190 €

Benvenuto!

Residenza Zanardelli is an intimate, family-run, 4 star hotel located in the historical center of Rome. Many well-known sites and monuments, including St. Peter's Basilica, the Pantheon, the Trevi Fountain, and the Spanish Steps, are within walking distance.

The hotel is a palazzo constructed in the "Barocchetto Romano" style, one of the architectural designs most characteristic of the late 19th century in Rome.

Newly renovated and beautifully furnished rooms await our guests. Each room has its own private bathroom, satellite plasma TV, telephone and air conditioning.

Several of the rooms have a direct view of the Palazzo Altemps, which has a wonderful collection of ancient sculpture.

Residenza Zanardelli

ESSENTIALS

PLANNING YOUR TRIP

ENTRANCE REQUIREMENTS
Passport (see next page). Required for all non-EU citizens.
Visa (see next page). Italy does not require visas for EU citizens and residents of Australia, Canada, Ireland, New Zealand, the US, and many more countries for up to 90 days. To find out if you need a visa, check your respective Italian Embassy.
Study or Work Permit (p. 14). Required for all foreigners planning to study or work in Italy. See the **Beyond Tourism** chapter (p. 79) for more info.

EMBASSIES AND CONSULATES

ITALIAN CONSULAR SERVICES ABROAD

Australia: Embassy of Italy, 12 Grey St., Deakin, Canberra, ACT 2600 (☎+61 262 733 333; www.ambcanberra.esteri.it/Ambasciata_Canberra). **Consulate General of Italy,** 509 St. Kilda Rd., Melbourne, VIC 3004 (☎+61 039 867 5744; www.consmelbourne. esteri.it). **Consulate General of Italy,** The Gateway, Level 45, 1 Macquarie Pl., Sydney, NSW 2000 (☎+61 029 392 7900; www.conssydney.esteri.it).

Canada: Embassy of Italy, 275 Slater St., 21st fl., Ottawa, ON K1P 5H9 (☎+1-613-232-2401; www.ambottawa.esteri.it). **Consulate General of Italy,** 3489 Drummond St., Montréal, QC H3G 1X6 (☎+1-514-849-8351; www.consmontreal.esteri.it).

Ireland: Embassy of Italy, 63/65 Northumberland Rd., Dublin (☎+353 16 60 17 44; www.ambdublino.esteri.it).

New Zealand: Embassy of Italy, 34-38 Grant Rd., P.O. Box 463, Thorndon, Wellington (☎+64 44 735 339; www.ambwellington.esteri.it). **Consulate General of Italy,** 102 Kitchener Rd., PO Box 31 121 Auckland (☎+64 649 489 9632).

UK: Embassy of Italy, 14 Three Kings Yard, London W1K 4EH (☎+44 207 312 2200; www.amblondra.esteri.it). **Consulate General of Italy,** 32 Melville St., Edinburgh EH3 7HA (☎+44 131 226 3631; www.consedimburgo.esteri.it). **Consul General of Italy,** Rodwell Tower, 111 Piccadilly, Manchester M1 2HY (☎+44 161 236 9024; www.consmanchester.esteri.it).

US: Embassy of Italy, 3000 Whitehaven St., N.W., Washington, DC 20008 (☎+1-202-612-4400; www.ambwashingtondc.esteri.it). **Consulate General of Italy,** 600 Atlantic Ave., Boston, MA 02110 (☎+1-617-722-9201; www.consboston.esteri. it). **Consulate General of Italy,** 500 N. Michigan Ave., Ste. 1850, Chicago, IL 60611 (☎+1-312-467-1550; www.conschicago.esteri.it). **Consulate General of Italy,** 690 Park Ave., New York, NY 10021 (☎+1-212-439-8600; www.consnewyork.esteri.it).

CONSULAR SERVICES IN ITALY

Australia: V. Antonio Bosio 5, Rome 00161 (☎06 85 27 21, emergency ☎800 87 77 90; www.italy.embassy.gov.au). Open M-F 9am-5pm.

Canada: V. Zara 30, Rome 00198 (☎06 85 44 41; www.dfait-maeci.gc.ca/canada-europa/italy/menu-en.asp). Open M-Th 8:30-11:30am.

Ireland: P. di Campitelli 3, Rome 00186 (☎06 69 79 121; www.ambasciata-irlanda.it). Open M-F 10am-12:30pm and 3-4:30pm.

New Zealand: V. Clitunno 44, Rome 00198 (☎06 85 37 501; www.nzembassy.com). Open M-F 8:30am-12:45pm and 1:45-5pm.

UK: V. XX Settembre 80a, Rome 00187 (☎06 42 20 00 01; www.britain.it). Open M-F Sept.-May 9am-5pm; June-Aug. 8am-2pm. Closed UK and Italian holidays.

US: V. Vittorio Veneto 119/A, Rome 00187 (☎06 46 741; www.usembassy.it). Consular services open M-F 8:30am-12:30pm. Closed US and Italian holidays.

TOURIST OFFICES

The **Italian Government Tourist Board (ENIT; l'Ente Nazionale Italiano per il Turismo)** provides information on Italy's culture, natural resources, history, and leisure activities. Visit their website, www.italiantourism.com, for info. Call ☎+1-212-245-4822 for a free copy of *General Information for Travelers to Italy*.

Australia: 46 Market St., Sydney, NSW 2000 (☎+61 02 92621666; http://www.enit.it/dovesiamo.asp?Lang=UK&sede=australia).

Canada: 175 E. Bloor St., Ste. 907 South Tower, Toronto, ON M4W 3R8 (☎+1-416-925-4882; http://www.enit.it/dovesiamo.asp?Lang=UK&sede=canada).

UK: 1 Princes St., London W1B 2AY (☎+44 20 7408 1254; www.italiantouristboard.co.uk).

US: 630 5th Ave., Ste. 1565, New York, NY 10111 (☎+1-212-245-5618; www.italiantourism.com).

DOCUMENTS AND FORMALITIES

PASSPORTS

REQUIREMENTS

Citizens of Australia, Canada, Ireland, New Zealand, the UK, and the US need valid passports to enter Italy and to re-enter their home countries. Italy does not allow entrance if the holder's passport expires in under three months beyond the stay; returning home with an expired passport is illegal and may result in a fine. Your passport will prove your most convenient method of identification and, if the photo was taken long ago, a source of humorous conversation.

NEW PASSPORTS

Citizens of Australia, Canada, Ireland, New Zealand, the UK, and the US can apply for a passport at any passport office or at selected post offices and courts of law. Citizens of these countries may also download passport applications from the official website of their country's government or passport office. Any new passport or renewal applications must be filed well in advance of the departure date, though most passport offices offer rush services for a steep fee. Note, however, that "rushed" passports still take up to two weeks to arrive.

ONE EUROPE. European unity has come a long way since 1957, when the **European Economic Community (EEC)** was created to promote European solidarity and cooperation. Since then, the EEC has become the **European Union (EU),** a mighty political, legal, and economic institution. On May 1, 2004, 10 South, Central, and Eastern European countries—Cyprus, the Czech Republic, Estonia, Hungary, Latvia, Lithuania, Malta, Poland, Slovakia, and Slovenia—were admitted into the EU, joining 15 other member states: Austria, Belgium, Denmark, Finland, France, Germany, Greece, Ireland, Italy, Luxembourg, the Netherlands, Portugal, Spain, Sweden, and the UK. On January 1, 2007, two others, Bulgaria and Romania, came into the fold, bringing the tally of member states to 27.

What does this have to do with the average non-EU tourist? The EU's policy of freedom of movement means that most border controls have been abolished and visa policies harmonized. Under this treaty, formally known as the **Schengen Agreement,** you're still required to carry a passport (or government-issued ID card for EU citizens) when crossing an internal border, but, once you've been admitted into one country, you're free to travel to other participating states. Most EU states are already members of Schengen (minus Cyprus) as are Iceland and Norway. EU newcomers Bulgaria and Romania are still in the process of implementing the free travel agreement. The UK and Ireland have opted out of the agreement, but have created their own Common Travel Area, whose regulations match those of Schengen.

For more important consequences of the EU for travelers, see **The Euro** (p. 16) and **Customs in the EU** (p. 15).

ESSENTIALS

PASSPORT MAINTENANCE

Photocopy the page of your passport with your photo as well as your visas, traveler's check serial numbers, and any other important documents. Carry one set of copies in a safe place, apart from the originals, and leave another set at home. Consulates also recommend that you carry an expired passport or an official copy of your birth certificate in a part of your baggage separate from other documents.

If you lose your passport, immediately notify the local police and your home country's nearest embassy or consulate. To expedite its replacement, you must show ID and proof of citizenship; it also helps to know all information previously recorded in the passport. In some cases, a replacement may take weeks to process, and it may be valid only for a limited time. Any visas stamped in your old passport will be lost forever. In an emergency, ask for immediate temporary traveling papers that will permit you to re-enter your home country.

VISAS, INVITATIONS, AND WORK PERMITS

VISAS

EU citizens do not need a visa. Citizens of Australia, Canada, New Zealand, and the US do not need a visa for stays of up to 90 days, but this three-month period begins upon entry into any of the countries that belong to the EU's **freedom of movement** zone. For more information, see **One Europe** (p. 13). Those staying longer than 90 days may purchase a visa at an Italian consulate or embassy. A visa costs about €75 and allows the holder to spend between 90 and 365 days in Italy, depending on the type of visa. Double-check entrance requirements at the nearest Italian embassy or consulate (p. 11) for up-to-date info before departure. US citizens can also consult http://travel.state.gov.

Foreign nationals planning to spend over 90 days in Italy should apply within eight working days of arrival for a *permesso di soggiorno* (permit of stay). Generally, non-EU tourists are required to get a permit at a police station or foreign office *(questura)* if staying longer than 20 days or taking up residence in a location other than a hotel or boarding house. If staying in a hotel or hostel, ask the staff to fill out the registration requirements for you and have the fee waived. There are steep fines for any failure to comply.

Entering Italy to study requires a special visa. For more information, see the **Beyond Tourism** chapter (p. 79).

WORK PERMITS

Admittance to a country as a traveler does not include the right to work, which is authorized only by a work permit. For more information, see the **Beyond Tourism** chapter (p. 79).

IDENTIFICATION

When you travel, always carry at least two forms of identification on your person, including a photo ID. A passport and a driver's license will usually suffice. Never carry all of your IDs together; split them up in case of theft or loss and keep photocopies in your luggage and at home.

STUDENT AND YOUTH IDENTIFICATION

The **International Student Identity Card (ISIC),** the most widely accepted form of student ID, provides discounts on some sights, accommodations, food, and transportation, access to a 24hr. emergency help line, and insurance benefits for US cardholders (see **Insurance,** p. 22). Applicants must be full-time secondary or post-secondary school students at least 12 years old. Because of the proliferation of fake ISICs, some services (particularly airlines) require additional proof of student identity. For travelers who are under 26 years old but are not students, the **International Youth Travel Card (IYTC)** also offers many of the same benefits as the ISIC.

Each of these identity cards costs US$22. ISICs and IYTCs are valid for one year from the date of issue. To learn more about ISICs and IYTCs, try www.myisic.com. Many student travel agencies (p. 14) issue the cards; for a list of issuing agencies or more information, see the **International Student Travel Confederation (ISTC)** website (www.istc.org).

The **International Student Exchange Card (ISE Card)** is a similar identification card available to students, faculty, and children aged 12 to 26. The card provides discounts, medical benefits, access to a 24hr. emergency help line, and the ability to purchase student airfares. An ISE Card costs US$25; call ☎+1-800-255-8000 (in North America) or ☎+1-480-951-1177 (from all other continents). For more info visit www.isecard.com.

CUSTOMS

Upon entering Italy, you must declare certain items from abroad and pay a duty on the value of those articles if they exceed the allowance established by Italy's customs service. Goods and gifts purchased at duty-free shops abroad are not exempt from duty or sales tax; "duty-free" means that you won't pay tax in the country of purchase. Duty-free allowances were abolished for travel between EU member states on June 30, 1999, but still exist for those arriving from outside the EU. Upon returning home, you must likewise declare all articles acquired abroad and pay a duty on the value of articles in excess of your home country's allowance. Jot down a list of any valuables brought from home and register them with customs before traveling abroad. It's a good idea to **keep receipts for all goods acquired abroad.**

CUSTOMS IN THE EU. As well as freedom of movement of people (p. 13), travelers in the European Union can also take advantage of the freedom of movement of goods. This means that there are no customs controls at internal EU borders and travelers are free to transport whatever legal substances they like as long as it is for their own personal (non-commercial) use. Duty-free allowances were abolished on June 30, 1999, for travel between the original 15 EU member states; this now also applies to Cyprus and Malta. However, travelers between the EU and the rest of the world still get a duty-free allowance when passing through customs.

MONEY

CURRENCY AND EXCHANGE

The currency chart below is based on August 2009 exchange rates. Check the currency converter on websites like www.xe.com or www.bloomberg.com for the latest exchange rates.

EURO (€)		
AUS$1 = €0.59	€1 = AUS$1.71
CDN$1 = €0.64	€1 = CDN$1.56
NZ$1 = €0.48	€1 = NZ$2.10
UK£1 = €1.16	€1 = UK£0.86
US$1 = €0.71	€1 = US$1.42

As a general rule, it's cheaper to convert money in Italy than at home. While currency exchange will probably be available in your arrival airport, it's wise to bring enough foreign currency to last for at least 24-72hr.

When changing money abroad, try to go only to banks or money changers *(cambio casas)* that have at most a 5% margin between their buy and sell prices. Since you lose money with every transaction, it makes sense to convert large sums at one time.

If you use traveler's checks or bills, carry some in small denominations (the equivalent of US$50 or less) for times when you are forced to exchange money at poor rates, but bring a range of denominations since charges may be applied per check cashed. Store your money in a variety of forms; ideally, at any given time you will be carrying some cash, some traveler's checks, and an ATM and/ or credit card. All travelers should also consider carrying some US dollars (about US$50 worth), which are often preferred by local tellers.

> **THE EURO.** As of January 1, 2009, the official currency of 16 members of the European Union—Austria, Belgium, Cyprus, Finland, France, Germany, Greece, Ireland, Italy, Luxembourg, Malta, the Netherlands, Portugal, Slovakia, Slovenia, and Spain—has become the euro.
>
> The currency has important—and positive—consequences for travelers hitting more than one Eurozone country. For one thing, money changers across the eurozone are obliged to exchange money at the official, fixed rate (below) and at no commission (though they may charge a small service fee). Second, euro-denominated traveler's checks allow you to pay for goods and services across the eurozone, again at the official rate and commission-free. At the time of printing, €1 = US$1.42 = CDN$1.56 = NZ$2.10 etc. For more info, check a currency converter (such as www.xe.com) or www.europa.eu.int.

TRAVELER'S CHECKS

Traveler's checks are one of the safest and most convenient means of carrying funds. However, they can also be one of the most frustrating means of spending money since fewer and fewer shops outside of tourist areas accept traveler's checks. **American Express** and **Visa** are the most-recognized brands. Many banks and agencies sell them for a small commission. Check issuers provide refunds if the checks are lost or stolen, and many provide additional services, such as toll-free refund hotlines abroad, emergency message services and assistance with lost and stolen credit cards or passports. Ask about toll-free refund hotlines and the location of refund centers when purchasing checks, and always carry emergency cash.

American Express: Checks available with commission at AmEx offices and select banks (www.americanexpress.com). AmEx cardholders can purchase checks by phone (☎+1-800-528-4800). Cheques for Two can be signed by either of 2 people traveling together. For purchase locations or more info, contact AmEx's service centers: in Australia ☎+61 2 9271 8666, in Canada and the US +1-800-528-4800, in New Zealand +64 9 583 8300, and in the UK +44 1273 571 600. In Italy, call ☎+39 067 2282.

Visa: Checks available at banks worldwide. For the location of the nearest office, call the Visa Travelers Cheque Global Refund and Assistance Center: in the UK ☎+44 800 895 078, in the US +1-800-227-6811; elsewhere, call the UK collect at +44 2079 378 091. Checks available in American, British, Canadian, European, and Japanese currencies, among others. Visa also offers TravelMoney, a prepaid debit card that can be reloaded online or by phone. For more information on Visa travel services, see http://usa.visa.com/personal/using_visa/travel_with_visa.html.

CREDIT, DEBIT, AND ATM CARDS

Where they are accepted, credit cards often offer superior exchange rates—up to 5% better than the retail rate used by banks and other currency-exchange establishments. Credit cards may also offer services such as insurance or emergency help and are sometimes required to reserve hotel rooms or rental cars. **MasterCard** (a.k.a. **EuroCard** in Italy) and **Visa** (e.g. **Carte Bleue** in Italy) are the most frequently accepted; **American Express** cards work at some ATMs and at AmEx offices and major airports.

The use of ATM cards is widespread in Italy. Depending on the system that your home bank uses, you can most likely access your personal bank account from abroad. ATMs get the same wholesale exchange rate as credit cards, but

there is often a limit on the amount of money you can withdraw per day (usually around US$500). There is also typically a surcharge of US$1-5 per with-
drawal, so it pays to be efficient.

Debit cards are as convenient as credit cards but withdraw money directly
from the holder's checking account. A debit card can be used wherever its
associated credit card company (usually MasterCard or Visa) is accepted.

The two major international money networks are **MasterCard/Maestro/Cirrus**
(for ATM locations ☎+1-800-424-7787; www.mastercard.com) and **Visa/PLUS**
(for ATM locations visit http://visa.via.infonow.net/locator/global/). Most ATMs
charge a transaction fee that is paid to the bank that owns the ATM. It is a good
idea to contact your bank or credit card company before going abroad; frequent charges in a foreign country can sometimes prompt a fraud alert, which
will freeze your account.

PINS AND ATMS. To use a cash or credit card to withdraw money from
a cash machine (ATM) in Europe, you must have a four-digit Personal Identification Number (PIN). If your PIN is longer than four digits, ask your bank
whether you can just use the first four or whether you'll need a new one.
Credit cards don't usually come with PINs, so, if you intend to hit up ATMs in
Europe with a credit card to get cash advances, call your credit card company
before leaving to request one.

Travelers with alphabetic, rather than numerical, PINs may also be thrown
off by the lack of letters on European cash machines. The following are the
corresponding numbers to use: 1 = QZ; 2 = ABC; 3 = DEF; 4 = GHI; 5 = JKL;
6 = MNO; 7 = PRS; 8 = TUV; 9 = WXY. Note that if you mistakenly punch the
wrong code into the machine three times, it will swallow your card for good.

GETTING MONEY FROM HOME

If you run out of money while traveling, the easiest and cheapest solution is to
have someone back home make a deposit to your bank account. Otherwise,
consider one of the following options.

WIRING MONEY

It is possible to arrange a **bank money transfer,** which means asking a bank back
home to wire money to a bank in Italy. This is the cheapest way to transfer
cash, but it's also the slowest, usually taking several days or more. Note that
some banks may only release your funds in local currency, potentially sticking
you with a poor exchange rate; inquire about this in advance. Money transfer
services like **Western Union** are faster and more convenient than bank transfers—but also much pricier. Western Union has many locations worldwide.
To find one, visit www.westernunion.com or call in Australia ☎+61 1 800 173
833, in Canada and the US+1 800-325-6000, in the UK+44 0800 735 1815, or in
Italy at 800 788 935. To wire money using a credit card, call in Canada and the
US ☎+1 800-CALL-CASH, in the UK+44 0800 833 833. Money transfers services, like remittances and access to emergency funds, are available to **American
Express** cardholders in Italy; check www.amextravelresources.com before leaving. **Thomas Cook** also provides resources for international money transfers. See
www.thomascook.com for more information.

US STATE DEPARTMENT (US CITIZENS ONLY)

In serious emergencies only, the US State Department will forward money within hours to the nearest consular office, which will then disburse it according to instructions for a US$30 fee. If you wish to use this service, you must contact the Overseas Citizens Services division of the US State Department (☎+1-202-501-4444, from US 888-407-4747).

COSTS

The cost of your trip will vary considerably, depending on where you visit, how you travel, and where you stay. The most significant expenses will probably be your round-trip (return) airfare to Rome (see **Getting to Rome: By Plane,** p. 25) and a railpass or bus pass.

STAYING ON A BUDGET

To give you a general idea, a bare-bones day in Rome (sleeping in hostels/guesthouses, buying food at supermarkets) would cost about US$50 (€32); a slightly more comfortable day (sleeping in hostels/guesthouses and the occasional budget hotel, eating one meal per day at a restaurant, going out at night) would cost about US$90 (€57); and, for a luxurious day, the sky's the limit. Don't forget to factor in emergency reserve funds (at least US$200) when planning how much money you'll need.

TIPPING AND BARGAINING

At many Italian restaurants, a service charge *(servizio)* or cover *(coperto)* is included in the bill. Locals sometimes do not give tips, but it is appropriate for foreign visitors to leave an additional 5-10% at restaurants for the waiter. A euro or two will usually suffice. Taxi drivers expect about a 5-10% tip, though Italians rarely tip them. Bargaining is common in Italy, but use discretion. Haggling is appropriate at markets with vendors, and unmetered taxi fares (settle the price before getting in), but elsewhere, it is usually inappropriate. Hotel negotiation is more successful in uncrowded *pensioni* (Italian accommodations, which are sort of a middle ground between hotels and hostels). To get lower prices, show little interest. Don't offer what you can't pay; you're expected to buy once the merchant accepts your price.

TAXES

The **Value Added Tax** (**VAT**; *imposto sul valore aggiunta*, or IVA) is a sales tax levied in the EU. Foreigners making any purchase over €155 are entitled to an additional 20% VAT refund. Some stores take off 20% on-site. Others require that you fill out forms at the customs desk upon leaving the EU and send receipts from home within six months. Not all storefront "Tax-Free" stickers imply an immediate, on-site refund, so ask before making a purchase.

PACKING

Pack lightly: lay out only what you think you absolutely need, then pack half of the clothes and twice the money. The **Travelite FAQ** (www.travelite.org) is a good resource for tips on traveling light. The online **Universal Packing List** (http://upl.codeq.info) will generate a customized list of suggested items based on your trip length, the expected climate, your planned activities, and other factors.

Converters and Adapters: In Italy, electricity is 230 volts AC, enough to fry any 120V North American appliance. 220/240V electrical appliances won't work with a 120V current, either. Americans and Canadians should buy an **adapter** (which changes the shape of the plug; US$10-20) and a **converter** (which changes the voltage; US$10-20). Don't make the mistake of using only an adapter (unless appliance instructions explicitly state otherwise). Australians and New Zealanders (who use 230V at home) won't need a converter but will need a set of adapters to use anything electrical. For more on all things adaptable, check out http://kropla.com/electric.htm.

LIQUIDS IN THE AIR. Travelers should note new EU and US travel restrictions on liquids—including drinks, toiletries, and gels—on airplanes. At the time of printing, liquids could be transported only in containers of 100mL (3 fl. oz. in the US) or less. Each passenger could carry only as many containers as fit in a 1L (1 quart in the US) clear plastic bag. To avoid hassles, put as many of your liquids as possible in your checked luggage. Contact Rome's international airport (p. 29) for the latest policy.

Important documents: Don't forget your passport, traveler's checks, ATM and/or credit cards, adequate ID, and photocopies of all of the aforementioned in case these documents are lost or stolen (p. 12). Also check that you have any of the following that might apply to you: a hosteling membership card (p. 14); driver's license (p. 14); travel insurance forms (p. 22); ISIC (p. 14); and/or railpass or bus pass (p. 28).

SAFETY AND HEALTH

GENERAL ADVICE

In any type of crisis, the most important thing to do is **stay calm.** Your country's embassy abroad (p. 12) is usually your best resource in an emergency; registering with that embassy upon arrival in the country is a good idea. The government offices listed in the **Travel Advisories** box (p. 20) can provide information on the services they offer their citizens in case of emergencies abroad.

LOCAL LAWS AND POLICE

In Italy, you will mainly encounter two types of police: the *polizia* (☎113) and the *carabinieri* (☎112). The *polizia* are a civil force under the command of the Ministry of the Interior, whereas the *carabinieri* fall under the jurisdiction of the Ministry of Defense and are considered a military force. Both, however, generally serve the same purpose—to maintain security and order in the country. In the case of attack or robbery, both will respond to inquiries for help.

DRUGS AND ALCOHOL

Needless to say, **illegal drugs** are best avoided altogether. In Italy, drugs including marijuana, cocaine, and heroin are illegal. An increase in cocaine and heroin addiction and trafficking have led Italian authorities to respond harshly to drug-related offenses. If you carry **prescription drugs,** bring copies of the prescriptions and a note from a doctor, and have them accessible at international borders. The drinking age in Italy is 16. Drinking and driving is prohibited and can result in a prison sentence. The legal blood alcohol content (BAC) for driving is under 0.05%.

SPECIFIC CONCERNS

DEMONSTRATIONS AND POLITICAL GATHERINGS

Americans should be mindful while traveling in Italy, as there is some anti-American sentiment. It is best to err on the side of caution and sidestep any political discussions. In general, use discretion and avoid being too vocal about your citizenship.

FOOTBALL AFICIONADOS

Rome is home to two rival Serie A football clubs, **A.S. Roma** and **S.S. Lazio,** and there is a history of conflict—and even rioting—between the teams. If you dare to wear anything that supports either of them, especially during the **Rome Derby** (when the two play each other), make sure you don't bump into supporters of the other club, or you may be subject to confrontation. Play it safe and refrain from openly supporting either club.

TERRORISM

Terrorism has not been as serious a problem in Italy as in other European countries, though the general threat of terrorism still exists. Exercise common sense and caution when in crowded, public areas like train or bus stations and open spaces like *piazze* in larger cities. The box below lists offices to contact and websites to visit to get the most updated list of your government's advisories about travel.

TRAVEL ADVISORIES. The following government offices provide travel information and advisories by telephone, by fax, or via the web:

Australian Department of Foreign Affairs and Trade: ☎+61 2 6261 1111; www.dfat.gov.au.

Canadian Department of Foreign Affairs and International Trade (DFAIT): ☎+1-800-267-8376; www.dfait-maeci.gc.ca. Call or visit the website for the free booklet *Bon Voyage...But.*

New Zealand Ministry of Foreign Affairs: ☎+64 4 439 8000; www.mfat.govt.nz.

United Kingdom Foreign and Commonwealth Office: ☎+44 20 7008 1500; www.fco.gov.uk.

US Department of State: ☎+1-888-407-4747, 202-501-4444 from abroad; http://travel.state.gov.

PERSONAL SAFETY

EXPLORING AND TRAVELING

To avoid unwanted attention, try to blend in as much as possible. Respecting local customs (in many cases, dressing more conservatively than you would at home) may ward off would-be hecklers. Familiarize yourself with your surroundings before setting out, and carry yourself with confidence. Check maps in shops and restaurants rather than on the street. If you are traveling alone, be sure someone at home knows your itinerary and never tell anyone you meet that you're by yourself. When walking at night, stick to busy, well-lit streets and avoid dark alleyways. If you ever feel uncomfortable, leave the area as quickly and directly as you can. There is no sure-fire way to avoid all the threatening situations that you might encounter while traveling, but a good **self-defense**

course will give you concrete ways to react to unwanted advances. **Impact, Prepare,** and **Model Mugging** (www.modelmugging.org) can refer you to local self-defense courses in Australia, Canada, Switzerland, and the US.

If you are using a **car,** learn local driving signals and wear a seat belt. Children under 40 lb. should ride only in specially designed car seats, available for a fee from most car-rental agencies. Study route maps before you hit the road and, if you plan on spending a lot of time driving, consider bringing spare parts. For long drives in desolate areas, invest in a cell phone and a roadside assistance program (p. 34). Park your vehicle in a garage or well-traveled area and use a steering-wheel locking device in larger cities. Sleeping in your car is the most dangerous way to get your rest, and it's illegal in many countries.

No one should hitchhike without careful consideration of the risks involved. Hitching means entrusting your life to a random person who happens to stop beside you on the road, and hitchers always risk theft, assault, sexual harassment, and unsafe driving.

POSSESSIONS AND VALUABLES

Never leave your belongings unattended; crime can occur in even the safest-looking hostel or hotel. Bring your own padlock for hostel lockers and don't ever store valuables in a locker. Be particularly careful on **buses** and **trains;** horror stories abound about determined thieves who wait for travelers to fall asleep. Carry your bag or purse in front of you where you can see it. When traveling with others, sleep in alternate shifts. When alone, be careful in selecting a train compartment: never stay in an empty one and always use a lock to secure your pack to the luggage rack. Use extra caution if traveling at night or on overnight trains. Try to sleep on top bunks with your luggage stored above you (if not in bed with you) and keep important documents and other valuables on you at all times.

There are a few steps you can take to minimize the financial risk associated with traveling. First, **bring as little with you as possible.** Second, buy a few combination **padlocks** to secure your belongings either in your pack or in a hostel or train-station locker. Third, **carry as little cash as possible.** Keep your traveler's checks and ATM/credit cards in a **money belt**—not a "fanny pack"—along with your passport and ID cards. Fourth, **keep a small cash reserve separate from your primary stash.** This should be about US$50 (US dollars or euro are best) sewn into or stored in the depths of your pack, along with your traveler's check numbers and photocopies of your important documents.

In Rome, **con artists** often work in groups and may involve children in their schemes. Beware of certain classics: sob stories that require money, rolls of bills "found" on the street, mustard spilled (or saliva spit) onto your shoulder to distract you while they snatch your bag. **Never let your passport or your bags out of your sight.** Hostel workers will sometimes stand at bus and train arrival points to recruit tired and disoriented travelers to their hostel; never believe strangers who tell you that theirs is the only hostel open. Beware of **pickpockets** in city crowds, especially on public transportation. Also, be alert in public telephone booths. If you must say your calling-card number, do so very quietly; if you punch it in, make sure no one can look over your shoulder.

If you will be traveling with electronic devices, such as a laptop computer or MP3 player, check whether your homeowner's insurance covers loss, theft, or damage when you travel. If not, you might consider purchasing a low-cost separate insurance policy. **Safeware** (☎+1-800-800-1492; www.safeware.com) specializes in covering computers and charges US$90 for 90-day comprehensive international travel coverage up to US$4000.

PRE-DEPARTURE HEALTH

In your passport, write the names of any people you wish to be contacted in case of a **medical emergency** and list any **allergies** or **medical conditions.** Matching a prescription to a foreign equivalent is not always easy, safe, or possible, so, if you take **prescription drugs,** carry up-to-date prescriptions or a statement from your doctor stating the medications' trade names, manufacturers, chemical names, and dosages. While traveling, be sure to keep all medication with you in your carry-on luggage.

While it may be difficult to find brand name medications like Tylenol or Advil, these products can easily be identified by their common Italian drug names such as *acetaminofene* (acetaminophen), *paracetamolo* (paracetamol), and *ibuprofen* (ibuprofen).

IMMUNIZATIONS AND PRECAUTIONS

Travelers over two years old should make sure that the following vaccines are up to date: MMR (for measles, mumps, and rubella); DTaP or Td (for diphtheria, tetanus, and pertussis); IPV (for polio); Hib (for *Haemophilus influenzae* B); and HepB (for Hepatitis B). For recommendations on immunizations and prophylaxis, consult the Centers for Disease Control and Prevention (CDC; below) in the US or the equivalent in your home country and check with a doctor for guidance.

USEFUL ORGANIZATIONS AND PUBLICATIONS

The American **Center for Disease Control and Prevention** (**CDC;** ☎+1-800-CDC-INFO/232-4636; www.cdc.gov/travel) maintains an international travelers' hotline and an informative website. Consult the appropriate government agency of your home country for consular information sheets on health, entry requirements, and other issues for various countries (see the listings in the box on **Travel Advisories,** p. 20). For quick information on health and other travel warnings, call the **Overseas Citizens Services** (☎+1-202-647-5225) or contact a passport agency, embassy, or consulate abroad. For information on medical evacuation services and travel insurance firms, see the US government's website at http://travel.state.gov/travel/abroad_health.html or the **British Foreign and Commonwealth Office** (www.fco.gov.uk). For general health information, contact the **American Red Cross** (☎+1-202-303-5000; www.redcross.org).

STAYING HEALTHY

Common sense is the simplest prescription for good health while you travel. Drink lots of fluids to prevent dehydration and constipation and wear sturdy, broken-in shoes and clean socks.

ONCE IN ROME

ENVIRONMENTAL HAZARDS

Arid summer weather creates prime conditions for heat exhaustion and dehydration, so drink plenty of liquid.

Heat exhaustion and dehydration: Heat exhaustion leads to nausea, excessive thirst, headaches, and dizziness. Avoid it by drinking plenty of fluids, eating salty foods (e.g., crackers), abstaining from dehydrating beverages (e.g., alcohol and caffeinated beverages), and wearing sunscreen. Continuous heat stress can eventually lead to **heatstroke,** characterized by a rising temperature, severe headache, delirium, and cessation of sweating. Victims should be cooled off with wet towels and taken to a doctor.

INSECT-BORNE DISEASES

Many diseases are transmitted by insects—mainly mosquitoes, fleas, ticks, and lice. Be aware of insects in wet or forested areas. Use insect repellents such as DEET and soak or spray your gear with permethrin (licensed in the US only for use on clothing). **Mosquitoes**—responsible for malaria, dengue fever, and yellow fever—can be particularly abundant in wet, swampy, or wooded areas and during Roman summers. **Ticks**—which can carry Lyme and other diseases—can be particularly dangerous in rural and forested regions outside of Rome.

> **Lyme disease:** A bacterial infection carried by ticks and marked by a circular bull's-eye rash of 2 in. or more. Later symptoms include fever, headache, fatigue, and aches and pains. Antibiotics are effective if administered early. Left untreated, Lyme can cause problems in joints, the heart, and the nervous system. If you find a tick attached to your skin, grasp the head with tweezers as close to your skin as possible and apply slow, steady traction. Removing a tick within 24hr. greatly reduces the risk of infection. Do not try to remove ticks with petroleum jelly, nail polish remover, or a hot match. Ticks usually inhabit moist, shaded environments and heavily wooded areas.

FOOD- AND WATERBORNE DISEASES

Prevention is the best cure: be sure that your food is properly cooked and that the water you drink is clean. Watch out for food from markets or street vendors that may have been cooked in unhygienic conditions. Other culprits are raw shellfish, unpasteurized milk, and sauces containing raw eggs. Buy bottled water or purify your own water by bringing it to a rolling boil or treating it with **iodine tablets;** note, however, that boiling is more reliable. While Italy's water is relatively clean (the ancient Roman aqueduct water still provides Rome with a reliable water source), it is important to be wary in places like trains where water is not clean. The sign *"acqua non potabile"* means the water is not drinkable; *"acqua potabile"* means the water is sanitary. Even as a developed nation, Italy experienced an outbreak of stomach flu due to contaminated drinking water in Taranto in 2006.

> **Traveler's diarrhea:** Results from drinking fecally contaminated water or eating uncooked and contaminated foods. Symptoms include nausea, bloating, and urgency. Try quick-energy, non-sugary foods with protein and carbohydrates to keep your strength up. Over-the-counter anti-diarrheals (e.g., Imodium®) may counteract the problem. The most dangerous side effect is dehydration; drink 8 oz. of water with ½ tsp. of sugar or honey and a pinch of salt, try uncaffeinated soft drinks, or eat salted crackers. If you develop a fever or your symptoms don't go away after 4-5 days, consult a doctor. Consult a doctor immediately for treatment of diarrhea in children.

OTHER INFECTIOUS DISEASES

The following diseases exist all over the world. Travelers should know how to recognize them and what to do if they suspect they have been infected.

AIDS and HIV: For detailed information on Acquired Immune Deficiency Syndrome (AIDS) in Italy, call the CDC's 24hr. National AIDS Hotline at ☎+1-800-232-4636. Note that Italy screens incoming travelers for AIDS, primarily those planning extended visits for work or study, and denies entrance to those who test HIV-positive. Contact the consulate of Italy (p. 11) for info.

Sexually transmitted infections (STIs): Gonorrhea, chlamydia, genital warts, syphilis, herpes, HPV, and other STIs are easier to catch than HIV and can be just as serious. Though condoms may protect you from some STIs, oral or even tactile contact can lead to transmission. If you think you may have contracted an STI, see a doctor immediately.

OTHER HEALTH CONCERNS

MEDICAL CARE ON THE ROAD

Rome conforms overall to the standards of modern Western health care. Medical facilities tend to be better in private hospitals and clinics. Most Roman doctors speak English; if they don't, they may be able to arrange for a translator. *Let's Go* lists info on how to access medical help in the **Practical Information** section (p. 91).

If you are concerned about obtaining medical assistance while traveling, you may wish to employ special support services. The **International Association for Medical Assistance to Travelers (IAMAT;** US ☎+1-716-754-4883, Canada +1-416-652-0137; www.iamat.org) has free membership, lists English-speaking doctors worldwide, and offers details on immunization requirements and sanitation. For those whose insurance doesn't apply abroad, you can purchase additional coverage (p. 22).

Those with medical conditions (such as diabetes, allergies to antibiotics, epilepsy, or heart conditions) may want to obtain a **MedicAlert** membership (US$40 per year), which includes, among other things, a stainless-steel ID tag and a 24hr. collect-call number. Contact the MedicAlert Foundation International (from US ☎888-633-4298, outside US +1-209-668-3333; www.medicalert.org).

WOMEN'S HEALTH

Women traveling in unsanitary conditions are vulnerable to **urinary tract (including bladder and kidney) infections.** Bring supplies from home if you are prone to infection, as they may be difficult to find on the road. **Tampons, pads,** and **contraceptive devices** are widely available, though your preferred brand may not be stocked—bring extras of anything you can't live without. Abortion (*aborto* or *interruzione volontaria di gravidanza*) is legal and may be performed in the first 90 days of pregnancy for free in a public hospital or for a fee in an authorized private facility. Except in urgent cases, a week-long reflection period is required. Women under 18 must obtain parental permission or a judge's consent. Availability may be limited in some areas, especially in the south, due to a "conscience clause" that allows physicians who oppose abortion to opt out of performing the procedure. The election of Pope Benedict XVI has sparked controversy over abortion, but no immediate policy changes are expected.

GETTING TO ROME

BY PLANE

When it comes to airfare, a little effort can save you a bundle. For those with flexibility *and* patience, **standby flights** are one way to save; be prepared to spend all day at the airport for a week or more before finally boarding a plane. Call major airline companies for details (see **Commercial Airlines, p. 26**). The key is to hunt around, be flexible, and ask about discounts. Students, seniors, and those under 26 should almost never pay full price for a ticket.

AIRFARES

Airfares to Rome peak between April and October, and holidays are also expensive. The cheapest times to travel are early spring and late fall. Midweek (M-Th morning) round-trip flights run cheaper than weekend flights, but they are generally more crowded and less likely to permit frequent-flier upgrades. Not fixing a return date ("open return") or arriving in and departing from different cities ("open-jaw") can be pricier than round-trip flights. Patching one-way flights together is the most expensive way to travel. Flights into Rome tend to be cheaper than into other Italian cities.

If Rome is only one stop on a more extensive globe-hop, consider a round-the-world (RTW) ticket. Tickets usually include at least five stops and are valid for about a year; prices range US$3000-8000. Try the airline consortiums **Oneworld** (www.oneworld.com), **Skyteam** (www.skyteam.com), and **Star Alliance** (www.staralliance.com).

Fares for round-trip flights to Rome from the US or Canadian east coast cost US$700-1200, US$500-700 in the low season (from mid-October. to mid-Dec. and Jan.-Mar.); from the US or Canadian west coast US$800-1600/600-1000; from the UK, UK£175-300/125-200; from Australia AUS$1700-2600/1320-2000; from New Zealand NZ$2000-3000/1800-2400.

BUDGET AND STUDENT TRAVEL AGENCIES

While knowledgeable agents specializing in flights to Rome can make your life easy, they may not spend the time to find you the lowest possible fare—they get paid on commission. Travelers holding ISICs and IYTCs (p. 14) qualify for big discounts from student travel agencies. Most flights from budget agencies are on major airlines, but in high season some may sell seats on less reliable chartered aircraft.

The Adventure Travel Company, 124 MacDougal St., New York, NY 10021, USA (☎+1-212-674-2887; www.theadventuretravelcompany.com). Offices across Canada and the US including New York City, San Diego, San Francisco, and Seattle.

STA Travel, 2871 Broadway, New York, NY 10025, USA (24hr. reservations and info ☎+1-800-781-4040; www.statravel.com). A student and youth travel organization with offices worldwide, including US offices in Los Angeles, New York City, Seattle, Washington, DC and a number of other college towns. Ticket booking, travel insurance, railpasses, and more. Walk-in offices are located throughout Australia (☎+61 134 782), New Zealand (☎+64 0800 474 400), and the UK (☎+44 8712 230 0040).

ESSENTIALS

FLIGHT PLANNING ON THE INTERNET. The Internet may be the budget traveler's dream when it comes to finding and booking bargain fares, but the array of options can be overwhelming. Many airline sites offer special last-minute deals on the web. Look for sale fares on www.alitalia.com and www.flyairone.it. **STA** (www.statravel.com) and **StudentUniverse** (www.studentuniverse.com) provide quotes on student tickets, while **Orbitz** (www.orbitz.com), **Expedia** (www.expedia.com), and **Travelocity** (www.travelocity.com) offer full travel services. **Priceline** (www.priceline.com) lets you specify a price and obligates you to buy any ticket that meets or beats it; **Hotwire** (www.hotwire.com) offers bargain fares but won't reveal the airline or flight times until you buy. Other sites that compile deals include www.bestfares.com, www.flights.com, www.lowestfare.com, www.onetravel.com, www.cheaptickets.com and www.travelzoo.com.

Cheapflights (www.cheapflights.com) is a useful search engine for finding—you guessed it—cheap flights. **Booking Buddy** (www.bookingbuddy.com), **Kayak** (www.kayak.com), and **SideStep** (www.sidestep.com) are online tools that let you enter your trip information and search multiple sites at once. *Let's Go* does not endorse any of these websites. As always, be cautious and research companies before you hand over your credit card number. **SideStep** (www.sidestep.com) and **Booking Buddy** (www.bookingbuddy.com) are online tools that help sift through multiple offers.

Air Traveler's Handbook (www.faqs.org/faqs/travel/air/handbook) is an indispensable resource on the internet; it has a comprehensive listing of links to everything you need to know before you board a plane.

COMMERCIAL AIRLINES

TRAVELING FROM NORTH AMERICA

Crossing the pond? Standard commercial carriers like **American** (☎+1-800-433-7300; www.aa.com), **United** (☎+1-800-538-2929; www.ual.com), and **Northwest** (☎+1-800-225-2525; www.nwa.com) will probably offer the most convenient flights, but they may not be the cheapest. Check **Air France** (☎+1-800-237-2747; www.airfrance.us), **Alitalia** (☎+1-800-223-5730; www.alitaliausa.com), **British Airways** (☎+1-800-247-9297; www.britishairways.com), and **Lufthansa** (☎+1-800-399-5838; www.lufthansa.com) for cheap tickets from destinations throughout the US to Rome. You might find an even better deal on one of the following airlines, if any of their limited departure points is convenient for you.

Finnair (☎+1-800-950-5000; www.finnair.com). Cheap round-trips from Los Angeles, New York, and Toronto to Rome; connections throughout Europe ($300).

KLM (☎+44 8712 227 474; www.klmuk.com). Cheap tickets from London, Dublin, and elsewhere to Rome ($250).

TRAVELING FROM IRELAND AND THE UK

Cheapflights (www.cheapflights.co.uk) publishes bargains on airfare from the British Isles, but British and Irish globetrotters really looking to save should always fly on budget airlines. The following commercial carriers occasionally offer discounted fares or specials.

Aer Lingus (in Ireland ☎+353 818 365 000; www.aerlingus.ie). Flights from Dublin, Cork, Kerry, and Shannon to Rome (€30-200).

KLM (☎+44 8712 227 474; www.klmuk.com). Cheap tickets from London, Dublin, and elsewhere to Rome (UK£60-200).

TRAVELING FROM AUSTRALIA AND NEW ZEALAND

Qantas Air (in Australia ☎+61 13 13 13, in New Zealand +64 800 808 767; www.qantas.com.au). Flights from Australia and New Zealand to Rome (AUS$1400-2600).

Air New Zealand (☎+64 800 737 000; www.airnewzealand.com). Flights from Auckland, Christchurch, Melbourne, Perth, and Sydney to Rome (NZD$2000-3600).

Singapore Air (in Australia ☎+61 13 10 11, in New Zealand 800 808 909; www.singaporeair.com). Flights from Auckland, Christchurch, Melbourne, Perth, and Sydney to Rome (AUS$1900-2400).

Thai Airways (in Australia ☎+61 1300 65 19 60, in New Zealand +64 9 256 8518; www.thaiair.com). Auckland, Melbourne, Perth, and Sydney to Rome (AUS$1600-2600).

BUDGET AIRLINES

For travelers who don't place a premium on convenience, we recommend ▓budget airlines (p. 27) as the best way to jet around Europe. Travelers can often snag these tickets for illogically low prices (i.e., less than the price of a meal in the airport food court), but you get what you pay for: namely, minimalist service and no frills. In addition, many budget airlines fly out of smaller regional airports several kilometers out of town. You'll have to buy shuttle tickets to reach the airports of many of these airlines, so plan on adding an hour or so to your travel time. After round-trip shuttle tickets and fees for services that might come standard on other airlines, that €1 sale fare can suddenly jump to €20-100. Still, it's possible save money even if you live outside the continent by hopping a cheap flight to anywhere in Europe and using budget airlines to reach your final destination. Prices vary dramatically; shop around, book months ahead, pack light, and stay flexible to nab the best fares. For a more detailed list of these airlines by country, check out www.whichbudget.com.

easyJet (☎+44 871 244 2366, UK£0.10 per min.; www.easyjet.com). From London, Liverpool, Glasgow, and Edinburgh to Rome (UK£25-200).

Ryanair (in Ireland ☎+353 0818 30 30 30, in UK 0871 246 0000, elsewhere +35 3124 80856; www.ryanair.com). The cheapest flights (from £10 with taxes) from Dublin, Glasgow, Liverpool, London, and Shannon to Rome.

SkyEurope (in UK ☎+44 0905 722 2747, elsewhere +421 2 3301 7301; www.skyeurope.com). 40 destinations in 19 countries around Europe. Flights from Bucharest, Prague, and Bratislava to Rome (€33).

Sterling (in Denmark ☎+45 70 10 84 84, in UK 0870 787 8038; www.sterling.dk). The 1st Scandinavian-based budget airline. Connects Denmark, Norway, and Sweden to 47 European destinations, including Rome (€50).

Transavia (in UK ☎+44 020 7365 4997; www.transavia.com). From Copenhagen and Rotterdam to Rome (€45).

Wizz Air (in UK ☎+44 090 475 9500, UK£0.65 per min.; www.wizzair.com). From Budapest and Warsaw to Rome (€45).

BY TRAIN

Traveling to Rome by train from within Europe can be as expensive as a flight, but allows travelers to watch the country unfold before them and grants the possibility of spontaneous stopovers before reaching the ultimate destination. Prices and number of trips per day vary according to destination, day of the week, season, and other criteria. To find prices, schedules, and locations check www.raileurope.com or www.voyages-sncf.com.

Stazione Termini is the train and subway hub, though it's closed midnight-5:30am. During this time, trains usually arrive at Stazione Tiburtina or Stazione Ostiense; bus N2 will get you from either station to Termini. (Just make sure you're going in the right direction.) Termini's services include: shopping; ATMs; hotel reservations, across from track 13; luggage storage, underneath track 24; police, across from track 13. Termini's bathrooms (€0.70) beneath track 1, are a surreal black-lit wonderland; the ones under track 24 are less thrilling but will do. Trains (Direct, or D, is the slowest; IC is the intercity train; ES, or Eurostar, is the fastest and most expensive) leave Termini for: **Bologna** (IC 3hr., €33; ES 2hr., €42); **Florence** (D 3hr., €14; IC 2hr., €24; ES 1hr., €33); **Milan** (D 8hr., €30; IC 6hr., €41; ES 4hr., €50); **Naples** (D 2hr., €10; IC 2hr., €19; ES 1hr., €25); **Venice** (D overnight, €33; IC 5hr., €39; ES 4hr., €50). Hours and prices are updated every six months; check **www. ferroviedellostato.it** for the most up-to-date schedules and prices.

It's easiest to purchase intercity and some international train tickets using Termini's automated ticket booths. Dozens of these are located by the station's main entrance at P. dei Cinquecento. If you know what you're looking for, the process only takes a few minutes, and can generally be done right before boarding. An exception is for seats that must be reserved in advance, like some first-class tickets, tickets to popular international destinations, or tickets on the only train of the day to or from a destination; these can generally be booked a couple of days in advance with no problems. You might consult the Ferrovie dello Stato website for information on seat availability, but reserving online can be tricky—the process is lengthy and convoluted, and some international credit cards won't allow you to make the purchase. It may be easier just to stop at Termini for five minutes and pick up the things you need. You can buy tickets and get information on trains from a real human being at the full-service Trenitalia kiosk in Termini, also by the P. del Cinquecento entrance. The line here can become substantial, so if you prefer this option, get to the station a little early. Remember, for some trains you must **validate your ticket.** If you need to, you'll be informed when you buy it.

BY BUS

Though European trains are popular, in some cases buses prove a better option. Often cheaper than railpasses, international bus passes allow unlimited travel on a hop-on, hop-off basis between major European cities. Amsterdam, Athens, Istanbul, London, Munich, and Oslo are centers for lines offering long-distance rides across Europe. Bus travel within Italy has its own benefits and disadvantages; in remote parts of the country, private companies offer cheap fares and are often the only option, though schedules may be unreliable.

Eurolines, 4 Vicarage Rd., Edgbaston, Birmingham B15 3ES, UK (☎+44 8705 80 80 80; www. eurolines.com). The largest operator of Europe-wide coach services. Unlimited 15-day (high season UK£195, under 26 and over 60 UK£165; low season UK£149/129); 30-day (high season UK£290/235; low season UK£209/169); or 60-day (high season UK£333/259; low season UK£265/211) travel passes that offer unlimited transit between 35 major European cities.

BY CAR

Driving to Rome is quite easy; as they say, all roads lead to Rome. The city is ringed by a motorway, **Grande Raccordo Anulare (GRA).** If you are going to the very center of the city, any road leading off the GRA will get you there. If you are going anywhere else, however, a GPS or a good map is essential. Signs on the GRA indicate the road leading to the center (e.g. Via Appia Nuova, Via Aurelia, Via Tiburtina) but this is often helpful only for Romans in the know.

BORDER CROSSINGS

The surrounding countries of France, Switzerland, and Austria can make great daytrips from Italy's border cities. Multiple-country rail passes are available through **RailEurope (www.raileurope.com).**

As a part of the EU, Italy only requires that travelers present a valid passport and ID to travel between EU nations. When traveling to France and Austria, no currency exchange is necessary.

GETTING INTO ROME

AIRPORTS

DA VINCI INTERNATIONAL (FIUMICINO)

Most international flights arrive at **Da Vinci International Airport,** known as **Fiumicino (FCO; ☎ 06 65 951).**

TRAIN

After exiting customs, follow the signs for **Stazione Trenitalia/Railway Station.** The **Termini line** (the colorful Leonardo Express) runs nonstop to Rome's main train station, **Termini** (30min., 2 per hr. 6:35am-11:35pm, €11). Buy a ticket at the Trenitalia ticket counter, the *tabaccheria* on the right, or from one of the machines in the station. Beware of scam artists attempting to sell fake tickets. A train leaves Termini for Fiumicino every 30min. (30min., 5:50am-10:50pm; €11); the very first train of the morning leaves from track 23 and all others leave from track 25. Buy your tickets at the Leonardo Express kiosk on track 25 or from one of the machines in the station. Be warned: track 25 is quite a walk from the entrance to the station on P. dei Cinquecento; try to leave a good 10min. just to get to the departure point. The **Railway Information Center** across from track 4 can provide you with helpful information on transportation options (open 7am-9:45pm).

If you're willing to put up with some inconveniences, you can save a few euro by leaving for Fiumicino from **Rome Ostiense** instead of Termini. (30 min.; €5.50. This local train also stops at **Roma Trastevere.**) You'll have to take the Metro to Ⓜ B-Piramide and walk a few blocks south to Ostiense station—be sure to budget in plenty of time so you don't miss your train. Note also that the absolute earliest airport train of the morning leaves from Ostiense. It's at 5:18am, and it'll get you to the airport by 5:48am, more than half an hour before the first train from Termini will. You'll have to take a cab or bus N2 to Ostiense, though, as the Metro doesn't function at that hour.

No matter which station you pick, failure to **validate your ticket** before boarding could lead to a €50-100 fine. Insert it into one of the little yellow boxes you see near the tracks to get that crucial stamp of approval.

BUS, SHUTTLE, AND TAXI

For flights that arrive after 10:30pm or leave before 8am, the most reliable option to go between Rome and the airport is a **taxi.** (Request one at the kiosk in the airport or call ☎06 49 94 or 66 45.) **Agree on a price with the driver before getting into the cab**—it should be around €40. Factors such as the amount of luggage and the time of day will affect the price. The cheapest option is to take the blue **COTRAL bus** (☎800 174 471) outside the main exit doors after customs to Tiburtina (1:15, 2:15, 3:30, 5am; €5 onboard). From Tiburtina, take bus N2 to Termini. To get to Fiumicino from Rome late at night or early in the morning, take bus N2 from Termini to Tiburtina (every 20-30min.), then catch the blue COTRAL bus to Fiumicino from the *piazza* (12:30, 1:15, 2:30, 3:45am; €5). The **24hr. airport shuttle service** (☎06 47 40 451 or 42 01 34 69; www.airportshuttle.it) is a good deal for two or more. Call or visit the website to reserve a spot. (€28 from Fiumicino to the city center, each additional passenger €6; early mornings, nights, and holidays prices rise 30%.)

CIAMPINO AIRPORT

Most charter flights and a few international ones, including **Ryanair,** arrive at **Ciampino Airport** (**CIA;** ☎06 65 951).

BUS, SHUTTLE, AND TAXI

To get to Rome from Ciampino, take the **COTRAL bus** (every 30min. 6:10am-11:40pm, €1) to Anagnina station on Metro A. The public shuttle buses (☎06 59 16 826; www.sitbusshuttle.com) or the **Terravision Shuttle** (☎06 79 34 17 22; www.terravision.it) are slightly more convenient options, especially for late or early flights. They both go to V. Marsala, outside Termini, at the Hotel Royal Santina (40min.; 25 per day per carrier, first shuttles to Ciampino 4:30am, last shuttles to Rome around midnight; public shuttle €6, Terravision around €5-6). Online booking available. Schedules are online and at the hotel. After 11pm and before 7am, take a **taxi** (€35-40).

GETTING AROUND ROME

BY PUBLIC TRANSPORTATION

BUS AND TRAM

The network of routes may seem daunting, but Rome's **buses** are an efficient means of getting around the city, especially since the Metro doesn't serve the *centro storico.* The **Agenzia del Trasporto Autoferrotranviario del Comune di Roma** has booths throughout the city, including one in Termini. (**ATAC;** ☎06 80 04 31 784; www.atac.roma.it. Open M-Sa 7am-8pm, Su 8am-7pm.) There are also full-service ATAC booths in nine other Metro stations: Anagnina, Battistini, Cornelia,

Lepanto, Ottaviano, and Spagna on the A line; EUR Fermi, Laurentina, and Ponte Mammolo on the B line. (All are open M-Sa 7am-8pm. On Sunday and holidays, Cornelia is closed; Spagna and Battistini are open 8am-7pm; all others open 8am-8pm.) At any of these *biglietterie*, you can grab a map (€1) or purchase monthly, yearly, or discounted Metro passes. Single-use ATAC tickets (€1) are valid for the Metro and buses, and are sold at *tabaccherie*, newsstands, vending machines, and some bars. Vending machines are in Metro stations, on street corners, and at major bus stops; look for ATAC labels. Tickets are valid for one Metro ride or 75 minutes of unlimited bus travel. A **biglietto integrato giornaliero,** or daily ticket (€4), covers unlimited bus or train travel in the metropolitan area (including Ostia but not Fiumicino) until midnight the day of purchase; a **carta integrale settimanale** (€16) is good for a week; a three-day tourist ticket is €11.

Each bus stop *(fermata)* is marked by yellow signs, which list all routes that stop there and the key stops along those routes. Some buses run only on weekdays *(feriali)* or weekends *(festive)* while others have different routes on different days. Most buses run from about 5:30am-midnight, after which the less reliable night buses *(notturni)* take over and run at ½-1hr. intervals. The ATAC website has information on specific bus lines and their hours. It also has a handy route planner that will plot your trip by Metro and bus to practically any place in the city. The page is also available in English.

Enter buses through the front and back doors; exit through the middle door. Try not to block entries and exits as this is considered quite rude. A few useful bus routes are: **#40/64,** Vatican area, C. V. Emanuele, Largo Argentina, P. Venezia, Termini; **#81,** P. Malatesta, San Giovanni, Colosseo, Bocca della Verità, P. Venezia, Largo Argentina, V. del Corso, P. Cavour, V. Cola di Rienzo, Vatican; **#116T,** Vatican area, Via Giulia, Campo dei Fiori area, Piazza Navona area, V. del Corso, V. Veneto; **#170,** Termini, V. Nazionale, P. Venezia, Bocca della Verità, Testaccio, Stazione Trastevere, V. Marconi, P. Agricoltura; **#492,** Tiburtina, Termini, P. Barberini, P. Venezia, C. Rinascimento, P. Cavour, P. Risorgimento; **#175,** Termini, P. Barberini, V. del Corso, P. Venezia; **Linea H,** Termini to Trastevere; **#910,** Termini to Villa Borghese. Some helpful tram routes: **tram 8,** Largo di Torre d'Argentina to Trastevere; **tram 3,** Trastevere, Colosseo, San Lorenzo, Villa Borghese; and **tram 9,** P. Risorgimento, Villa Borghese, San Lorenzo. Note: some trams (the 3, for example) run as buses for significant parts of the day.

ATAC also offers *Giro Turistico*, a relaxing 3hr. circuit of the city. They provide a map and some explanation in Italian and quasi-English, whirling you around the city for a comprehensive peek at the city's primary monuments.

A popular alternative to city and tour buses are the hop-on/hop-off, open-top double-decker buses. In the last few years there has been an explosion in the number of such tours. An all-day ticket runs about €18-20, can be purchased as you board at any stop, and provides unlimited access to available seats and headphones to plug into outlets for running commentary on approaching sights in nearly every European language. Most companies follow more or less the same route, starting at Termini Station, but there are also "Christian Rome" buses and the Archeobus, which will take you to the catacombs along the Appian Way.

METRO AND COMMUTER RAIL

Mi Scusi! Mi Scusi! Romans often prepare for their descent from the bus or subway well in advance. If you are not getting off at the next stop, step away from the doors and allow people to move to the front as early as the preceding stop. They may ask you, *"Scende la prossima fermata?"* (Are you getting off at the next stop?) to which you should respond "si" or "no."

Every time they tried to dig more tracks for their subway system, the Romans discovered more ancient ruins. As a result, Rome's subway system is subpar for a city of its size. Many of Rome's sights are a trek from the nearest stop, but for covering large distances quickly, the subway beats the bus—it's comparatively fast and reliable. The two lines (A and B) of the **Metropolitana** intersect at Termini and can be reached by several entrances, including the stairway between the station and P. del Cinquecento. Entrances to Metro stations elsewhere are marked by poles with a white "M" on a red square. The subway usually runs daily 5:30am-1:30am, but due to construction of the forthcoming C line, the subway occasionally closes at 10pm. At night, bus N1 replaces Metro A and N2 replaces Metro B.

You don't have to validate your ticket to pass through the turnstiles on the subway; however, ATAC's ticket inspectors prowl stations and trains, and checks are increasingly common, so validating your ticket is wise.

There is a network of suburban rail lines that mostly connect to smaller towns to Rome. However, most of Rome is well covered by the ATAC buses, the Metro, and trams.

BY TAXI

Taxis in Rome are convenient but expensive. You can flag them down in the street, but they are easily found at stands near Termini and in major *piazze*. Ride only in yellow or white taxis, and make sure your taxi has a meter (if not, settle on a price before you get in the car). Expect to pay around €10-12 for a ride from Termini to the Vatican during the day; prices rise significantly at night. The meter starts at €2.33 (M-Sa 7am-10pm), €3.36 (Su and holidays 7am-10pm), or €4.91 (daily 10pm-7am). Surcharges are levied when heading to or from Fiumicino (€7.23) and Ciampino (€5.50), with a €1 charge per suitcase larger than 35cm by 25cm by 50cm. Standard tip is 10%. **RadioTaxi** (☎06 35 70) responds to calls, but be aware that the meter starts the moment the taxi is dispatched.

BY CAR

Driving in Rome is a bad idea. Roman drivers are aggressive, and those who drive mopeds appear ignorant of human mortality. Parking is expensive and very difficult to find, and if you don't keep your eyes peeled, you may drive into a car-free zone—certain streets are reserved for public transportation and the police—and incur a fine. Rome is also plagued with people who demand money to direct you to a parking space, even on the rare occasions when there are many spots available. Car theft and robberies are rampant, even during the day in busy areas. As if that weren't enough, gas *(benzina* in Italian*)* is exorbitantly priced at approximately €1.30 per liter.

If you are considering renting a car to travel away from Rome to explore the rest of Italy, however, you are in luck. With a vast network of narrow, winding roads, and loosely enforced speed limits, touring Italy by car is a memorable experience. Despite the initial intimidation that may come from cruising bumper to bumper on a cliffside road along the Amalfi coast, with a little bit of courage and a decent helping of driving competence, car travel opens up corners of Italy that are not easily accessible.

Rome is linked to the north and south of Italy by a great north-south highway called the **A1,** which feeds into the **Grande Raccordo Anulare (GRA),** the beltway that encircles Rome. Tolls on these roads are high; a trip to Florence can cost around €11. Avoid V. Cassia, V. Tiburtina, and V. del Mare at all costs; the ancient two-chariot lanes can't cope with modern-day traffic.

For an informal primer on European road signs and conventions, check out www.travlang.com/signs. The **Association for Safe International Road Travel (ASIRT;** ☎ +1-301-983-5252; www.asirt.org) can provide more specific information about road conditions. ASIRT considers road travel (by car or bus) to be relatively safe in Italy.

DRIVING PERMITS AND CAR INSURANCE

INTERNATIONAL DRIVING PERMIT (IDP)

If you plan to drive a car while in Italy, you must be over 18 and have an **International Driving Permit (IDP),** though certain regions will allow travelers to drive with a valid American or Canadian license for a limited number of months.

Your IDP, valid for one year, must be issued in your own country before you depart. An application for an IDP usually requires one or two photos, a current local license, an additional form of identification, and a fee. To apply, contact your home country's automobile association. Be vigilant when purchasing an IDP online or anywhere other than your home automobile association. Many vendors sell permits of questionable legitimacy for higher prices.

CAR INSURANCE

Most credit cards cover standard insurance. If you rent, lease, or borrow a car, you will need a **green card,** or **International Insurance Certificate,** to certify that you have liability insurance and that it applies abroad. Green cards can be obtained at car rental agencies, car dealers (for those leasing cars), some travel agents, and some border crossings. Rental agencies may require you to purchase theft insurance in countries that they consider to have a high risk of auto theft.

RENTING A CAR

A single traveler won't save by renting a car (especially considering the high gas prices), but four usually will. It is always significantly less expensive to reserve a car from the US than from Europe. If you can't decide between train and car travel, you may benefit from a combination of the two; RailEurope and other railpass vendors offer **rail-and-drive** packages. **Fly-and-drive** packages are often available from travel agents or airline-rental agency partnerships.

Expect to pay €260 per week (€45-90 per day). By reserving in advance, non-residents of Italy are eligible for discounts of up to 60%. Insurance is required, augmenting the rates by as much as €55 a week. Paying by credit card may give you free insurance on rentals; check with your credit card company. All agencies require either a credit card or a cash deposit of at least €155, and most take only plastic.

Reserve ahead and pay in advance if at all possible. Always check if prices quoted include tax and collision insurance; some credit card companies provide insurance, allowing their customers to decline the collision damage waiver. Ask about discounts and check the terms of insurance, particularly the size of the deductible. To rent a car from most establishments in Italy, you need to be at least 18 years old. Some agencies require renters to be 25, and most charge those 18-24 an additional insurance fee of €12 per day. Be sure to ask about the insurance coverage and deductible, and always check the fine print. At most agencies, all that's needed to rent a car is a license from home, proof that you've had it for a year, and preferably an International Driver's Permit (see above).

You can make arrangements to pick up cars at Termini, the airports, or in the city offices. You may return your car at any rental location in Italy (with an additional charge of roughly €25 north of Rome and a monumental €155 or more to the south. Before making a reservation, ask your airline or travel agent about special deals. Rental agencies in Italy include:

Alamo (in US ☎+1-877-222-9075, in Rome +39 0665 010 678; www.alamo.com).

Auto Europe (in North America ☎+1-888-223-5555, in Italy +39 172 1011; www.autoeurope.com).

Avis (in Italy ☎+ 39 199 100 133; www.avis.com).

Budget (in US ☎+1-800-527-0700, outside US +1-800-472-3325; www.budgetrentacar.com).

Europcar International (in Rome ☎+39 468 303 717; www.europcar.com).

Europe by Car (☎+1-800-223-1516; www.europebycar.com).

Hertz (in US ☎+1-800-654-3131, outside US +1-800-654-3001; www.hertz.com).

Kemwel (☎+1-800-678-0668, reservations +1-877-820-0668; www.kemwel.com).

ON THE ROAD

Italian roads range from the *autostrade*—superhighways with a 130kph (80 mph) speed limit, increased to 150kph (93 mph) in some areas—to the narrow and sometimes unpaved *strade comunali* (local roads). Highways usually charge expensive tolls, often best paid by credit card. In cities, the speed limit is usually 50kph (31 mph). Headlights must be on when driving on the *autostrada*. For driving rules and regulations, check **Moto Europa** (www.ideamerge.com/motoeuropa) or **In Italy Online** (www.initaly.com/travel/info/driving.htm).

DANGERS

Mountain roads can have steep cliffs and narrow curves; exercise caution if you must drive in the Dolomites or the Apennines. Be careful on minor roads in the countryside, as many are not well maintained and best taken at a slow and steady pace.

CAR ASSISTANCE

The **Automobile Club d'Italia (ACI)** is at the service of all drivers in Italy, with offices located throughout the country (www.aci.it). In case of breakdown, call ☎116 for assistance from the nearest ACI. On superhighways use the emergency telephones placed every 2km. For long drives in desolate areas, invest in a roadside assistance program and a cell phone, but be aware that use of phones while driving is only permitted with a hands-free device.

BY BIKE AND MOPED

Rome's cobblestone streets, dense traffic, and reckless drivers make the city a challenge for bikes and mopeds. Funerals are generally more expensive than cabs, so if you're in a real bind we'd pick the latter, but legions of Vespa-riding natives do seem to get around each day without mishap. If you're anywhere near central Rome, ATAC's new **bike** rental service is by far your cheapest and most convenient option. You can purchase a reloadable bike-sharing card at ⓂA-Lepanto, ⓂA-Spagna, or Ⓜ-Termini (all open M-Sa 7am-8pm, Su and holidays 8am-8pm). The spiffy green bikes—with baskets, naturally—can be found at nineteen stations at major sights and streets around the center. Once you remove one from its rack, you'll pay just €0.50 per half-hour or a fraction thereof. Bikes can be returned to any rack and are available 24/7. (See www. atac-bikesharing.it or call ☎06 57 003 for locations and other information.) The price of **motorini (scooters)** changes based on their size but is around €35-55 per day. Be aware that the length of a "day" sometimes depends on the shop's closing time. Try **Treno e Scooter,** on the right-hand side of P. dei Cinquecento from Termini (☎06 48 90 58 23; www.trenoescooter.191.it. Open daily 9am-2pm and 4-7pm. AmEx/MC/V). There's also **Bici & Baci,** V. del Viminale 5, in front of Termini (☎06 48 28 443 or 48 98 61 62; www.bicibaci.com. Open daily 8am-7pm. AmEx/MC/V). The minimum rental age is 16. Helmets, included with rental, are strictly required by law. Prices often include a 20% sales tax. For those just interested in an afternoon on a bike, **Enjoy Rome** offers an informative, if harrowing, tour of the city. Villa Borghese is another popular destination for biking. If you've never ridden a moped before, Rome's seven hills are not the place to start.

BY FOOT

Some of Italy's grandest scenery and Rome's historical streets can be seen only by foot. Let's Go features many daytrips, but native inhabitants and fellow travelers are the best source for tips. Professionally-run hiking and walking tours are often your best bet for navigating *la bell'Italia*. Hiking tours generally range from six to nine days long and cost US$2800-4000. The **Backpack Europe** website (www.backpackeurope.com) provides links to hiking, walking, and kayaking options throughout Italy.

KEEPING IN TOUCH

BY EMAIL AND INTERNET

While Internet is a relatively common amenity throughout Italy, Wi-Fi is not, and as a general rule, the prevalence of both decreases the further you travel from urban areas. In Rome, it may be possible to find Internet but not Wi-Fi. In smaller towns, even a basic Internet connection may be hard to come by. Rates range from €2-6 per hour. While it's possible in some places to forge a remote link with your home server, in most cases this is a much slower (and more expensive) option than using free **web-based email accounts** (e.g., ▨www.gmail.com). **Internet cafes** and the occasional free Internet terminal at a public library or university are listed in **Practical Information.** For additional cybercafes in Italy, check out http://cafe.ecs.net and www.cybercaptive.com.

 Laptop users can occasionally find internet cafes that will allow them to connect their laptops to the internet. Travelers with wireless-enabled computers may be able to take advantage of an increasing number of internet "hot spots," where they can get online for free or for a small fee. Newer computers can detect these hot spots automatically; otherwise, websites like www.jiwire.com, www.wififreespot.com, and www.wi-fihotspotlist.com can help you find them. For information on insuring your laptop while traveling, see p. 21.

WARY WI-FI. Wireless hot spots make Internet access possible in public and remote places. Unfortunately, they also pose **security risks.** Hot spots are public, open networks that use unencrypted, unsecured connections. They are susceptible to hacks and "packet sniffing"—ways of stealing passwords and other private information. To prevent problems, disable ad hoc mode, turn off file sharing and network discovery, encrypt your email, turn on your firewall, beware of phony networks, and watch for over-the-shoulder creeps.

BY TELEPHONE

CALLING HOME FROM ITALY

Prepaid phone cards are a common and relatively inexpensive means of calling abroad. Each comes with a Personal Identification Number (PIN) and a toll-free access number. You call the access number and then follow the directions to enter your PIN. To buy prepaid phone cards, check online for the best rates; www.callingcards.com is a good place to start. Online providers generally send your access number and PIN via email, with no actual "card" involved. You can also call home with prepaid phone cards purchased in Italy (see **Calling Within Italy,** see this page).

PLACING INTERNATIONAL CALLS. To call Italy from home or to call home from Italy, dial:
1. The **international dialing prefix.** To call from **Australia,** dial 0011; **Canada** or the **US,** 011; **Ireland, New Zealand,** or the **UK,** 00; **Italy,** 00.
2. The **country code** of the country you want to call. To call **Australia,** dial 61; **Canada** or the **US,** 1; **Ireland,** 353; **New Zealand,** 64; the **UK,** 44; **Italy,** 39.
3. The **city/area code.** *Let's Go* lists the city/area codes for cities and towns in Italy opposite the city or town name, next to a ☎, as well as in every phone number. If the first digit is a zero (e.g., 020 for London), omit the zero when calling from abroad (e.g., dial 20 from **Canada** to reach **London**).
4. The **local number.**

Another option is to purchase a **calling card,** linked to a major national telecommunications service in your home country. Calls are billed collect or to your account. To call home with a calling card, contact the operator for your service provider in Italy by dialing the appropriate toll-free access number.

Placing a collect call through an international operator can be expensive, but may be necessary in case of an emergency. You can frequently call collect without even possessing a company's calling card just by calling its access number and following the instructions.

CALLING WITHIN ITALY

The simplest way to call within the country is to use a coin-operated phone. Prepaid phone cards (available at newspaper kiosks and tobacco stores, or *tabaccherie*), usually save time and money in the long run.

CELLULAR PHONES

Cellular phones *(telefonini)* are a convenient and inexpensive option for those planning longer visits to Italy. Pay phones are increasingly hard to come by, making cell phones a good alternative for tourists. You won't necessarily have to deal with cell phone plans and bills; prepaid minutes are widely available and phones can be purchased cheaply or even rented, avoiding the hassle of pay phones and phone cards.

The international standard for cell phones is **Global System for Mobile Communication (GSM).** To make and receive calls in Italy you will need a GSM-compatible phone and a **SIM (Subscriber Identity Module) card,** a country-specific, thumbnail-sized chip that gives you a local phone number and plugs you into the local network. Many SIM cards are prepaid, and incoming calls are often free. You can buy additional cards or vouchers (usually available at convenience stores) to "top up" your phone. For more info on GSM phones, check out www.telestial.com, www.orange.co.uk, www.roadpost.com, or www.planetomni.com. Companies like **Cellular Abroad** (www.cellularabroad.com) rent cell phones that work in a variety of destinations around the world.

GSM PHONES. Just having a GSM phone doesn't mean you're necessarily good to go when you travel abroad. The majority of GSM phones sold in the United States operate on a different frequency (1900) than international phones (900/1800) and will not work abroad. Tri-band phones work on all three frequencies (900/1800/1900) and will operate through most of the world. Additionally, some GSM phones are SIM-locked and will only accept SIM cards from a single carrier. You'll need a SIM-unlocked phone to use a SIM card from a local carrier when you travel.

TIME DIFFERENCES

Italy is 1hr. ahead of Greenwich Mean Time (GMT) and observes Daylight Saving Time.

BY MAIL

SENDING MAIL HOME FROM ITALY

Airmail is the best way to send mail home from Italy. **Aerogrammes,** printed sheets that fold into envelopes and travel via airmail, are available at post offices. Write "airmail" or *"per posta aerea"* on the front. Most post offices charge exorbitant fees or simply refuse to send aerogrammes with enclosures. Surface mail is by far the cheapest and slowest way to send mail. It takes one to two months to cross the Atlantic and one to three to cross the Pacific—good for heavy items you won't need for a while, such as souvenirs. Delivery times and package shipping costs vary; inquire at the post office *(ufficio postale).*

SENDING MAIL TO ITALY

To ensure timely delivery, mark envelopes "airmail," *"par avion,"* or *"per posta aerea."* In addition to the standard postage system whose rates are listed below, **Federal Express** (in Australia ☎+61 13 26 10, in Canada and the US +1-800-463-3339, in Ireland +353 800 535 800, in New Zealand +64 800 733 339, in the UK +44 8456 0708 09; www.fedex.com) handles express mail services to Italy. Sending a postcard within Italy costs €0.20 while sending letters (up to 20 kg) domestically requires €7.

There are several ways to arrange pick up of letters sent to you while you are abroad. Mail can be sent via **Fermo Posta** (General Delivery) to almost any city or town in Italy with a post office, and it is generally reliable, if occasionally untimely. Address **Fermo Posta** letters like so:

Julius CEASAR

c/o Ufficio Postale Centrale

FERMO POSTA

48100 Rome

Italy

The mail will go to a special desk in the central post office, unless you specify a post office by street address or postal code. Note that the postal service may ignore this specification. It is usually safer and quicker, though more expensive, to send mail express or registered. Bring your passport (or other photo ID) for pickup; there may be a small fee. If the clerks insist that there is nothing for you, ask them to check under your first name as well. *Let's Go* lists post offices in the **Practical Information** section.

American Express's travel offices throughout the world offer a free **Client Letter Service** (mail held up to 30 days and forwarded upon request) for cardholders who contact them in advance. Some offices provide these services to non-cardholders (especially AmEx Travelers Cheque holders), but call ahead to make sure. Let's Go lists AmEx locations in **Practical Information;** for a complete list, call ☎+1-800-528-4800 or visit www.americanexpress.com/travel.

ACCOMMODATIONS

HOSTELS

Many hostels are laid out dorm-style, often with large single-sex rooms and bunk beds, although private rooms that sleep from two to four are becoming more common. They sometimes have kitchens and utensils for your use, breakfast and other meals, storage areas, laundry facilities, internet, transportation to airports, and bike or moped rentals. However, there can be drawbacks: some hostels impose a maximum stay, close during certain daytime "lockout" hours, have a curfew, don't accept reservations, or, less frequently, require that you do chores. In Italy, a dorm bed in a hostel will average around €15-25 and a private room around €25-30 per day.

A HOSTELER'S BILL OF RIGHTS. There are certain standard features that we do not include in our hostel listings. Unless we state otherwise, you can expect that every hostel has no lockout, no curfew, free hot showers, some system of secure luggage storage, and no key deposit.

HOSTELLING INTERNATIONAL

Joining the youth hostel association in your own country (listed below) automatically grants you membership privileges in **Hostelling International (HI),** a federation of national hostelling associations. Non-HI members may be allowed to stay in some hostels, but they will have to pay extra to do so. HI hostels are scattered throughout Italy and are typically less expensive than private hostels. HI's umbrella organization's website (www.hihostels.com), which lists the web addresses and phone numbers of all national associations, can be a great place to begin researching hostelling in a specific region. Other hostelling websites include www.hostels.com and www.hostelplanet.com.

Most HI hostels also honor **guest memberships**—you'll get a blank card with space for six validation stamps. Each night you'll pay a nonmember supplement and earn one guest stamp; six stamps make you a member. This system works well most of the time, but in some cases you may need to remind the hostel reception. A new membership benefit is the **FreeNites program,** which allows hostelers to gain points toward free rooms. Most student travel agencies (p. 25) sell HI cards, as do all of the national hostelling organizations listed below. All prices listed below are valid for a one-year membership.

Australian Youth Hostels Association (AYHA), 422 Kent St., Sydney, NSW 2000 (☎+61 2 9261 1111; www.yha.com.au). AUS$42, under 26 AUS$32.

Hostelling International-Canada (HI-C), 205 Catherine St., Ste. 400, Ottawa, ON K2P 1C3 (☎+1-613-237-7884; www.hihostels.ca). CDN$35, under 18 free.

Hostelling International Northern Ireland (HINI), 22-32 Donegall Rd., Belfast BT12 5JN (☎+44 28 9032 4733; www.hini.org.uk). UK£15, under 25 UK£10.

Youth Hostels Association (England and Wales), Trevelyan House, Dimple Rd., Matlock, Derbyshire DE4 3YH (☎+44 1629 592 600; www.yha.org.uk). UK£16, under 26 UK£10.

Youth Hostels Association of New Zealand Inc. (YHANZ), Level 1, 166 Moorhouse Ave., P.O. Box 436, Christchurch (☎+64 3 379 9970, in NZ 0800 278 299; www.yha.org.nz). NZ$40, under 18 free.

Hostelling International-USA, 8401 Colesville Rd., Ste. 600, Silver Spring, MD 20910 (☎+1-301-495-1240; www.hiayh.org). US$28, under 18 free.

OTHER TYPES OF ACCOMMODATIONS

HOTELS, GUESTHOUSES, AND PENSIONS

Hotel singles in Italy cost about US$40-80 (€25-50) per night, doubles US$ 60-140 (€40-90). In many lower budget establishments, you'll typically share a hall bathroom; a private bathroom will cost extra. Some hotels offer "full pension" (all meals) and "half pension" (no lunch). Smaller guesthouses and pensions are often cheaper than hotels. If you make **reservations** in writing, indicate your night of arrival and the number of nights you plan to stay. The hotel will send you a confirmation and may request payment for the first night.

BED AND BREAKFASTS (B&BS)

For a cozy alternative to impersonal hotel rooms, B&Bs (private homes with rooms available to travelers) range from acceptable to sublime. Rooms in B&Bs generally cost US$30-70 (€20-50) for a single and US$100-130 (€70-90) for a double in Italy. Many websites provide listings for B&Bs; check out **Bed & Breakfast Inns Online** (www.bbonline.com), **BedandBreakfast.com** (www. bedandbreakfast.com), or **BNBFinder.com** (www.bnbfinder.com).

AGRITURISMO

Frequently omitted by mainstream travel guides and ignored by local tourist offices, *agriturismo* is a pleasurable, leisurely, and inexpensive way to visit the Italian countryside. Local families open their homes to guests and provide reasonably-priced meals. The host family and guests gather around the table each night, sharing bottles of homemade wine, fresh vegetables from the garden, and stories that last far into the night. These houses, however, are usually only accessible by car—a tranquil remoteness that simply adds to their charm, provided that you can reach them. If you're looking to truly experience the laid-back Italian lifestyle, hearty cuisine, local wines, and sweeping countryside vistas, *agriturismo* is the best way to spend your time and money. To find *agriturismo* options in your region, consult local tourist offices or check out the **Associazione Nazionale per l'Agriturismo, l'Ambiente e il Territorio (National Association of Agrotourism, Environment and Territory;** www.agriturist.it**).**

UNIVERSITY DORMS

Many **colleges** and **universities** open their residence halls to travelers when school is not in session; some do so even during term time. Getting a room may take a couple of phone calls and advanced planning, but rates tend to be low, and many offer free local calls and Internet access. For a list of student housing opportunities in Italian cities, write to The **Italian Ministry of Education,** Vle. Trastevere 76/A, 00153 Rome (☎+39 06 58 491; www.pubblica.istruzione. it), and ask for a *Guide for Foreign Students.*

HOME EXCHANGES AND HOSPITALITY CLUBS

Home exchange offers the traveler various types of homes (houses, apartments, condominiums, villas, even castles in some cases), plus the opportunity to live like a native and cut down on accommodation fees. For more information, contact **HomeExchange.com Inc.** (☎+1-310-798-3864 or toll-free 800-877-8723; www. homeexchange.com) or **Intervac International Home Exchange** (☎05 19 17 841; www.intervac.com).

   Hospitality clubs link their members with individuals or families abroad who are willing to host travelers for free or for a small fee to promote cultural exchange and general good karma. In exchange, members usually must be willing to host travelers in their own homes. **The Hospitality Club** (www.hospitalityclub.org) is a good place to start. **Servas** (www.servas.org) is an established, more formal, peace-based organization, and requires a fee and an interview to join. An Internet search will find many similar organizations, some of which cater to special interests (e.g., women, GLBT travelers, or members of certain professions). As always, use common sense when planning to stay with or host someone you do not know.

LONG-TERM ACCOMMODATIONS

Travelers planning to stay in Italy for extended time periods may find it most cost-effective to locate an **apartment** for rent *(affittasi)*. A basic one-bedroom or studio apartment in Rome will range €500-2000 per month. Besides the rent itself, prospective tenants are frequently required to front a security deposit (usually one month's rent and the last month's rent).

   A good place to check for apartments is Rome's **craigslist** (http://rome. it.craigslist.it/), a forum for renters and rentees where you can see others' listings or post your own housing needs. For regional listings, try http://affittistudenti.studenti.it and www.secondamano.it. Also check out http://liveinrome. com and www.romepower.com for more apartment listings.

SPECIFIC CONCERNS

SUSTAINABLE TRAVEL

Italy's government has focused on cultural restoration, while natural resources are overlooked and underappreciated. As the number of travelers on the road rises, the detrimental effect they can have on natural environments is an increasing concern. *Let's Go* promotes the philosophy of sustainable travel. Through a sensitivity to issues of ecology and sustainability, today's travelers can be a powerful force in preserving and restoring the places they visit.

Ecotourism, a rising trend in sustainable travel, focuses on the conservation of natural habitats—mainly, on how to use them to build up the economy without exploitation or overdevelopment. Travelers can make a difference by doing advance research, by supporting organizations and establishments that pay attention to their carbon "footprint," and by patronizing establishments that strive to be environmentally friendly. Recently, ecotourism has been getting more creative, interesting and diverse. Opportunities in Italy can be found at **www.ecoturismo-italia.it,** an Italian nonprofit that works in conjunction with other international organizations. For information on environmental conservation, see the resources below or the **Beyond Tourism** (p. 79) section of this book.

ECOTOURISM RESOURCES. For more information on environmentally responsible tourism, contact one of the organizations below:

Conservation International, 2011 Crystal Dr., Ste. 500, Arlington, VA 22202, USA (☎+1-800-429-5660 or 703-341-2400; www.conservation.org).

Green Globe 21, Green Globe vof, Verbenalaan 1, 2111 ZL Aerdenhout, the Netherlands (☎+31 23 544 0306; www.greenglobe.com).

International Ecotourism Society, 1301 Clifton St. NW, Ste. 200, Washington, DC 20009, USA (☎+1-202-506-5033; www.ecotourism.org).

United Nations Environment Program (**UNEP;** www.unep.org).

WOMEN TRAVELERS

Women exploring on their own inevitably face some additional safety concerns. Single women can consider staying in hostels that offer single rooms that lock from the inside or in religious organizations with single-sex rooms. It's a good idea to stick to centrally located accommodations and to avoid solitary late-night treks or Metro rides. Always carry extra cash for a phone call, bus, or taxi. **Hitchhiking is never safe** for lone women or even for two women traveling together. Look as if you know where you're going and approach older women or couples for directions if you're lost or feeling uncomfortable in your surroundings. Generally, the less you look like a tourist, the better off you'll be. Dress conservatively, especially when visiting Roman churches and religious sites. Wearing a conspicuous wedding band sometimes helps to prevent unwanted advances.

Your best answer to verbal harassment is no answer at all; feigning deafness, sitting motionless, and staring straight ahead at nothing in particular will usually do the trick. The extremely persistent can sometimes be dissuaded by a firm, loud, and very public *"Vai via"* or *"Vattene"* ("Go Away!"). Don't hesitate to seek out a *poliziotto* (police officer) or a passerby if you are being harassed.

Memorize the emergency numbers in places you visit, and consider carrying a whistle on your keychain. A self-defense course will both prepare you for a potential attack and raise your level of awareness of your surroundings (see **Personal Safety,** p. 20). Also, it might be a good idea to talk with your doctor about the health concerns that women face when traveling (p. 24).

GLBT TRAVELERS

It is difficult to characterize the Italian attitude toward gay, lesbian, bisexual, and transgender (GLBT) travelers. Homophobia is still in issue in some regions, but Rome has easily accessible gay scenes. Away from the larger cities, however, gay social life may be difficult to find. The online newspaper **365gay.com** has a travel section. **Babilonia** and **Guida Gay Italia** can be found at newsstands, and **Pride** and **GayClubbing** (both free) can be found at most gay venues. Rome also offers a variety of gay *discoteche* (nightclubs) and bars. Listed below are contact organizations, mail-order catalogs, and publishers that offer materials addressing some specific concerns. **Out and About** (www.planetout.com) offers a website and a weekly newsletter addressing gay travel concerns.

Arcigay, V. Don Minzoni 18, 40121 Bologna (☎051 64 93 055; www.arcigay.it). Provides resources for homosexuals and helps combat homophobia throughout the peninsula. Holds dances and other special events. Website contains addresses and phone numbers of city centers.

Gay.It, V. Ravizza 22/E, 56121 Pisa (www.gay.it). Provides info on gay life in Italy. Associated website in English (www.gayfriendlyitaly.com) gives regional info on nightlife, homophobia, gay events, and more.

Giovanni's Room, 345 S. 12th St., Philadelphia, PA 19107, USA (☎+1-215-923-2960; www.giovannisroom.com). An international lesbian and gay bookstore with mail-order service (carries many of the publications listed below).

International Lesbian and Gay Association (ILGA), 17 Rue de la Charité, 1210 Brussels, Belgium (☎+32 2 502 2471; www.ilga.org). Provides political information, such as homosexuality laws of individual countries.

TRAVELERS WITH DISABILITIES

Travelers with disabilities should inform airlines and hotels of their disabilities when making reservations, as some time may be needed to prepare special accommodations. Call ahead to restaurants, museums, and other facilities to find out if they're wheelchair accessible. Guide-dog owners should inquire as to the quarantine policies of each destination country.

Rail is probably the most convenient form of transport for disabled travelers in Europe: many stations have ramps, and some trains have wheelchair lifts, special seating areas, and specially equipped toilets. All Eurostar, some InterCity (IC), and some EuroCity (EC) trains are **wheelchair-accessible,** and CityNightLine trains and Conrail trains feature special compartments. For those who wish to rent cars, some major **car-rental** agencies (e.g., Hertz) offer hand-controlled vehicles. Look for pamphlets on accessibility from local tourist offices; a list of publications and where to find them can be found at **www.coinsociale.it.** A good wheelchair accessible tour of Rome is available at **www.slowtrav.com/italy/accessible/rome.**

Accessible Italy, Via C. Manetti 34, 47891 Dogana, Repubblica di San Marino (☎+39 378 05 49 94 11 11; www.accessibleitaly.com). Provides tours to Italy for travelers with disabilities. Proceeds go toward improving handicap-access to attractions in Italy. Also organizes handicap-accessible weddings in Italy.

Accessible Journeys, 35 W. Sellers Ave., Ridley Park, PA 19078, USA (☎+1-800-846-4537; www.disabilitytravel.com). Designs tours for wheelchair users and slow walkers. The site has tips and forums for all travelers.

Mobility International USA (MIUSA), 132 E. Broadway, Ste. 343, Eugene, OR 97401, USA (☎+1-541-343-1284; www.miusa.org). Provides a variety of books and other publications containing information for travelers with disabilities.

Society for Accessible Travel and Hospitality (SATH), 347 5th Ave., Ste. 605, New York, NY 10016, USA (☎+1-212-447-7284; www.sath.org). An advocacy group that publishes free online travel information. Annual membership US$49, students and seniors US$29.

MINORITY TRAVELERS

Like much of Western Europe, Italy has experienced a wave of immigration from Africa, Eastern Europe, and South America in recent years that has spurred some racial tension, especially over competition in the local economy. Particularly in southern Italy, travelers belonging to racial minorities or members of non-Christian religions may feel unwelcome or experience some hostility. Tension has always existed in Italy regarding gypsies from Romania and other parts of Eastern Europe. In terms of safety, there is no easy answer. Men and women should always travel in groups and avoid unsafe parts of town. The best answer to verbal harassment is often not to acknowledge it. A number of advocacy groups for immigrant rights have sprouted up throughout Italy, including **Associazione Almaterra** (☎+39 01 12 46 70 02; www.arpnet.it) and **NOSOTRAS** (☎+39 05 52 77 63 26; www.nosotras.it). The following organizations work to combat discrimination in Rome and can give advice and help in the event of an encounter with racism.

Associazione Arci, V. dei Monti di Pietralata 16, 00157 Rome (☎+39 06 41 50 95 00; www.attivarci.it). Extensive organization that promotes citizen rights, democracy, and inclusivity. Fights to end discrimination and racism on the peninsula.

Casa dei Diritti Sociali FOCUS, V. dei Mille 6, 00185 Rome (☎+39 06 44 64 61 13; www.dirittisociali.org). Volunteer organization promoting solidarity with and among immigrant populations and multiculturalism through youth outreach and political advocacy.

DIETARY CONCERNS

With all of Italy's delicious carnivorous offerings, vegetarians may feel left out. While there are not many strictly vegetarian restaurants in Italy, it is not difficult to find vegetarian meals. To avoid confusion in restaurants, make sure you tell your waiter *"Non mangio carne"* ("I don't eat meat") or say that you would like your pizza or pasta sauce *"senza carne, per favore"* ("without meat, please"). Before you head to Italy, check out the **Italian Vegetarian Association (AVI),** V. XXV Aprile 41, 20026 Novate Milanese, Milano (www.vegetariani.it), which also offers *Good Vegetarian Food* (Italian Vegetarian Association, 2004; €12), a guide to vegetarian tourism in Italy.

Vegetarians will also find numerous resources in the travel section of **The Vegetarian Resource Group's** website, at www.vrg.org, as well as www.vegdining. com, www.happycow.net, and www.vegetariansabroad.com.

Lactose intolerance also does not have to be an obstacle to eating well in Italy. Though it may seem like everybody but you is devouring pizza and gelato, there are myriad ways for the lactose intolerant to indulge in local cuisine. In restaurants ask for items without *latte* (milk), *formaggio* (cheese), *burro* (butter), or *crema* (cream); or order the cheeseless delicacy, *pizza marinara*.

Travelers who keep **kosher** should contact synagogues in larger cities for info on kosher restaurants. Your own synagogue or college Hillel should have access to lists of Jewish institutions across the nation. Check out **www.shamash. org/kosher/** for an extensive database of kosher establishments in Italy. If you are strict in your observance, you may have to prepare your own food on the road. A good resource is the *Jewish Travel Guide*, edited by Michael Zaidner (Vallentine Mitchell; US$18). Travelers looking for **halal** restaurants may find www.zabihah.com a useful resource.

LET'S GO ONLINE. Plan your next trip on our newly redesigned website, **www.letsgo.com.** It features the latest travel info on your favorite destinations as well as tons of interactive features: make your own itinerary, read blogs from our trusty Researchers, browse our photo library, watch exclusive videos, check out our newsletter, find travel deals, and buy new guides. We're always updating and adding new features, so check back often!

A Dead Language Lives
A Young Classicist Experiences Italy Yesterday and Today

Although I had heard of Father Reginald Foster as a child, it was only seven years later as a Classics major that I made the pilgrimage to Rome to study with Fr. Reggie, one of the Vatican's chief Latinists. I had traveled to Italy several times before and thought I would immerse myself exclusively in the old lingua franca. But I soon found that the more I read and spoke Latin, the more I came to understand and appreciate the modern Italian language and culture around me.

Since class did not begin until 2pm, I spent the mornings wandering. The irresistible scents wafting from the bakery on a side street off Vle. di Trastevere, the midday street festival in the Jewish Ghetto, or the cats prowling around the Mausoleum of Augustus are the city's best attractions—and are conveniently free.

In the afternoon, I journeyed back to the basement schoolroom at the top of the Gianicolo Hill. Fr. Reggie teaches Latin as if it were a living language. He often began with musings—in Latin, naturally—on his arduous commute to work in the Vatican that morning in the face of the two-week-long taxi strike or on the intricacies of the national rail service. He devoted a portion of class every week to translating acta diurna (headlines) from English-language news magazines into Latin. We read everything from Thomas More to 1999 Papal marriage court decisions.

After three 1½hr. sessions, we would break for an evening of casual Latin conversation or reading sub arboribus (under the trees) in the garden of the Carmelite monastery.

Because of the length and pace of the course, I engaged Rome as a resident rather than as a tourist. Every day, during the break after the first class, I would wander down the street to the Star Café, where Remo, the jovial owner, would give me an espresso with an extra cookie. I spent the second recess selecting fruits from the neighborhood vendor. I got to know my neighborhood, Trastevere, through regular excursions to the nearby cheese shop and Standa supermarket and morning runs up the slopes of the Gianicolo hill and through the Doria Pamphilj Gardens. This routine helped ensure that I was not just studying a "dead language" and insulating myself from the very living city.

My Latin and Italian experiences came together while watching the final match of the World Cup with 200,000 fans in the Circus Maximus, the old Roman racetrack. The triumphant march of the azzurri through the tournament fostered a camaraderie that manifested itself in distinctly Italian ways. With gleeful grins, the owners of a local pizzeria not far from Fr. Reggie's class carved up watermelons and offered them gratis to us after the semifinal win over Germany. The victory over France even inspired T-shirts with a Latin slogan—a welcome sight despite a grammatical error.

> "I wasn't studying a 'dead language' and tuning out the living city around me"

A traveler to Rome armed with knowledge of Latin can unlock mysteries of the Eternal City that would remain otherwise indecipherable. Latin inscriptions everywhere tell stories of ceremony, betrayal, victory, and defeat. Engaging the language in Fr. Reggie's way—as a living embodiment of a humanistic tradition—gives the traveler a sense of how Italy has evolved into what it is today. It doesn't take long to realize that Rome is a city with an amazing past; Latin and its connection to Italian bridges that gap between the Rome of Caesar and chariots and the Rome of Prodi and Vespas.

Clem Wood has spent summers in both Florence and Rome. He graduated from Harvard in the spring of 2008 with an A.B. in Classics and plans to return to Italy for further adventures and studies in the near future.

LIFE AND TIMES

HISTORY

IN PRINCIPIO ERAT ROMA

Arms, and the man I sing, who, forc'd by fate,
And haughty Juno's unrelenting hate,
    Expell'd and exil'd, left the Trojan shore.
    Long labors, both by sea and land, he bore,
    And in the doubtful war, before he won
    The Latian realm, and built the destin'd town.
Virgil, *The Aeneid* (translated by John Dryden)

Once upon a pagan time, **Aeneas** (the son of Venus, according to his dad) found himself more than a little fed up with the wave of certain undesirable elements (i.e., Greeks) streaming into his native Troy. Thinking fast, he threw his aging father in a backpack and took off, stopping just long enough to sleep with Dido, Queen of Carthage before settling down in the sunny land of the Latins. Pleased with the climate, friendly peoples, and lax rules about who gets to be king, he married a nearby princess and stole everything the locals owned—including their language, Latin. At this point, Virgil's *Aeneid* leaves off, but that's scarcely all there is to say on the matter.

A few generations later, according to the ancient Roman historian **Livy**, a Vestal "Virgin" named Rhea Silvia, a distant descendant of Aeneas, gave birth to a bouncing pair of baby boys allegedly fathered by Mars, the god of war. Unexpected pregnancies weren't really an option for someone in her profession (no maternity leave), and so her cruel uncle set her twins **Romulus** and **Remus** adrift in the Tiber. Luckily, the boys were found by a motherly she-wolf who had just lost her cubs, and thought the tiny refugees suitable substitutes. The party was soon broken up, however, when a shepherd came along and "rescued" the twins. (Italian archaeologists reported in 2007 that they'd found the cave where the she-wolf reputedly kept the kids, which shows just how much history lies underground around here.) Despite their troubled childhood, the twins managed to found a city on the Palatine Hill on April 21, 753 BC. A quick spat over the merits of various names for the new 'burg—"Rome" vs. "Reme"—left Remus dead and Romulus as the city's first fratricidal king.

Though the stories about gods and wolf-boys are probably a bit off, the timeline is about right. Most archaeologists agree that the city of Rome was probably founded some time in the eighth century BC, or a little earlier. The people who first ruled Rome were probably the **Sabine tribe;** three

753 BC Rome is founded. History begins.

625 BC Ancus Marcius builds the first prison in Rome, giving him a place to put captives from the local conquered tribes while he decides what to do with them.

616 BC The Etruscan kings come to power in Rome and become known for tyranny.

509 BC The Roman Republic is founded and becomes known for tyranny.

390 BC In one of France's most recent military triumphs, the Gauls sack Rome. Romans build a better wall around the city.

legendary Sabine kings (Numa Pompilius, Tullus Hostilius, and Ancus Martius) are credited with starting most of the city's oldest traditions, like conquering everyone nearby.

The Sabine kings were followed by the **Etruscans,** a tribe from farther north that had been ruling a pretty decent territory even before Rome got started. (See **Cerveteri,** p. 255, and **Tarquinia,** p. 255.) Responsible for the adaptation of the Latin language and the Latinization of the Greek gods, Etruscan kings inaugurated their control of Rome by building the **Circus Maximus** to give the city a place to watch horse-races. Some remains of their civilization can still be seen: notably, the Etruscans built the **Cloaca Maxima** (p. 142), the pride and joy of the Roman sewer system. Their rule came to an end when Sextus, the son of the king Tarquinius Superbus, raped the chaste Roman matron Lucretia, driving her to suicide. Outraged, her father and his friend Lucius Junius Brutus led the Roman populace to kick out the Tarquins and found the **first Roman Republic.**

Free from Etruscan rule, the Romans began to breastfeed their bouncing baby republic. Originally, the government was an oligarchy in which land-owning patricians gathered in the Senate to make laws, hear trials, and declare war. A complex bureaucracy quickly grew up, in which *praetores* (judicial officers), *quaestores* (tax collectors), *aediles* (magistrates), and tribunes oversaw the city's burgeoning infrastructure. Meanwhile, *censores* watched over the public morals (thus modern "censorship" was born). From its power base in the Tiber valley, the city expanded, conquering neighbors with astounding efficiency. In 395 BC, Etruscan power was put down for good when the Romans captured Veii, the Etruscans' chief city. Southern Italy was made safe for Romans in 275 BC, when Pyrrhus, the Greek ruler of Tarentum, was halted at the **Battle of Beneventum.**

133 BC Tiberius Gracchus is murdered for advocating land reform.

121 BC Tiberius' brother Gaius Gracchus, a slow learner, is murdered for advocating land reform.

73 BC Spartacus inspires a great Stanley Kubrick movie.

45 BC Julius Caesar names himself Dictator for Life. "Life" lasts one more year.

GROWING UP AS A REPUBLIC...

After the conquest of Italy, the republic waged a series of **Punic Wars** (264-146 BC), against Carthage (modern-day Tunisia) for control of key Mediterranean trade routes and territory in Spain and Sicily. It was during the second of these wars that the Carthaginian **Hannibal**—no relation to Lecter—famously marched his elephants and army up through Spain and across the Alps. He swooped down the peninsula, surprising a series of Roman generals, and made it all the way to the walls of Rome, but failed to breach them. The campaign devolved into a cat-and-mouse game with Roman general Fabius Maximus, who eluded the overeager Hannibal for several years until the starving Carthaginians refused to play anymore and took their tired elephants home. Carthage was decisively defeated at Zama, in Africa, in 202 BC by another great Roman general, Scipio Africanus. Pressing the advantage, Cato the Elder encouraged Romans to raze the powerless Carthage in the **Third Punic War** of 146 BC, ending every speech (no matter what it was about) with *Carthago delenda est* ("Carthage must be destroyed!"). Rumor has it that the victorious Roman soldiers sowed the Carthaginian fields with salt, killing the plants forever, to keep the city from causing trouble again.

Traditionally, Roman society had been austere and pious, but drunk with a heady mix of bloodlust and riches, it became a veritable swamp of greed and corruption. Yeoman farmers were pushed off their land by avaricious owners and driven into slavery or starvation. Less than grateful, the locals protested; popular demands for land redistribution led to riots against the corrupt patricians. At the same time, the local Italian tribes grew tired of being drafted into the Roman army and demanded full citizenship. These claims culminated in the **Social War** (91-87 BC), as tribes throughout the peninsula fought successfully for the right to vote like a Roman.

Fed up, **Sulla,** the general who led Roman troops during the conflict, marched on Rome (traditionally a demilitarized zone) and seized control of the city in a military coup. Over 1500 nobles and senators were ordered executed without trial. Sulla's strong-arm tactics set a dangerous precedent for the Republic, as generals began to amass private armies funded by huge personal fortunes. In 73 BC, **Spartacus,** rebellious gladiatorial slave, led an army of as many as 120,000 slaves and farmers in a two-year rampage down the peninsula. When the dust cleared, 6000 slaves had been crucified, and **Pompey the Great,** an associate of Sulla, took control of Rome.

Disallowed by the Senate from ruling alone, Pompey ran the city with **Julius Caesar** and **Crassus,** forming the **First Triumvirate.** The threesome went sour—as they so often do—and Caesar, the charismatic conqueror of the Gauls, emerged victorious, having Pompey assassinated in 48 BC. Meanwhile, legend says, Crassus had molten gold poured down his throat somewhere in Asia Minor. Caesar's reign was brief but memorable; a small senatorial faction led by his erstwhile friend **Brutus** assassinated him on the **Ides of March** in 44 BC, adding *"Et tu, Brute?"* ("You too, Brutus?") to popular vernacular. In the ensuing power vacuum, a **Second Triumvirate** was formed. This time the ruling all-stars were made up of Caesar's grand-nephew and adopted son, **Octavian; Marc Antony** (soon to be tangled up with that royal hussy **Cleopatra** and sent off to Africa); and **Lepidus,** a no-account rascal. Octavian soon declared war on Marc Antony and Cleopatra, and spanked them soundly—so soundly, in fact, that they killed themselves in 30 BC.

... AND BECOMING AN EMPIRE

Under his new name **Augustus,** Octavian consolidated power and began assembling an imperial government in 27 BC. His reign (27 BC-AD 14) is considered the golden age of

42 BC Antony and Cleopatra start gettin' it on.

19 BC Virgil finishes his *Aeneid.* Classics professors everywhere rejoice that they have something to read other than the Iliad and Odyssey.

LIFE AND TIMES

8 BC Augustus names the month of August after himself. (Julius Caesar had already taken July.)

AD 37-41 Caligula rules Rome, attempts to make his horse Incitatus a consul and priest, dresses up as various male and female gods, tells his soldiers to steal seashells to symbolize his "defeat of the ocean," and is generally insane.

AD 69 After Nero's death leaves it unclear who's on top, four separate emperors take the throne within a year. Vespasian finally sets things back up right.

AD 79 Mount Vesuvius erupts, destroying Pompeii and Herculaneum, and showing modern archaeologists exactly what a Roman town looked like right before a volcanic eruption.

80 The Colosseum hosts its inaugural games.

Rome, a flourishing of culture ushering in the 200 years of the **Pax Romana (Roman Peace).** Literature flourished, including the heroic sort (Virgil's *Aeneid*) and the racy sort (Ovid's *Ars Amoris*). Augustus's power was not only political: he declared himself a god, paving the way for all sorts of mischief among future emperors. Nonetheless, Rome benefited from a huge building boom, which produced a new **forum** (p. 131) and the first **Pantheon** (p. 156). Even in peacetime, though, the army got plenty of exercise, as the emperor's generals busied themselves hacking up the Germans.

The descendants of Augustus proved unequal to the task of world government. Drunk with megalomania, they slipped into fevers of debauchery and insanity. **Tiberius** (AD 14-37), who allegedly turned the island of Capri into a hedonic paradise, ushered in an era of decadence. Deranged **Caligula** (who once made his horse consul), drooling **Claudius,** and sadistically wacky **Nero** each drained the treasury to support their lifestyles. In AD 64, much of Rome was burned to the ground in a great fire; Nero may or may not have been responsible for the blaze, but he certainly took advantage of the situation by building himself a new house, the **Domus Aurea** (p. 147). Moreover, Nero found a fine set of scapegoats for the fire in the early Christians. Common Romans were entertained and appeased watching Christians dressed in the hides of animals getting torn to shreds by savage beasts.

Tired of his quirks, the Senate "persuaded" Nero to commit suicide in 68. **Vespasian** (69-79) cleaned up Nero's mess, tearing down the Domus Aurea and starting to build the **Colosseum** (p. 134); his sons **Titus** (79-81) and **Domitian** (81-96) continued in Vespasian's footsteps. The Antonine emperors, starting with **Nerva** (96-98), marked the apex of the Empire. Spanish-born emperor **Trajan** (98-117) expanded the Empire to its greatest size, conquering Dacia (modern Romania) and the Danube region with feats of engineering and tactical brilliance. Trajan died while conquering Persia, and the general **Hadrian** (118-138) managed to *carpe diem* his way right into the throne. Hadrian preferred philosophy to war and decided to focus his energies on redecorating Rome with his own architectural designs, including another **Pantheon** (p. 156) and his colossal mausoleum, now **Castel Sant'Angelo** (p. 165).

Unfortunately, it was all downhill after Hadrian. The city clung to its status as *Caput Mundi* (head of the world) until the death of the philosopher-emperor **Marcus Aurelius** in 180, by which time the Empire had grown too large to defend. Emperors, forced to relegate power and money to generals in the field, lay vulnerable to military coups. The tumultuous third century saw no fewer than 30 emperors—only one of them lucky enough to die of natural causes. Despite some enlightened administrations, the brutality and depravity of despots like **Commodus** (see the movie *Gladiator* for an embellished account), **Caracalla** (see **Baths of Caracalla**, p. 153), and the confused **Elagabalus** (who believed he was the sun god), did much to undermine the stability of the Empire. Even Russell Crowe couldn't have held the city together at this point.

CHRIST RISEN, ROME FALLEN

By the third century, Rome was in poor shape. **Aurelian** (270-275) thought that the surest way to solve the city's military and economic crises was to build a wall around it. **Diocletian** (284-305) secured control of the fragmented Empire in 284, established order, and subdivided the Empire into four more manageable parts. He also intensified the persecution of Christians, but found the growing religion more than he could handle. By the end of Diocletian's reign, approximately 30,000 Christians lived in Rome.

After Diocletian, the fortunes of Christianity took a turn for the better. Gallerius, ruling the western part of the Empire, granted freedom of worship to Christians in 311. In 312, while battling it out with Maxentius for the imperial throne, **Constantine** (312-337) saw a huge cross in the sky along with the phrase *"In hoc signo vinces"* ("By this sign you shall conquer"). Figuring he had nothing to lose, Constantine quickly put crosses on all his soldiers' shields; sure enough, victory followed, and the next year Constantine's **Edict of Milan** promised not to kill anyone for their religion. Despite the attempts of **Julian the Apostate** (361-363) to revive old Roman rituals, Christianity became the dominant religion. In 391, **Theodosius** (379-395) issued an edict against paganism.

Constantine hastened the end of Rome's supremacy by moving the capital east to **Byzantium** (which he humbly renamed **Constantinople**) in 330. Right on cue, armies of northern barbarians knocked politely on Rome's crumbling fortifications, then proceeded to steal anything not nailed down. Alaric, king of the **Visigoths,** sacked the city. In 410, another sacker-extraordinaire, **Attila the Hun,** arrived on tour in 452, but fast-talking **Pope Leo I** convinced him to pillage elsewhere. Unfortunately for the city, three years later **Genseric the Vandal** did less listening and more pillaging. In 476, the Western Roman Empire was finally done in when **Odoacer the Goth** ousted Romulus Augustulus. Gothic rule wasn't such a bad thing, though: under Odoacer and his son Theodoric, Roman life proceeded peacefully.

DARK TIMES

The Byzantine emperor **Justinian** brutally conquered much of the western division between 535 and 554, and imposed the *corpus juris*, or codified law of the Empire, which served as Europe's legal model for 500 years. By the sixth century, the Eternal City, once home to nearly a million people, supported only several thousand. When **King Totila** of the Goths pillaged the aqueducts in 546, the city's fate was sealed. The hills of Rome, once the place for Roman domiciles, gave way to the suddenly more appealing neighborhoods on the Tiber.

313 The Edict of Milan grants everyone, especially Christians, freedom of worship.

410 Celebrating the 800-year anniversary of the Gaul's sack of Rome, the Visigoths sack Rome.

476 Rome falls. History ends, temporarily.

554 The Byzantine Empire under Justinian finally conquers Italy at the Battle of Casilinum. (Or "re-conquers Italy," depending on your point of view.)

LIFE AND TIMES

756 The Donation of Pepin makes the Pope head of a brand-new Catholic theocracy.

904-964 The Church of Rome beats Hugh Hefner by a thousand years in the race to establish the world's first "pornocracy."

In these days some of the most famous neighborhoods of Rome—**Trastevere, Campo de' Fiori,** and the area around **Piazza Navona**—were settled. Starvation and plague ran rampant in ramshackle alleyways near the river, while periodic invasions by barbarians lowered property values.

Rome owed its salvation from the turbulence of the Dark Ages in large part to wealthy popes who attracted cash-laden pilgrims and invoked the wrath of God to intimidate would-be invaders. **Pope Gregory the Great** (590-604) devised efficient strategies for distributing food and spreading the word of God across Europe; centuries later, John Calvin (not a fan of the Catholics in general) was still impressed enough with Gregory's work to call him "the last good Pope."

POWER POLITICS AND PHILANDERING POPES

From the sixth century on, the Popes walked a dangerous tight-rope between the power of the Byzantine Empire in the south and the German Lombards to the north. Fortunately, no one plays power politics like a Pope. When the Lombards started getting too strong, **Pope Stephen II** invited the Frankish warlord **Pepin the Short** to invade. Naturally, Pepin won and as a thank-you for the invite gave the Pope control over the land from Rome to Ravenna. That **"Donation of Pepin"** started up the independent **Papal States,** which would remain a separate nation ruled by the Pope until 1870.

The Popes and the Franks stayed close; on Christmas Day, 800, Pope Leo III slipped a crown on the head of Pepin's son **Charlemagne** and declared him "Emperor of the Romans." Unfortunately, Charlemagne's death in 814 set off another 200 years of anarchy as his descendants killed each other for the dubious privilege of ruling Europe.

In 846, Muslim **Saracens** rowed up the Tiber and plundered several basilicas. Many felt this was God's retribution for clerical misbehavior—not surprising, given the degree of licentiousness and vice in the medieval Church. The post-humous trial of **Pope Formosus** gives a pretty good idea of how weird things were getting. Claiming that Formosus had violated canonical law, Formosus's successor **Pope Stephen VI** dug up his buried body and dressed him in ecclesiastical robes to attend a "cadaver synod." After a poor defense, the corpse was convicted on all counts, including coveting the papacy, and, confusingly, perjury. Its three blessing fingers were severed (one can never be too careful), and the corpse formerly known as Formosus was chucked into the Tiber. Pope Stephen himself was later murdered, the next pope was overthrown, and the pope after that was also done-in.

The papacy hit rock-bottom when **Pope Sergius III** was appointed in 904. His mistress **Marioza**—yes, mistress—had so much influence in the city that later historians took to calling the period a "pornocracy" or **Rule of Harlots.** We're not kidding. Marioza's grandson became Pope in 955 as **John XII,** thus carrying on a proud family tradition of bringing vice to the papacy. Getting his priorities straight, John installed a harem at the Vatican shortly after his father's death, then suffered a stroke while in bed with a married woman in 964. On the plus side, John crowned German monarch **Otto I** as **Holy Roman Emperor;** Otto, however, changed his mind and conquered Rome. For the next century, the pope was picked by the Emperor, which at least calmed things down for a while.

In 1075, **Pope Hildebrand** demanded an end to the Holy Roman Emperor's interference with the Church, forcing Emperor **Henry VI,** whom he had excommunicated, to beg in the snow for forgiveness. His pleading turned out to be deceitful; the next time the Emperor was excommunicated, he laid siege to Rome, and Hildebrand's followers jumped ship. In 1084, Norman conqueror **Robert Guiscard** remembered—ahead of schedule—that Rome was due for its tercentennial sacking and made convincing work of it.

KEEPIN' IT PAPAL

Romans received a measure of self-rule in the 1122 **Concordat of Worms,** which transferred the balance of power from the Emperor to the Church. Tipsy on its gains, the Church soon came to a predictably advanced state of corruption. A secular senate was formed in 1143, but a few hangings later, in 1155, power over the city returned to the only English pope ever picked, **Adrian IV.**

In 1188, during the papacy of **Clement III** (a Roman by birth), the rebellious Senate and the Church struck a bargain. The papacy's (super)powers were accepted, and members of the senate swore their loyalty to the pope. In exchange, the Church agreed to recognize the city of Rome as a commune, with the power to declare war or peace. This agreement let the Popes come home to Rome and paved the way for the unprecedented power of **Pope Innocent III.** Innocent excommunicated England's **King John,** declared the Magna Carta null and void, and fought heresy with a vengeance. He further declared the Pope to be Vicar of Christ on Earth, "set midway between God and Man," in charge of "the whole world." Innocent's power over the city itself, however, was weak: the citizens maintained earlier reforms, leading to a period of widespread prosperity, if not peace.

Boniface VIII, elected in 1294, antagonized nearly every ruler in Europe with a string of excommunications and the papal edict *Unam Sanctam,* which decreed that it was necessary for salvation that every living thing be subject to the Pope. Fed up, the French assaulted Boniface in his home and accused him of such crimes as sodomy and keeping a pet demon; poor Boniface died of shock. No word on who took the pet demon. His successor, the Frenchman **Clement V,** moved the papacy to **Avignon,** France, where it stayed for most of the 14th century, giving Rome a well-deserved break. Freed from the Church, the city struggled to find peace, but

1305 Pope Clement V moves the Papal Court to Avignon. Rome takes a deep breath.

1378 Pope Gregory IX brings the Papal Court back from Avignon. Rome heaves a deep sigh.

LIFE AND TIMES

feuding between the Orsini and Colonna families and the outbreak of the **Black Death** in 1348 kept Rome exciting.

At the behest of St. Catherine of Siena, Pope Gregory XI agreed to return the papacy to Rome in 1377, restoring the city's greatest source of income. Not everyone was happy with the decision, though, and for a while the **Great Schism** (1378-1417) split the church between two Popes: one in Rome and one in Avignon. A third popped up in Pisa for a while, but that didn't last long. Finally, the **Council of Constance** (1414-1418) tidied matters up and settled the Popes in Rome for good. Good call, Constance.

1506 Pope Julius II starts the building of St. Peter's Basilica in Rome, which would take 120 years to complete.

1527 Seeing no reason the Gauls and Visigoths should have all the fun, the Holy Roman Emperor sacks Rome.

1633 In one of the less scientifically-minded episodes of the Inquisition, Pope Urban VII puts Galileo on trial for heresy.

LIFE AND TIMES

RENAISSANCE AND BAROQUE

Taking charge in 1417, **Pope Martin V** initiated a period of Renaissance urbanity and absolute rule in Rome that lasted until 1870. No-nonsense Martin widened and paved roads, and buildings in new Renaissance styles went up. **Julius II** (1503-13) began an ambitious building program, setting out plans for Rome in general and for St. Peter's in particular—ever heard of the **Sistine Chapel?** (p. 198). He hired **Bramante,** who demolished medieval Rome with such enthusiasm and intent that Raphael nicknamed him *il Ruinante*.

When young priest **Martin Luther** made a visit to Rome in 1510, he was sorely disappointed by the city's aesthetic indulgence and spiritual dissolution. He was revolted by the sight of Raphael's ornate *Stanze in the Vatican*, in which Christian and pagan symbols mingled—in the buff, no less. While the pope went "triumphing about with fair-decked stallions [and] the priests gabbled Mass," Luther went about writing the 95 Theses that kicked off the **Protestant Reformation.** After excommunicating Luther, **Pope Leo X** (1513-1521) asserted his interest in the humanities, drawing up plans for a new St. Peter's dome and commissioning artists Michelangelo and Raphael. To support their caviar tastes, Renaissance popes taxed Romans and their country cousins; Lazio and Umbria soon filed for bankruptcy, and much of the distressed agricultural population up and left.

Things got violent with another sack of Rome, this one an intense eight-day pillage by German warriors, Spanish marauders, and 15,000 angry Lutherans in May 1527. After political conflict between **Pope Clement VII** and Holy Roman Emperor **Charles V,** the Emperor's bloodthirsty troops stormed through the city, destroying everyone and everything in sight. Religion got no respect; one priest was murdered because he refused to kneel and give Holy Communion to a donkey. Clement VII only escaped by holing himself up for six months in Castel Sant'Angelo (p. 165) until Charles V managed to get his men under control.

Pope Paul III, disappointed by the sack, set up the **Inquisition** in 1542. It took hold remarkably well, and the burning of books, infidels, and freethinkers carried on until the mid-17th century, when all of Rome was clearly in line and behaving.

Powerful families and the papacy were still hopelessly corrupt, but they didn't seem to be hurting anyone. Having created such havoc, the popes lost much of their political credibility and relevance in the play among European powers during the **Thirty Years' War,** and most of the 17th and 18th centuries were relatively quiet for Rome.

REVOLUTIONS AND REPUBLICS

The **French Revolution** caused some problems, as **Pope Pius VI** amiably mishandled diplomatic relations with the new secular French government. Effigies of Pius were set on fire and a severed head landed in the lap of the Papal Nuncio as he was traveling in his coach. Romans, in turn, attacked a French delegation on the Corso in 1793. Homes of French sympathizers were vandalized and the French Academy set on fire with shouts of "Long live the Catholic religion!"

Napoleon Bonaparte, then only a general in the French Army, arrived on the scene in 1796 to deal with the problem and refill French coffers with the treasures of Italy. Napoleon refused to depose the pope for strategic reasons, but he brought the Church to its knees, extorting millions in tribute and carrying off precious works of art. Romans watched as 500 wagons left the city loaded with booty; some of the most important pieces of Italian and Roman art are still found in Parisian museums. In 1798, French **General Berthier** followed up on Napoleon's work: he stormed the Vatican, kidnapped the pope, and established a brand-new Roman Republic. When Napoleon's empire crumbled, however, the 1815 **Congress of Vienna** returned the papacy to temporal power in Rome.

In 1849, with the liberal **Risorgimento** raging, Rome voted to abolish the papal state and establish yet another Roman Republic. Pope Pius IX appealed to Catholic heads of state to keep his crown, with success; Napoleon III came down from France to put the Pope back in power, defeating Italian revolutionaries Giuseppe Mazzini and Giuseppe Garibaldi.

Despite the French interference, regional Italian rulers slowly managed to unite the country over the next twenty years; they declared Rome the capital, and there crowned the first Italian king **Vittorio Emanuele II.** In 1870, when the French left for war with Prussia, there was no one to stop the Italian forces from crashing through the Vatican. The pope, who had just declared the doctrine of **papal infallibility,** "imprisoned" himself, refused to give up, and urged all Italians to support him; he died alone in 1878.

FASCISM AND MODERNITY

The 20th century didn't see much respite for Italy. The tenuously united country hit a rough spot right off with WWI; despite picking the winning team, they didn't make much out of the peace settlement and found their economy just

1796 Following in the footsteps of their Gaulish ancestors, the French sack Rome again, though in a more civilized fashion and with better accents.

1870 The Pope finally loses his Papal States.

LIFE AND TIMES

as depressing as it was before. A return to the symbolism of a great Roman past did a little to raise self-esteem, but at the cost of starting WWII. Today, Rome stands at the center of a deeply divided nation, without the political or religious control of its heyday.

IL DUCE

The life of **Benito Mussolini** is a tribute to the bigness of which the littlest man is capable. After stints as a schoolteacher, a journalist, and even a pacifist, Mussolini (or *Il Duce*, "the Leader") started his political career with the militant left, but soon added a dash of Nationalism to his Marx. At the tender age of 25, Mussolini called for the appointment of a "ruthless and energetic" dictator to clean up Italy. Three months later, he conceded that he might be the man for the job.

In 1919, Mussolini assembled paramilitary combat groups (*i fasci di combattimenti*), known as the **Blackshirts,** who waged a fierce campaign for power. They broke labor strikes for corrupt industrialists, raided newspapers soft on Bolshevism, and established mini-dictatorships in small cities on the pattern of the Communist rise to power. Mussolini had grown so powerful in Italy that the 1922 **March on Rome** was just for show, as were the reports that 3000 Fascist martyrs had died. When Vittorio Emanuele III named him Prime Minister, Mussolini forged a totalitarian state, suppressing opposition parties, regulating the press, and demolishing labor unions. His few pieces of constructive legislation included revamping the train system to increase efficiency and the **Lateran Pact of 1929,** regulating Vatican-Italian relations.

In 1929, Mussolini moved his office to **Palazzo Venezia** (p. 154), where he delivered his imperial orations. He fancied himself an emperor in the grandest tradition, and was determined to mark his territory by a series of unfinished, gargantuan architectural schemes. Under his aegis, the government spent more than 33 billion lire on public works; he plowed down medieval, Renaissance, and Baroque works—as well as over three-quarters of the ruins he claimed to be preserving—to create a wide processional street, **Via dei Fori Imperiali.** To symbolize his achievement, Mussolini envisioned a huge forum that would make St. Peter's and the Colosseum look like Legoland. For the centerpiece of his *Foro Mussoliano,* he commissioned a 263 ft. statue of himself as Hercules. One hundred tons of metal later, with only an enormous foot and head to show for it, the project lost its balance and collapsed.

Impressed by German efficiency, Mussolini entered WWII with Hitler in 1939. Used to relying on propaganda rather than strength, Mussolini squandered his army in France, Russia, and Greece until a coup and the Allied forces deposed *Il Duce,* who was rather ingloriously hanged. Rome's sizable resistance movement made up for Italy's dreadful military performance, protecting Jews and anti-Fascists from the occupying Germans. Serious damage to the city was averted;

LIFE AND TIMES

1922 Benito Mussolini orchestrates a coup and is named Prime Minister. This has been generally recognized by historians as a bad thing.

1929 Mussolini and Pope Pius XI sign the Lateran Treaty, establishing Vatican City as the world's smallest independent country.

1939 Italy picks the wrong side in WWII.

1944 After the collapse of the Italian and German armies, Rome is declared an "open city" and liberated without massive destruction.

Hitler had the sense to declare Rome an "open city" as liberating Allies approached in June 1944. The dreary **EUR** (Esposizione Universale Roma; p. 184) is a reminder of Mussolini's unsettling vision and his ultimate failure.

THE ITALIAN NATION

The end of WWII led to sweeping changes in Italian government. The **Italian Constitution of 1948** established a Republic with a president, a parliament with a 315-member Senate and 630-member Chamber of Deputies, and an independent judiciary. Within this framework, the **Christian Democratic Party,** bolstered by American aid (and rumored Mafia collusion), bested the Socialists. Domination by a single party did not stabilize the country; political turmoil has reigned, along with over 50 different governments since WWII.

Postwar instability and industrialization led to violence in the 1970s. The *autunno caldo* (hot autumn) of 1969, a season of strikes, demonstrations, and riots, opened a decade of unrest. The most disturbing event was the 1978 murder of ex-Prime Minister **Aldo Moro,** who is remembered by a plaque in the Jewish Ghetto (p. 159) where his body was dumped by the leftist Brigade Rosse. Things have calmed down a bit since then, but even today city and regional bonds often prove stronger than nationalist sentiment. The most pronounced split exists between the north's wealthy industrial areas and the south's agrarian territories.

RECENT EVENTS

The daily events of Italian politics read like a soap opera, though occasionally more disturbing than amusing. In 1992, **Oscar Luigi Scalfaro** was elected president on a platform of governmental reform; his campaign for clean government uncovered the scandal of *"Tangentopoli"* (Kickback City), leading to over 1200 convictions for bribery. Organized crime reacted to the crackdown with acts of violence like the 1993 bombings of the Uffizi Gallery in Florence and several sites in Rome, including the Church of San Giorgio in Velabro (p. 152). Other fallout led to the "suicides" of 10 indicted officials over the past four years, and open Mafia retaliation against investigators.

In 1994, **Silvio Berlusconi**—a self-made billionaire who owned three television channels, a major newspaper, and (most importantly) the AC Milan soccer team—was elected Prime Minister at the head of a right-wing political coalition called the "Freedom Alliance." Eight months later, though, the reactionary *Lega Nord* (Northern League) pulled out of the ruling coalition, calling for the north of Italy to secede and form an independent "Republic of Padania." (It hasn't happened yet.) Berlusconi was forced to resign, and the elections of 1996 brought the center left-coalition, the **L'Ulivo** (Olive Tree), to power. The following years brought some stability to Italian politics; prime ministers **Romano Prodi, Massimo D'Alema** (a former communist), and "Dr. Subtle" **Giuliano**

1948 Feeling hopeful, Italy is re-established as a constitutional democratic republic.

1969-1980 The autunno caldo is followed by the anni di piombo ("years of lead"), named for the frequent political bombings and shootings. Italy feels less hopeful.

1990 Berlusconi declared guilty of perjury, but only after having been amnestied.

1998 Berlusconi is convicted of bribery twice in a single week. Both cases were appealed, resulting in acquittal when the statute of limitations expired.

2005 Berlusconi is acquitted on charges of false accounting, because a new law passed by his government makes false accounting legal as long as no one is harmed.

LIFE AND TIMES

2008 Berlusconi declares himself "universal record-holder for the number of trials in the entire history of man."

Amato managed to get through the job without epically disgracing themselves.

Afraid that Italian politics might become boring, Berlusconi ran again for Prime Minister in 2001—and despite a record of multiple convictions for corruption (all later reversed), he won. Politicos mostly credit his success to his pledged *Contratto con gli Italiani* or "Contract with the Italians," modeled on Newt Gingrich's 1994 "Contract with America." Also, he still owns **AC Milan**. Once in office, he headed up a conservative agenda by courting US President George W. Bush and sending 2700 Italian troops to Iraq to assist the US-led invasion in 2003—much to left-wing dismay. Berlusconi also managed to briefly sour relations with Germany with a particularly unfortunate, off-hand comment that one of the German members of the European parliament would be "perfect" for a movie role as a Nazi concentration camp guard.

Fortunately for political comedians, Berlusconi's unpopularity mounted as the war in Iraq dragged on. His government floundered after elections in April 2005 and he resigned, only to return with a new coalition five days later and pick up right where he left off. In 2006, he was defeated again by his old rival Romano Prodi, just as he had been ten years before. This time, however, Prodi's coalition (newly named "The Union"—olive trees are so mid-90s) had more trouble keeping things together; despite pulling the Italian troops out of Iraq, Prodi lost ground in controversies over funding for operations in Afghanistan and the US military base in Vicenza. In January 2008, Prodi lost a vote of no confidence in the Senate and resigned. May 2008 elections brought overwhelming returns in favor of—you guessed it—Silvio Berlusconi, back in charge of Italy's 62nd government since the end of WWII.

After being held by center-leftists from 1993 up until 2008, the mayor's office in Rome is now in the hands of **Gianni Alemanno,** an ally of Berlusconi's. (He served as Minister of Agriculture in Berlusconi's second and third cabinets.) Alemanno's record is more right-wing than most; as a youth, he was a member of the neo-fascist **Italian Social Movement,** founded by Mussolini's supporters at the end of WWII. Though he has officially refused any connection to ultra-conservative parties since his election, the crowds celebrating Alemanno's mayoral victory included some far-right skinheads waving fascist salutes and chanting *"Duce! Duce!"* In November 2008, Alemanno allayed some of these fears by setting aside land in a Roman public park for a new museum memorializing the Holocaust, drawing praise from Rome's Jewish community.

RELIGION

Religion has been a major force in the shaping of Roman history, socially as much as politically. From the Pantheon to St. Peter's, a plethora of sights in Rome are or were connected with religion. This section aims to be a history of belief: for information on religion and politics, see **History** (p. 47).

GODS OF THE ROMANS

Early Roman religion is difficult to piece together, mostly because the ancient Romans themselves were directly involved in forgetting it by the first century BC. All that can be certain is that the Romans had the typical Indo-European **paterfamilias structure** of a male head of household who bore life-and-death power over the rest of the family, which empowered him to direct their religious beliefs to suit his personal whims. In early Rome, then, household gods proved most prominent. The **Lares** were gods attached to a particular household, worshipped by the family and its slaves. The **Penates** were also household gods, but were associated more with the storage cupboards and the care of the hearth. Unsurprisingly, the hearth was an area of strong religious importance, and the cult of **Vesta** (with her league of Vestal Virgins; see **House of the Vestal Virgins,** p. 142) was one of the most fundamental elements of early Roman religious practice.

Like the vast majority of inhabitants of the ancient world, the Romans practiced animal sacrifice, believing it important to achieve a state of *pax deorum* (peace of the gods). War rites of the early, less civilized Romans were even known to include human sacrifice in cases of dire crisis. Romans were introduced to the entire package of Greek gods and goddesses by the Etruscans (though the latter made their own alterations, resulting in the expansive and even contradictory mythologies of many Roman deities). The awed Romans soon adopted most of the Greek religious cast, simply transposing Hellenic names into Latinate versions for use at home. As the god of war, Mars was declared patron of belligerent Rome.

Roman polytheism was of a tolerant sort; religion was seen as a local practice, and foreign gods were frequently "interpreted" as versions of the Greco-Roman gods under other names. The Romans didn't impose their religion on anyone, and even the notorious "cult of the emperor"—which began with Julius Caesar and Augustus, who were deified posthumously—actually began by popular demand in one of the eastern provinces, where local inhabitants had a custom of deifying their rulers, most of whom had been treated as gods in their lifetimes. Many of the more educated Romans were non-religious, having absorbed the Stoic, Epicurean, and Platonic elements of Greek philosophy.

MITHRAISM

Mithraism, a religion with strong similarities to Christianity that flourished in the first few centuries AD, was the first successful monotheistic religion in the Empire. Imported from Persia, it centered around the god **Mithras,** who created the world by killing a sacred bull. Mithraism remains shrouded in mystery, mainly because it was a secretive cult based on the celebration of mysteries known by and passed down only to initiates. Their place of worship, the *mithraeum*, was usually built underground, and several Christian churches, notably the Basilicas of San Clemente (p. 178) and Santa Prisca, were constructed on top of them. Although only eight *mithraea* have been excavated in Rome, there may have been over 700 at the height of the movement. Several *mithraea* have also been excavated in Ostia Antica (see **Daytrips,** p. 247). The *mithraeum* was usually an artificial cave with stone benches facing a depiction of Mithras killing the sacred bull. The best-preserved artifact of the scene

POPE FICTION

One fine ninth-century day, as the Pope was riding by procession along Via Sacra, he asked to stop by the side of the road. His companions then watched in horror as the Pope, standing on the street, gave birth to a child. The Pope, it seemed, had a surprise hidden under his holy robes.

Vehemently denied by papal scholars (and most reputable historians) but eagerly endorsed by feminist revisionists, the story of Pope Joan has endured as too good to be true, but also too good to forget. According to legend, Pope Joan disguised herself as a man to rise through the ranks of the Catholic hierarchy and ultimately reign as pope for three years around 850. Joan's jig was up when she gave birth to her lover's child in the middle of a papal procession.

Conspiracy theorists find proof of Joan's existence in some bizarre practices of the Catholic Papacy. For example, the fact that Popes often sit on pierced chairs is seen as a vestige of the "physical inspections" that became routine after Joan's charade. Supposedly, the newly-elected Pope sat on "holey" chairs, while cardinals placed below would peep at the Pope's privates. Also, papal processions mysteriously avoid Via Sacra in favor of far less convenient routes, perhaps due to superstitions stemming back to the legend of Popess Joan.

is the bull sculpture in the Room of the Animals at the Vatican Museums.

CHRISTIANITY

Since Peter and Paul arrived shortly after Christ's death, Christianity has been big in Rome. However, finding harmony between Rome and religion hasn't been quite so simple. As early as AD 35, the Senate declared Christianity to be "strange and unlawful." Nonetheless, in 42, **Saint Peter,** the first Bishop of Rome, set up shop in the city. **Saint Paul,** the codifier of Christian thought, dropped by often, until he was beheaded in 62. Peter met *his* end through upside-down crucifixion near the site of the Vatican in 67. The duo are fittingly recognized as Rome's patron saints, ironically victims, rather than perpetrators, of violence.

Persecution of Christians began in earnest after the **Great Fire of Rome** in 64, and it continued sporadically for over 200 years. From 200 to 500, Christians used the catacombs outside of the center of Rome as cemeteries (p. 187).

Christian persecution in Rome ended with the **Edict of Milan,** a proclamation of toleration, made in 313. The **Nicaean Creed of 325** was the first cohesive statement of belief by the Pistic (Orthodox) church, nailing down the basics of Christianity. Soon, after the ban on paganism was decreed, Christianity monopolized the soul trade. A flurry of theological writings ensued: the Latin translation of the Bible standardized the word of God, while the *City of God* and *Confessions* provided the framework for Christian theology.

During this period, most of the major basilicas of Rome were started, though in forms vastly different from their current states. The **crucifix,** today the ubiquitous symbol of Christianity, only became widely used around the mid-500s. In 451, the **Council of Chalcedon** declared that Jesus was of both human and divine nature, answering a question that had spawned innumerable heretic sects (and, conveniently, invalidating many of them). From here the first major break in the church began to form, and in 1054, the Eastern and Western halves of the church separated in an event known as the **Great Schism.**

The Church's history during the Middle Ages was tumultuous. Papal succession was political, and greed and corruption were rampant. Pope Urban II kicked off the **First Crusade** in 1095 in order to unify the Church and squelch partisanship. While this crusade failed to retake the Holy Land and created all manner of havoc in the Middle East, it succeeded in bringing a rebirth to a religion in danger of stagnation. For similar reasons, Pope Gregory IX initiated the first incarnation of the **Papal Inquisition** in the 1230s.

The 14th century was only dress rehearsal for the confusion that would come with the Protestant Reformation of the 1500s. In 1517, **Martin Luther's** accusatory **95 Theses** threatened Rome's religious power. Ignatius of Loyola founded the **Jesuits** in 1534 to combat the Protestant menace; from 1534-1563, the Council of Trent met to plan the **Counter-Reformation** and further define what had become known as **Roman Catholicism.**

Since WWII, the Church has spread its message globally with renewed strength and vigor, particularly in Eastern Europe and the developing world. To this end, the **Second Vatican Council** (1962-1965) was an attempt to improve relations with other religions and to make the Church more accessible to the layperson.

Pope John Paul II's international approach to papacy has reflected the Church's intention to establish a more direct relationship with believers without the interference of politics. Since his election in 2005, **Pope Benedict XVI** has attempted to keep the global focus alive, but has taken the church in a more conservative direction, calling for an end to the acceptance of moral relativism and a return to fundamental Christian values.

ART AND ARCHITECTURE

ETRUSCAN ORIGINS

Before Rome was synonymous with empire, the **Etruscans** lived, worked, and made art that influenced the Roman conquerors who would later take over their territory. They are most famous for their subtle, reddish pottery, which took heavy inspiration from the Greeks and from Oriental, Phoenician, and Hittite sources. Their earliest known pottery (ninth century BC) took the form of funerary urns, mostly decorated with stippled or incised patterns. In the seventh century, the *bucchero* style—shiny black or gray funerary pottery that looks like metal—emerged in Cerveteri and quickly became a must-have for every Etruscan lady who lunched, the proto-"it" item. Just as typical, however, were the earthy terra-cotta bas reliefs that the Etruscans introduced and the Romans went on to claim for themselves.

CLASSIC ROME

The emerging Roman styles in art fall mainly into two large categories: propaganda art in service of the state and private household art, which originated, as much art did, from religion in the votive statues of household gods (the Lares and Penates) created by ancient Roman tribes. Household art was a democratic form, splashed across the interiors of houses, courtyards, and shops. Most private Roman art took the form of **frescoes,** Greek-influenced paintings that were daubed onto wet plaster so that both plaster and paint would dry together, forming a lasting and time-resistant patina. The **Sistine Chapel** in Vatican City houses some of Italy's most impressive frescoes, such as Botticelli's *The Temptation of Christ* (p. 198). Proud household owners often embellished their abodes with sneaky trompe l'oeil doors or columns to make their palatial homes look even larger. **Mosaic** was another popular genre from the Hellenistic period onward; a favorite subject was the watchdog, often executed on the vestibule floor, with the helpful inscription *cave canem* ("beware of dog"). Craftsmen-artists fashioned these mosaics by painting scenes into the floor (or occasionally wall) of a building, pressing finely shaded *tesserae* (bits of colored stone and glass) onto the painting's surface, and squeezing a soft bed of mortar in between the cracks to cement everything in place. An even more personalized art form—**graffiti**—was also widely practiced by citizens of the ancient Roman Empire. Look out for walls in Pompeii or excavated buried buildings to see the full range of uninhibited ancient self-expression—everything from love declarations to denunciations of Christianity as a cannibal religion, as well as such judiciously weighed sentiments as "Marcus Lucius has a very large ass."

Public art in Rome was commissioned by the Roman government and usually reflected the tastes and victories of whoever was in power at the time, as propaganda often does. At first the Romans simply exploited Greek design features for their buildings, but soon they developed the revolutionary technology of the arch from earlier Etruscan vaults. This, along with the happy invention of concrete, revolutionized their conceptions of architecture and made possible such monuments as the **Colosseum** (p. 134), triumphal arches celebrating military victories, aqueducts, amphitheaters, basilicas, and much more. The Romans then finessed the arch, lengthening it into a **barrel vault,** crossing two arches to make a **groin vault** (hehe), or rotating it in a tight circle to build **domes.** Monumental public buildings either reminded the spectator of a particular emperor's exploits in battle (like the artistically sublimated propaganda of **Trajan's Column,** p. 146) or functioned as frenzied arenas of mass entertainment intended to pacify an unruly populace, the fabulous bread and circuses. Some of the most famous constructions began around AD 80, when the normally affable ex-plebe emperor Vespasian built the blood-soaked arches and columns of the Colosseum, and when Titus had his triumphal **Arch of Titus** constructed to provide a suitable backdrop for him to parade his booty and slaves.

Religion, Marx noticed, has a way of keeping the people busy and out of trouble. The Roman government presciently took his word on this, making sure to spend money on the construction of religious temples and on festivals and rites to calm and patriotically inspire the populace by offering it a spectacle of spiritual unity and power. Temples were usually constructed along the Greek model, with a triangular **portico** supported by the classical row of columns and decorated with strips of friezes on strategic flat surfaces. In **capitals** (the decorative upper portion of a column), Romans used the Greek orders of **Doric, Ionic,** and **Corinthian,** making the latter more elaborate than ever by supplementing its crown of acanthus leaves with all manner of ornate curlicues. Later on, the Romans would begin to transfer column style and the full panoply of Greek architecture to almost any building.

The earliest and most sacred man-made monument in Rome was the **Temple of Vesta,** although its white simplicity was soon overshadowed by more pragmatic temples, such as those devoted to the deified Augustus and Julius Caesar. Rome's most important architect was also the world's first known engineer, **Vitruvius,** who originated the idea that harmonious buildings would base their measurements and proportions on the human body—a.k.a. the "measure of man." Later on, Romans became more interested in theaters and basilicas for distraction and contemplation. At this point, basilicas were still used as courthouses and shopping arcades, although the cool and climate-adapted design of a long rectangle with arch-and-column supports would be recycled by later Christian and Byzantine emperors as the first floor plans for early churches.

BYZANTINE DECADENCE

When Constantine transferred the capital of the Roman Empire in 330 from Rome to Constantinople (then known as Byzantium, now as modern-day Istanbul), artistic influences in Rome took a decidedly Asiatic twist. Born from the aesthetic traditions of the Christian catacombs and the Greek and Oriental styles, Byzantine art favored immobile, mystical, slender-fingered figures against flat gold or midnight-blue backgrounds, shadowy domes, and an atmosphere of enigmatic and flooding holiness—it should come as no surprised that Byzantine art was almost exclusively concerned with religious figures. Spread the world over by the **Emperor Justinian** and his powerful wife **Theodora,** the Byzantine style reveled in gorgeously ornate mosaics, some of which can still be seen in the churches of Santa Cecilia in Trastevere, Santa Prassede, and Santa Maria in Domenica, although the best examples of this style in Italy are all in Ravenna. Despite the fact that the religious Byzantine emperors erected countless costly palaces, only their religious buildings have survived subsequent sackings, medieval recycling, and modernization. These buildings were built on the model of Roman basilicas (law courts); instead of having a cathedral shape, they are rectangular and domed.

A TOUCH OF ROMANESQUE

Given the chaos of the third and fourth centuries, emperors' minds tended to turn to making war, not art. The gaze of the Christian art that eventually emerged in the Middle Ages was fixed firmly on heaven. From roughly 500 to 1200, Romanesque-style churches dominated Europe. In Rome, these fashions slowly overtook the older Byzantine style, retaining the basilica floor plan but updating it with rows of pillared round arches, low ceilings, oriel windows, peeling wooden statues of saints, and an elaborate and arcane bestiary of men and beasts cavorting in the caps of pillars and the reliefs above doorways. Wall frescoes and mosaics from this period abound in Rome, in **San Paolo fuori le Mura** (p. 183), which also hoards mosaics imported in toto from Byzantium, **Santa Maria Maggiore** (p. 171), and **Santa Prassede** (p. 172).

RENAISSANCE IN ROME

If cleanliness is next to godliness, it is a very distant neighbor to chiaroscuro.
   —Henry James

The succession of wealthy Renaissance popes eager to leave their mark on the city in the form of new buildings, paintings, and sculpture gave a sagging Rome its most striking stylistic tummy-tuck since its ancient days. This age heralded the split between science and faith, and the Church condemned both **Galileo** and **Giordano Bruno** for their astronomical assertions that the earth was not the center of the universe. Painters, sculptors, and architects relied heavily on subjective experience while at the same time employing the technical discoveries of the **Age of Science.** Although Rome was certainly not the center of the Italian Renaissance, it did manage to lure many of the most famous Florentine artists to come refurbish the imperial city's image, including Michelangelo, Brunelleschi, and Rafael.

   The supreme artist with the tortured soul, **Michelangelo Buonarroti** (1475-1564), grew up among the stonemasons of Tuscany. During this period, Michelangelo honed his knowledge of the human body after he swapped his handiwork (a hand-carved, wooden crucifix) for the privilege of dissecting corpses in the Cloisters of Santo Spirito. At the age of 21, he headed to the capital city to seek his fortune. Originally commissioned by the pope for some minor works, Michelangelo was deluged with requests once he became well known in Rome. It is for one of these commissions that he created the profoundly sorrowful and career-making **Pietà** in St. Peter's (p. 163).

In 1505, Pope Julius II sent for Michelangelo, now almost 30 and at the height of his career, to return once more to Rome to build the pope's **tomb** (in San Pietro in Vincoli). The relationship that was to last 10 years; between the demanding Julius II and the introverted and temperamental Michelangelo, it was hardly a meeting of like minds. The colossal tomb was left unfinished when Julius got carried away with plans for St. Peter's. Julius managed to sweet-talk the moody artist into returning to his patronage to paint the **Sistine Chapel** ceiling in 1508. Michelangelo spent the next four years slaving over—or, rather, under—the problem-ridden project, beginning by learning how to paint frescoes. In the following years, he threw away his original pictorial design, redesigned his plans, fired his assistants, and ended up doing the whole job himself. The ceiling was finished in 1512, four months before Julius's death, and Michelangelo escaped to Florence. Thirty years later, Michelangelo returned to Rome, greeted by the new Pope Paul II, who called the aged Michelangelo back to the Sistine Chapel for arguably his most important work, **The Last Judgment** (p. 198).

Michelangelo's Florentine contemporary **Raphael** (Raffaello Sanzio) also made the obligatory pilgrimage to Rome for prestige and generous papal commissions. Julius had him fresco his private rooms, now world-famous as the **Stanze di Raffaello** (p. 198). Raphael used his stay in the Vatican to covertly learn some of Michelangelo's techniques for creating realistic and dynamic art, much to Raphael's profit and Michelangelo's annoyance.

BERNINI + BORROMINI = BAROQUE

The **Baroque** in Rome can be summed up in the work of two artists: **Gian Lorenzo Bernini** and **Francesco Castelli Borromini.** The personality differences between effervescent, cavalier boy-genius Bernini and dark, temperamental Borromini are abundantly clear in their works. Known as the "greatest European" in his day, the architect, sculptor, painter, and dandy Bernini set the standard for the Baroque during his prolific career. Bernini's father, a Florentine sculptor, brought his son to Rome to start work; he was immediately signed on for training and didn't stop working until the age of 80. He died having worked for every pope who was in power during his lifetime.

Along with his *St. Teresa in Ecstasy* (in Santa Maria della Vittoria), Bernini's *Hellenistic David* (in the Galleria Borghese, p. 203) exhibits a style that stands in contrast to Michelangelo's classical sculptures. Sculpture, however, was only one facet of Bernini's career; he also made great contributions to Rome through architecture. The oval of the *piazza* of St. Peter's was the culmination of a life's work; he personally supervised the construction of each and every one of the 284 Doric columns of travertine marble. Bernini's churches and monuments (including the grand *baldacchino* at St. Peter's and his own favorite, the church of Sant'Andrea al Quirinale, p. 173) exemplify the exuberantly theatrical, illusory style that came to define the Baroque.

The non-conformist Swiss Borromini spent much of his career working against the showiness of the Baroque, focusing instead on melding Baroque convention with complex geometrical figures. Borromini was commissioned to design some of the details on Bernini's *baldacchino*, but it became apparent that Bernini and Borromini's styles were wholly incompatible. In works like the church of **San Carlo alle Quattro Fontane,** Borromini created an entirely new vocabulary that fused sculpture and architecture. Eventually the complexity of Borromini's work caught up with him; he became obsessed with his calculations and withdrew completely from society. Soon after the completion of the Falconieri Chapel, he impaled himself with a sword and was subsequently interred there.

NEOCLASSICAL RE-REVIVAL

In the late 1700s, southern Italy would provide the long-awaited reaction to the Baroque in the form of **Neoclassicism.** Morbidly infected by the excitement surrounding the excavations in Pompeii, Herculaneum, and Paestum, Neoclassical artists reasserted the values of Greco-Roman art that the Renaissance already had taken a shot at imitating via the Renaissance Classicist style. The greatest artists of this period weren't Roman, but they soon emigrated to Rome. Foremost among the Neoclassicists was **Jacques-Louis David** (1748-1825), who studied in Rome at the French Academy. In sculpture, the coldly pure lines of **Antonio Canova** also found fans, leading the Borghese to install some of his marble statues in their gardens.

Pope Benedict XIV preferred restoring Rome for tourists over conducting church business; street signs and historical markers appeared for the first time. He commissioned paintings for St. Peter's and mosaics for Santa Maria Maggiore (p. 171), redesigned by prominent architect Fernando Fuga. Baroque artists managed to resist the tide of Neoclassicism, and Nicola Salvi's **Trevi Fountain** (p. 206)—completed in 1762—exhibits Baroque's persistence. The tumultuous *Risorgimento* put a damper on construction in the mid-1800s; once the country was unified, large-scale building began to accommodate the new government. The undeveloped area east, southeast, and northeast of Termini was soon crowded with apartment buildings. A number of buildings were lost in expansion, including Henry James's favorite, the Villa Ludovisi.

FASCIST ART

Mussolini was one of the biggest builders of public works since the cadre of popes who built St. Peter's and the rest of the Vatican complex. Most of the monuments he erected, like his philosophy, are pompous, rigid, geometrical, and based on an artistic model that subjugates the individual to the public masses. Much of the Fascist legacy in Roman architecture can be found in the **EUR** (Esposizione Universale Roma) neighborhood on the outskirts of Rome (p. 184), including one building (the Palace of Labor) that architect Marcello Piancentini described proudly as a "square Colosseum." The **Foro Italico,** meant to be the monumental symbolic center for a heroic nation, is also a prime example of the Fascist notion of artistic expression—not too different from their notion of political expression. Note the excessive use of *"DUCE A NOI"* in the tile work, as well as the nude figures wrestling, swimming, laboring, and piloting biplanes.

FUSING OF THE OLD AND THE NEW

Things got a little more complicated and a lot less megalomaniacal after Mussolini was out of the picture. Although Italy and Rome are perhaps best known in modern times for their celluloid art (see **Film,** p. 69), Italian visual artists had some degree of fame. Several turned to more traditional forms for less than traditional purposes: neo-neo-Classicist Felice Casorotti kicked it with the old old school, while **Giorgio di Chirico** painted surrealist landscapes that combined ancient Roman architecture with signs of Italian modernity like trains and cars—Vespasian meets Vespa, so to speak. Textures and artistic materials also became more important, with Lucio Fontana exploring the aesthetics of the disgusting in sculpture and painting, and multimedia sculptor Alberto Burri melding masterpieces out of scraps of plastic, fabric, and cellophane. No tour of Roman museums is complete without ogling **Amedeo Modigliani's** paintings of voluptuously sexy nude women—they're always lurking around the corner.

LITERATURE

Anyone who has experienced the distinct pleasure of memorizing Latin verb conjugations will recall some of the heavy hitters of Republican and Imperial literature, from Cicero's masterful *"O tempora, o mores!"* to Tacitus's self-righteous glorification of the barbarian raiders in the Histories. By the Renaissance, however, Rome began to look outside its own literary heritage and attract writers from around the world. Foreign authors, especially in the 18th and 19th centuries, opened up a whole new world of literary imaginations, dealing with contemporary life in Rome in inventive and vivid ways. Today, it is impossible to appreciate what is arguably the most important city in the history of western civilization without some exposure to its literature. The following is required reading. There will be a test.

EPICS AND ELEGIES: ANCIENT ROME

CATULLUS. The masterful poet of the first century BC, Catullus was renowned for his wild use of hyperbole and alliteration, especially in declaration of his feelings for Lesbia. Despite occasional bouts of sexual frustration, his poetry sets a high standard for would-be parodists, while providing a great source of Latin obscenities for future generations of students.

JULIUS CAESAR. A skilled political leader and orator, the original JC not only penned *De Bello Gallico* about his first military campaigns in France, but conquered his own hometown (literally and literarily) with his first-hand account of the shredding of the Republic in *De Bello Civili*. Caesar was also a common subject of Catullus' poetic ramblings, in which he was accused of having an erotic relationship with his engineer. Who said the Romans didn't gossip?

VIRGIL. Virgil was so dedicated to his poetic craft that it literally killed him. After spending the last ten years of his life working on the *Aeneid*, he caught a fever and passed away before editing the final draft. Although now considered a piece of poetic brilliance, Virgil is still given a hard time for having left a few lines metrically incomplete. The story of Aeneid links the founding of Rome to the fall of Troy via the wandering of Aeneas.

OVID. Ovid's two favorite topics were love and sex, as seen in the *Amores* (about love between two poets) and *Metamorphoses* (about love between a plethora of gods and the occasional ill-fated mortal). Meanwhile, the *Ars Amatoria* is a tongue-in-cheek guide to love and lust providing step-by-step advice for finding a mate and seducing him or her. Though originally employed by Augustus, he was later banished to the Black Sea for sanctioning the escapades of Augustus's promiscuous daughter and grand-daughter, both named Julia.

MARCUS AURELIUS. Marcus Aurelius's philosophical musings, entitled *Meditations*, actually provide some valuable insight to the male psyche, especially for any woman who's wondered how men seem to deny their emotions. Feel fortunate that this pearl of wisdom was translated from Greek into English over a century ago.

BOONDOCK SAINTS: EARLY CHRISTIAN

SAINT CLEMENT. St. Clement, fourth bishop of Rome, liked to write letters. Someone slapped a title on them *(Epistles of St. Clement of Rome)* and published them. Now, wasn't that easy?

SAINT JEROME. St. Jerome updated the Bible, and in the process influenced the art and culture of the Middle Ages, Renaissance, and Reformation. The *Vulgate Bible* is essential reading for those planning to visit religious sites in Rome.

SAINT AUGUSTINE. St. Augustine's tales of naughtiness and conversion in *The Confessions* inspired centuries worth of purgations and asceticism.

MISCHIEVOUS MONKS AND SOME RENAISSANCE

DANTE ALIGHIERI. Dante Alighieri was father of the modern Italian language (the *volgare*) and the modern conception of heaven and hell. Michelangelo studied him extensively and used his *La Divina Commedia* as inspiration for *The Last Judgment* in the Sistine Chapel (p. 198).

PETRARCH. The father of Humanism, Petrarch can be credited with developing the sonnet as we known it today. He also wrote *Itinerarium*, a sort-of medieval guide-book for traveling, probably not too different from *Let's Go*.

GIOVANNI BOCCACCIO. Boccaccio's tale of naughty nuns and jousting nobles, *The Decameron*, ostensibly chronicles the adventures of ten Florentines fleeing their plague-ridden city. In reality, it is more of a literary landscape of Italy's regional foibles and peculiarities.

LOCAL LEGEND
THE ROMAN TWINS

Everyone knows the legendary history of Rome: the twins Romulus and Remus were abandoned and nursed by a she-wolf until they were found and raised by a shepherd. When they grew up, Romulus killed Remus in a power struggle and went on to become the founder of Rome in 753 BC.

It wasn't until 2007, though, that Italian archaeologist Irene Iacopi stumbled upon some of the first evidence in support of this popular myth. The cavern that Iacopi discovered is believed to be Lupercale, the mythical cave where the brothers were supposedly suckled by the she-wolf and where ancient Romans came centuries later to honor Romulus and Remus. Buried 50 ft. under the ruins of Augustus's palace on Palatine Hill, the cavern is decorated with extremely well-preserved marble mosaics, seashells, and a painted white eagle—symbol of the Roman empire—at the center of the vaulted ceiling.

Even if archaeologists can prove that the cave was a sanctuary revered during the time of Augustus, however, that does not prove the actual existence of Romulus and Remus. For the time being, the legend of the sons of Mars remains just that—a legend.

GIORDANO BRUNO. This philosopher's radical astrological and neo-Platonic observations earned him an execution in the Campo dei Fiori (p. 119).

ROMANTICISM

METASTASIO. Although born in Rome, Metastasio actually spent the 40 principle years of his career in the music world of Vienna, Austria. To remind people of Metastasio's actual heritage, the Romans erected a statue of this librettist in the P. della Chiesa Nuova.

CARLO GOLDONI. Goldoni transformed the stage through melodramas, and more significantly, through his *Commedia dell'Arte*, or improvised comedy, still performed today.

TWENTIETH CENTURY

GABRIELE D'ANNUNZIO. Gabriele D'Annunzio wrote it all—poems, stories, plays, and novels. Arguably Modernism's most flamboyant character, he wrote *Il Piacere* about his cavalier heroics and sexual escapades in Rome. Try to ignore that he was an avid supporter of fascism and developed many torture techniques alongside his brilliant words.

ALBERTO MORAVIA. Moravia's *Time of Indifference* attacks fascism in a straightforward style, and was promptly censored. Following its publication, in an effort to circumvent the probing (if Philistine) eye of the government, Moravia retreated into surrealism. If reading is not your thing, many of his novels, including *Il Conformista (The Conformist)*, have been made into movies.

ELSA MORANTE. The wife of Alberto Moravia, Elsa Morante was also a writer and is best known for her 1974 novel *La Storia*, published in English as *History: A Novel* and commended for its epic style.

NATALIA GINZBURG. The author of several psychological novels centered on family relationships and self, Ginzburg writes from Rome in *Famiglia* and *Borghesia*. She was also the secret editor of an anti-fascist newspaper in Rome until her husband was arrested and murdered for it.

DARIO FO. Dario Fo proves that being banned by the Catholic Church is and always will be a boost in sales. His *The Accidental Death of an Anarchist* and *We Won't Pay! We Won't Pay!* won him the Nobel Prize for Literature in 1997.

PIER PAOLO PASOLINI. Pasolini wrote about thieves, prostitutes, and other promiscuous characters of Rome's underbelly. His two most famous novels are *Ragazzi di Vita (The Ragazzi*, 1955) and *Una Vita Violenta (A Violent Life*, 1959), especially because Pasolini's murder is rumored to be attributed to one of his characters real-life counterparts.

ITALO CALVINO. Italo Calvino's novels and short stories are not easily classified as a particular genre. Some contain elements of magical realism while others elements of modern and postmodernism. His 1979 novel *If on a Winter's Night a Traveler* entertainingly questions the very act of reading and writing.

FILM

IN THE BEGINNING

Rome's premiere position within the film industry began in 1905, when Filoteo Alberini released *La Presa di Roma (The Taking of Rome)*. This dramatic story forever skyrocketed Rome into the heart of all Italian cinema, and also ushered in the Italian "super-spectacle:" extravagant, larger-than-life productions that replayed historical events with more-than -healthy doses of cosmetics and melodrama. Recognizing film's potential as propaganda in the late 30s, Mussolini revived an industry that had been in decline since the golden age of the silent era by creating *Cinecittà Studios*, Rome's answer to Hollywood. Yet the boost to the industry came at a price: Mussolini also enforced a few "imperial edicts" that dictated the production of films, one of which even forbade laughing at the Marx Brothers's 1933 film, *Duck Soup*. Films created under fascist rule between the years 1936 and 1943 glorified Italian military conquests and portrayed comfortable middle-class life. This era of Italian film is often referred to as the era of *telefoni bianchi* (white telephones) in reference to the common prop. Rare compared to their black cousins, these phones were a symbol of prosperity, and during the short-lived glory days of Italian Fascism, these films kept the chaos in other parts of Europe out of sight, out of mind. A few renegade leaders in the film industry opposed fascist rule, however. Mussolini's propaganda machine eventually ended at *Cinecittà Studios* as well, with the famous director and closet Marxist Luigi Chairini. Chiarini was instrumental in the founding of Italy's **Centro Sperimentale della Cinematografia,** the film school that slowly shifted away from propaganda and became the alma mater of many neorealist directors.

NEOREALISM

The fall of fascism brought the explosion of *neorealismo* in cinema in the 1940s, which rejected contrived sets and professional actors, emphasizing instead on-location shooting and "authentic" drama based in reality. These low-budget productions created a film revolution and brought Italian cinema international prestige. Neorealists first gained attention in Italy with **Luchino Visconti's** (1906-76) French-influenced *Ossessione* (1942). Because fascist censors suppressed this so-called "resistance" film, it wasn't until **Roberto Rossellini's** (1906-77) film *Roma, città aperta* (1945) that neorealist films gained international exposure. The film began his Neorealistic WWII trilogy, which also included *Paisà* (1946) and *Germania anno zero* (1948). **Vittorio De Sica's** 1948 *Ladri di biciclette (The Bicycle Thief)* was perhaps the most successful neorealist film. The film's simple plot explored the human struggle against fate. A demand for Italian comedy gave birth to *neorealismo rosa*, a more comic version of the intense and often dismally authentic glimpse into daily Italian life. Actor **Totò** (1898-1967), the illegitimate son of a Neapolitan duke, was Italy's Charlie Chaplin. With his dignified antics and clever lines, Totò charmed audiences and provided subtle commentary on Italian society.

THE GOLDEN AGE

The golden age of Italian cinema, which took place in the 1960s, began *la commedia all'italiana*, during which the prestige and economic success of Italian movies was at its height. Now in the international spotlight, Rome's film industry, nicknamed "Hollywood on the Tiber," was producing between 200 and 250 films a year, many of which are still considered classics today. **Mario Monicelli** (*I Soliti Ignoti*, 1958; *La Grande guerra*, 1959) brought a more cynical tone to the portrayal of daily Italian life, which was in a stage of rapid transformation and social unease. Italian comedy struggled to portray cultural stereotypes with as much wit as its public demanded. Actors **Marcello Mastroianni**, **Vittorio Gassman**, and **Alberto Sordi** gained fame portraying self-centered characters lovable for their frailties.

By the 60s, post-neorealist directors like **Federico Fellini** (1920-93) and **Michelangelo Antonioni** (1912-2007) valued careful cinematic construction over mere real-world experience, especially as two of Chiarini's students, **Roberto Rossellini** and Michelangelo Antonioni, rose to directorial fame after the war. Antonioni, to an even greater extent than his colleague Fellini, refused to conform to such "artificial constraints" as plot, form, conflict, resolution, and a cause-and-effect relationship between events. With the Oscar-winning *La Strada* (1954), Fellini went beyond neorealism, scripting the vagabond life of two street performers, Gelsomina and Zampanò, in the most poetic of terms. Fellini's *8½* (1963) interwove dreams with reality in a semi-autobiographical exploration of the demands of the artist that has earned a place in the international cinematic canon. His *La Dolce Vita* (1959) was condemned by both religious and political authorities for its portrayal of decadently stylish celebrities in 50s Rome on the V. Veneto. The film coined the term "paparazzi" and glamorized dancing in the Trevi, an act that is now illegal. Antonioni's haunting trilogy, *L'Avventura* (1959), *La Notte* (1960), and *L'Eclisse* (1962), presents a stark world of estranged couples and isolated aristocrats and follows the typical neo-Marxist pattern of condemning materialism. *Blow-Up* (1967), his only English-language script, was the story of a photographer in London who inadvertently captures a murder on film. Miming, murder, and mod London made for quite a hit. Meanwhile, controversial writer-director **Pier Paolo Pasolini** (1922-75) may have spent as much time on trial for his politics as he did making films. An ardent Marxist, he set his films in the underworld of shanty neighborhoods, poverty, and prostitution. His later films include scandalous adaptations of famous literary works, including *Il Decameron* (1971) and *The Arabian Nights* (1974).

A NEW ERA

More recently, *Commedia della Cinema* has replaced Marxism as the preferred form of expression, with directors like **Nanni Moretti** (*Caro Diario*, 1994) and **Lina Wertmuller** (*Ciao, Professore!;* 1993) providing an alternative to the canned Hollywood romantic comedy. In general, however, the novelty of Rome's neorealist film age has died down; Italy itself only produces between 80-100 films annually. The member of the group with the most international currency is **Roberto Benigni**, star of *Ciao, Professore!* The victorious stomp of his film *La Vita e Bella (Life is Beautiful)* through the 1999 Academy Awards is not likely to be forgotten in the film community anytime soon. So experience Rome, but learn from the mistakes of the cinematic legends who came before you—Gregory Peck (don't fall in love with a stranger), Spartacus (crucifixion isn't fun), Matt Damon (despite the face, Jude Law is not divine), etc.

MUSIC

IT'S PLAIN TO SEE

Even with the limited information known about Rome's musical history today, it is a fact that early Roman music would have made for a dull dance party. These Roman and Ambrosian rites (Italy's medieval liturgies), which originated in Jewish liturgy, were characterized by monophonic vocal plainchant, also known as **plainsong**. In other words, the song was only a single melody—no base and no backup drumbeat. Despite its rather "plain" quality, the Ambrosian chant and the Roman Gregorian chant can still be heard on occasion throughout the city at religious ceremonies and in churches. The **Gregorian Chant,** named for **Pope Gregory I** (c. 540-609) is characterized by a repeated reciting note, interrupted only by periodic deviations and is generally sung by an all-male clergy. Things may have gotten a bit more interesting when the Italian monk **Guido d'Arezzo** (c. 995-1050) came up with the modern system of staff-notation and explored the emerging concept of **polyphony,** or combining melodies in harmony. Organist and composer **Francesco Landini** (c. 1335-97) also made significant contributions to the development of the song during the 14th century **Ars Nova period** with the introduction of the Landini cadence. He was also a builder of organs, which was particularly impressive considering he was blind. Over time, *madrigales*, musical poems, and *caccia* (musical and poetic narratives describing hunting scenes) became popular during this age.

OPERA LIRICA: THE FAT LADY SINGS

Italy's most cherished musical art form was born in Florence in the mid-1590s, nurtured in Venice and Naples, and popularized in Milan's famed *Teatro alla Scala*. Conceived by the *Camerata*, a circle of Florentine writers, noblemen, and musicians including **Vincenzo Galilei** (famed music theorist and father of **Galileo,** c. 1525-91), *opera lirica* originated as an attempt to recreate the dramas of ancient Greece by setting lengthy poems to music. The earliest surviving opera is *Euridice* (1600), a collage of compositions by **Jacobo Peri** (1561-1633), **Ottavio Rinuccini** (1562-1621), and **Giulio Caccini** (c. 1550-1618). Opera found a perfect equilibrium between music and poetry for the first time in *L'Orfeo* (1607), a breakthrough piece by **Claudio Monteverdi** (1567-1643), who drew freely from history and juxtaposed high drama, love scenes, and uncouth humor. Still-popular **Alessandro Scarlatti** (1660-1725) was arguably the most talented composer of Italian operas, pioneering advances in the overture during the 17th century. Meanwhile, the simple and toneful *aria* became the dominant form of opera, and castrated men the singers of choice.

IF IT'S BAROQUE, FIX IT

Like the plainsongs, the success of Baroque music was directly due to the patronage of the Roman Catholic Church, which believed that the arts should embody religious influences and inspire the general masses. However, composers realized they would have to do more than have monks chanting monophonic melodies in order to get the people interested. Thus, the Baroque period, is known for its heavy ornamentation and emphasis on musical contrasts as well as the birth of the **string orchestra** (which replaced the monks).

A PREGNANT PAUSE

Rome was the ultimate enabler of my sweet tooth. My apartment was near the Jewish Ghetto, and Pasticceria Boccione became one of my favorite places to satisfy a sudden sugar craving. The ladies aren't much on conversation, but the almond paste cookies are killer.

I'd been to Boccione four or five times without any serious mishaps. Then one afternoon, I dropped in at about 5:30pm and nearly stepped into a pile of what looked like wood shavings. A pregnant woman guarding the door stopped me just in time. "They're cleaning," she told me. And, indeed, one of the bakers started spreading the shavings around the floor with a broom. Things only got weirder from there. As I waited outside to be let in, the first pregnant woman was joined by a second. Finally, one of the bakers ushered us into the store. We crunched around on whatever they had coated the floor in.

And then we waited. And waited. Or I waited. Time seemed to be barely squeaking by. One of the pregnant women asked for sunflower seeds. Two men came in and ordered cakes. They were going to serve me last of all, I could tell. "I'm Jewish, too," I wanted to tell them. "I belong here!"

As the breadth and complexity of string orchestras grew, Rome took a liking to the violin, whose form was perfected by **Antonio Stradivari** (1644-1737). With the combination of violins and Italian composers like **Vivaldi**, the Baroque era altered the path of Roman music forever, especially by influencing other musical genres, like opera.

VIVA LA VERDI!

Giuseppe Verdi (1813-1901), whose lyrical half-century domination of Italian opera emphasized human themes and the human voice, remains the crowning musical figure of 19th-century Italy and, along with his German contemporary Wagner, of all of opera. *Nabucco* (1842), a pointed and powerful *bel canto*, typifies Verdi's early works. The opera's chorus, *Vapensiero*, became the hymn of Italian freedom and unity during the *Risorgimento*. Verdi also produced the touching, personal dramas and memorable melodies of *Rigoletto* (1851), *La Traviata* (1853), and *Il Trovatore* (1853) in mid-career. His later work brought the grand and heroic conflicts of *Aïda* (1871), the dramatic thrust of *Otello* (1887), and the mercurial comedy *Falstaff* (1893). Verdi's support of the *Risorgimento* in the 1850s encouraged patriots to invoke his name—a convenient acronym for *"Vittorio Emanuele, Re d'Italia"* (King of Italy)—as their popular battle cry: *"Viva Verdi!"*

TWENTIETH-CENTURY OPERA

In the 20th century, **Ottorino Respighi** (1879-1936) explored his fascination with orchestral color in the popular **Roman Trilogy** (1924-29): *Fontane di Roma* (Fountains of Rome), *Pini di Roma* (Pines of Rome), and *Feste Romane* (Roman Festivals). As a teacher of composition at Rome's prestigious music school, Conservatorio de Santa Cecilia, he was best known for his musical achievements.

The Italian-American composer, **Gian Carlo Menotti** (1911-2007) wrote Pulitzer Prize-winning operas *The Consul* (1950) and *The Saint of Bleecker Street* (1954). **Luigi Dallapiccola** (1904-75) achieved success with surrealist choral works, including *Canti di prigionia* (*Songs of Prison*, 1941), which protested fascism. His student, avant-garde composer **Luciano Berio** (1925-2003), pioneered the composition of electronic music. Meanwhile, Grammy-winning tenor **Luciano Pavarotti** (1935-2007) made his world debit in the 60s and helped bring opera into mainstream popular culture with his televised operas in the 1990s. Since then, **Andrea Bocelli** (b. 1958) has continued to bridge the expanse between opera and pop with chart-topping songs such as "Con Te Partirò" in 1995. Today, visitors in Rome looking to experience Italian opera firsthand should attend a performance at **Teatro dell'Opera** (p. 224) or one of Italy's countless other opulent opera houses.

A RIVEDERCI, VERDI

More recent Italian music has reversed its centuries-long role as a ground-breaker, drawing inspiration instead from American pop culture. Melodic rockers of the 60s included **Enzo Iannacci**, a dentist-turned-musician; the crooning, politically-minded, **Genoese Fabrizio De Andre;** and **Adriano Celentano,** whose career spanned 40 years. Emerging in the 60s and 70s, **Lucio Battisti,** one of the most influential musicians in the Italian rock scene now enjoys a popularity rivaling that of the Beatles in his own country. Having produced a total of 18 albums during his career, you will often hear his songs played as covers by local up-and-coming Italian musicians. In the 70s and 80s, **Edoardo Bennato** used rock to spread a progressive political message and combined blues, pop, and even operatic tones. His successor **Vasco Rossi** drew an unprecedented 300,000-member crowd to a free concert he gave in 2004, and is still adding credits to his impressive career of 21 albums. Meanwhile, **Eros Ramazzotti** gained universal appeal by recording every album in Spanish as well as Italian, often teaming up with Cher, Tina Turner, and Ricky Martin (back in the day). Italians **Laura Pausini, Elisa,** and **L'Aura** followed suit by recording English albums. More recently, **Jovanotti's** rap has entered the global scene, along with socially conscious **Frankie-HI-NRG** and **99 Posse.**

CUSTOMS AND ETIQUETTE

IL GALATEO (CORRECT BEHAVIOR)

STEP IT UP. The Italian way can be summed up in a single word—refined. As soon as you step onto the streets of Rome, don't be surprised if you take

A lapsed Jew. Maybe they knew. Maybe the Boccione ladies were trying to smite me for my religious infidelities and were waiting until the store cleared out so that they could have a clear shot. After all, they wouldn't want to smite a pregnant woman accidentally. Fifteen minutes I had waited. Now I was really paranoid. Had I encountered a bunch of pastry makers doing the work of a wrathful god?

When I was finally called to the counter, I bought a couple of cornmeal biscuits and flew out the door, displacing wood shavings out into a crowded street.

—Emily Chertoff

The Pasticceria Ebraico Boccione is in the Jewish Ghetto at V. del Portico d'Ottavia 1. See p. 120 for the listing.

to walking a bit straighter or dressing a bit classier. It's not difficult to distinguish the tourists from the locals, so observing and picking up some of the colloquial customs is the best way to begin blending in. Don't forget to greet closer friends with two kisses, one on each cheek, and definitely don't smoke in public places, including the subway.

CONVERSAZIONE. The Italians are a social bunch, and as you stroll through the city in the evening, there is no doubt you will be tempted to strike up a conversation with some friendly passersby. To overcome the so-called language barrier, it is useful to commit basic words like hello and good-bye—*buongiorno* and *ciao*—to memory before you go. For everything else, a small phrase book can be handy—like ours! See the **Appendix, p. 298.** Even if your accent is abysmal, your new Roman companions will appreciate the effort and will likely correct your mistakes rather than mock them. When in doubt, good humor and animated conversation, sign-language and hand gestures included, can go far. Italians consider meeting new people and hanging out with good company among the most important ways to spend free time, so a new face in the crowd (yours!) is always welcome.

CATWALK COUTURE. Even if not decked out in Gucci and Ferragamo, Italians prioritize dress and appearance. Looking good means making a good impression, and it's simply inconceivable to be sloppy or unkempt. Wearing sweatpants or having unruly hair is effectively wearing a sign that screams "tourist." So, take off the fanny pack, comb your hair, and follow this rule: it's not so much what you wear, but how you wear it. Strive for elegance and simplicity. Even if you want to be comfortable in jeans, pair the ensemble with a cozy cardigan, designer trainers, or a trendy zip-up sweatshirt. Avoid excessive bagginess and holes (if you can help it). For women who want to add some dazzle, gold earrings, bracelets, or a pearl necklace are the most respectable choices. Even as a visitor, making an effort has its perks. Since people pay attention to clothes and appearance, don't be surprised if your clean-cut look turns a few heads or generates compliments from the crowds. *Ah, bella.*

WAKE UP AND SMELL THE CAFFÈ

THE ART OF ESPRESSO. Italians drink coffee at breakfast, lunch, dinner, and any time in between—and still manage to close shop in the afternoon for a snooze. But espresso in Italy isn't just a beverage; it's an experience, from the harvesting of the beans to the savoring of the beverage. High altitude Arabica beans compose 60-90% of most Italian blends, while the remaining 10-40% come from woody-flavored robusta beans. Italians are partial to a high concentration of robusta beans because they emit oils that produce a think, foamy *crema* under the heat and pressure of the espresso machine. All espresso beans are roasted longer than other coffee beans and give the drink fuller volume and richer flavor. After roasting, the beans are ground, tapped into a basket, and mixed with hot pressurized water. In a good cup of espresso, the foamy *crema* should be golden-brown and thick enough to support a spoonful of sugar for a good couple of seconds. Heavy *crema* prevents the drink's rich aroma from diffusing into the air and is a sign of a quality brew.

HOW TO ORDER. Any coffee lover should undoubtedly indulge in Italy's fantastic coffee culture. For a standard cup of espresso, request a *caffè*. Stir in sugar, if desired, and down it in one gulp like the locals. In many coffee shops, or bars, the choice can be overwhelming, so be sure to be specific when ordering. Here are some options you might see on the menu:

Un caffè	A small strong black espresso coffee
Un caffè ristretto	A smaller, stronger black espresso coffee
Un caffè doppio	A double-size espresso
Un caffè lungo	A "long" espresso weakened with water
Un caffè macchiato	A 'stained' espresso with a bit of milk
Un caffellatte	An espresso with a large amount of milk
Un cappuccino	An espresso with steamed, frothy milk
Un caffè corretto	A "corrected" espresso with a drop of grappa or brandy
Un caffè freddo	An iced coffee
Un caffè affogato	A dessert espresso "drowned" with a scoop of vanilla gelato
Un caffè americano	A very watery espresso (scorned by Italians)

COFFEE STAINED. While Italians oftentimes drink coffee with or following every meal, they do not drink cappuccino after 10am. If you order a cappuccino after lunch or dinner, you might as well open your map on the table and wave your country's flag; every Italian will know you're a tourist.

SIZE ME UP:

WOMEN'S CLOTHING										
US	2	4	6	8	10	12	14	16	18	20	22
ITALY	36	38	40	42	44	46	48	50	52	54	56

WOMEN'S SHOES										
US	5½	6½	7	7½	8	8½	9	10	10½	20	22
ITALY	35	36	37	38	38½	39	40	41	42	54	56

MEN'S CLOTHING										
US	34	36	38	40	42	44	46	48	18	20	22
ITALY	44	46	48	50	52	54	57	58	52	54	56

MEN'S SHIRTS										
US	14	14½	15	15½	16	16½	17	17½	18	20	22
ITALY	36	37	38	39	40	41	42	43	52	54	56

MEN'S SHOES										
US	6	6½	7	7½	8	8½	9	9½	10	10½	11-11½
ITALY	39	40	40½	41	41½	42	42½	43	43½	44-44½	45

SPORTS AND RECREATION

ANCIENT TIMES

The Romans, like many warlike cultures, liked their athletic spectacles swift, deadly, and performed by individuals other than themselves. Gladiatorial combat originated as part of a wartime funeral custom, but it quickly caught on and became an essential social ritual well into the era of Christian emperors. Elaborate arenas were built to house the ruthless death matches, including sites at **Pompeii** (p. 262) and, of course, the famed Roman **Colosseum** (p. 134). Romans also hosted *venationes* (staged hunts) and giant mock naval battles in such venues. Greek athletics, like wrestling, running, and javelin throwing, were slower to catch on in the Capital of the Ancient World—gambling, racing, and death sports were much more appealing to Mars' children.

FOOTBALL (SOCCER)

Slightly less violent though much more melodramatic, today's evolved form of the 16th century's *calcio* ("soccer" or, more commonly in Italy, "football") surpasses all other sports in popularity and competes with politics, wine, food, fashion, and religion as national obsession. However, Italian fans, or *tifosi*, are also divided by their undying devotion to local teams. During games between big-city rivals, don't be surprised to find hauntingly empty streets stifled with fans either commiserating or celebrating in communal agony or ecstasy. To become one with the mob, catch a game at Rome's **Stadio Olimpico** (p. 226) .

WORLD CUP 2006. Italy came. Italy saw. Italy conquered. The national team, the **Azzurri,** is a source of pride, and the Italian national team officially became the world's best soccer team in 2006, defeating France in penalty kicks. The players' receipt of the Italian Order of Merit of Cavaliere Ufficiale upon their victory serves as one testament to the sport's immense social importance.

FESTIVALS AND HOLIDAYS

Though most Italians work 35hr. per week, take 2hr. lunch breaks, close some businesses on Mondays, and take elaborate month-long coastal vacations each August, they still enjoy a seemingly constant stream of festivity, and the city of Rome offers no exception. Despite often religious origins, celebrations aren't necessarily pious. Revelry during **Carnevale** (its Italian equivalent) prepares Rome for Lent with massive celebrations to offset the oncoming religious sacrifices. Countless other quirky local and national festivals pay homage to medieval customs, often in the form of jousts and period costumes. Additionally, many modern festivals centered around modern art, trade, and fashion also dominate the Roman calendar. For a complete list of festivals, write to the **Rome Tourist Office** (p. 91).

DATE	FESTIVAL	LOCATION
January 1	Capodanno (New Year's Day)	Nationwide
January 5	Epiphany Fair at Piazza Navona	Rome
January 6	Epifania (Epiphany)	Nationwide
February 16, 2010	Carnevale (Fat Tuesday)	Nationwide
April	Sana a Roma (Mediterranean Trade Fair)	Rome
Palm Sunday to Easter Sunday (March 28 – April 4, 2010)	Settimana Santa (Holy Week)	Nationwide
April 2, 2010	Venerdi Santo (Good Friday)	Nationwide
April 4, 2010	Pasqua (Easter Sunday)	Nationwide
April 5, 2010	Pasquetta (Easter Monday)	Nationwide
April 25	Festa della Liberazione (Liberation Day)	Nationwide
May 1	Festa del Lavoro (Labor Day)	Nationwide
May 1	Primo Maggio Concert	Rome
1st Saturday in May (May 1, 2010) and September 19	Festa di San Gennaro	Naples (p. 283)
June	New Opera Festival of Rome	Rome
June to September	Estate Romana (Arts Festival)	Rome

DATE	FESTIVAL	LOCATION
June 2	Festa della Repubblica (Republic Day)	Nationwide
July	Summer Opera Season at Caracalla	Rome
July	Donna Sotto le Stelle (Fashion Festival)	Rome
August 15	Ferragosto (Feast of the Assumption)	Nationwide
September–October	Roma Europa Festival (Modern Art Festival)	Rome
September 19	Festa di San Gennaro	Naples (p. 283)
October	Festival Romics (Comics and Cartoon Festival)	Rome
October	Roma Jazz Festival	Rome
November 1	Ognissanti (All Saints' Day)	Nationwide
November 2	Giorno dei Morti (All Souls' Day)	Nationwide
December 8	Immacolata (Day of Immaculate Conception)	Nationwide
December 24	Le Farchie di Natale (Christmas Eve)	Nationwide
December 25	Natale (Christmas Day)	Nationwide
December 26	Festa di Santo Stefano (Saint Stephen's Day)	Nationwide
December 31	Festa di San Silvestro (New Year's Eve)	Nationwide

LIFE AND TIMES

BEYOND
TOURISM

A PHILOSOPHY FOR TRAVELERS

HIGHLIGHTS OF BEYOND TOURISM IN ROME

LEARN the **secrets** of the **Italian kitchen** (p. 85).

DIG among the **ruins** under **Monte Testaccio** (p. 82).

TEACH English to *bambini* at a rural **summer camp** (p. 88).

As a tourist, you are always a foreigner. Sure, hostel-hopping and sightseeing can be great fun, but connecting with a foreign country through studying, volunteering, or working can extend your travels beyond tourist traps. We don't like to brag, but this is what's different about a *Let's Go* traveler. Instead of feeling like a stranger in a strange land, you can understand Rome like a local. Instead of being that tourist asking for directions, you can be the one who gives them (and correctly!). All the while, you get the satisfaction of leaving Italy in better shape than you found it. It's not wishful thinking—it's Beyond Tourism.

As a **volunteer** in Rome, you can roll up your sleeves, cinch down your Captain Planet belt, and get your hands dirty doing anything from farming in a vineyard to restoring an ancient monument. This chapter is chock-full of ideas to get involved, whether you're looking to pitch in for a day or run away from home for a whole new life in Italian activism.

Ahh, to **study** abroad! It's a student's dream, and when you find yourself reading Dante while sipping an *espresso*, it actually makes you feel sorry for those poor tourists who don't get to do any homework while they're here. Courses range in topics from cooking to the Classics, all with the Eternal City as your classroom.

Working abroad is one of the best ways to immerse yourself in a new culture, meet locals, and learn to appreciate a non-US currency. Yes, we know you're on vacation, but we're not talking about normal desk jobs—we're talking about being an au pair or leading a pub crawl, in the name of funding another month of globe-trotting. Looking for employment in Rome can be a disheartening experience, but the prevalence of tourism means that anyone with foreign language skills can be a valuable commodity.

 SHARE YOUR EXPERIENCE. Have you had a particularly enjoyable volunteer, study, or work experience that you'd like to share with other travelers? Post it to our website, www.letsgo.com!

VOLUNTEERING

Feel like saving the world this week? Volunteering can be a powerful and fulfilling experience, especially when combined with the thrill of traveling in a new place. Italy lacks the history of a philanthropic tradition that other countries, such as the United States, have enjoyed; volunteer opportunities can be difficult to find. Most Italian volunteer programs focus on the more impoverished regions to the south of the peninsula, or those devastated by the recent Abruzzo earthquake. However, a current focus on issues like immigration and healthcare have resulted in a new push for public service outlets, especially for young people. And, of course, the prevalence of Catholicism provides some opportunities for social work.

Most people who volunteer in Rome do so on a short-term basis at organizations that make use of drop-in or once-a-week volunteers. For better or worse, volunteer work (like any kind of work in Rome) can be difficult to come by unless you have contacts. Some of the more popular sites for tourists might be looking for part-time docents to give tours in English or other foreign languages. You'll get better results if you go through their site offices directly, instead of through a placement agency. The best way to find opportunities that match your interests and schedule may be to check with community magazines and bulletin boards, such as the ones listed in the section below. As always, read up before heading out.

Those looking for longer, more intensive volunteer opportunities usually choose to go through a parent organization that takes care of logistical details and often provides a group environment and support system—for a fee. There are two main types of organizations, religious and secular, although there are rarely restrictions on participation for either. Websites like **www.volunteerabroad. com**, **www.servenet.org**, and **www.idealist.org** allow you to search for volunteer openings both in your country and abroad.

I HAVE TO PAY TO VOLUNTEER? Many volunteers are surprised to learn that some organizations require large fees or "donations," but don't go calling them scams just yet. While such fees may seem ridiculous at first, they often keep the organization afloat, covering airfare, room, board, and administrative expenses for the volunteers. (Other organizations must rely on private donations and government subsidies.) If you're concerned about how a program spends its fees, request an annual report or finance account. A reputable organization won't refuse to inform you of how volunteer money is spent. Pay-to-volunteer programs might be a good idea for young travelers who are looking for more support and structure (such as pre-arranged transportation and housing) or anyone who would rather not deal with the uncertainty of creating a volunteer experience from scratch.

ECOTOURISM

Italy's expansive coastline and mild mainland environment play host to thousands of visitors annually. Tourists and locals alike are able to play a role in preserving the environment that has made Italy such a popular travel destination. Taking advantage of opportunities to work with wildlife and restore local habitats can be a great way to experience Italian culture at its best.

Ecovolunteer: Common Dolphin Research, CTS-Centro Turistico Studentesco e Giovanile, Dept. Ambiente, V. Albalonga 3, Rome 00183 (☎06 64 96 03 27; www.ecovolunteer.org). Volunteers in the Gulf of Naples live on a research boat while tracking dolphins and other marine mammals. 1-week programs June-Oct. 18+. Program fee €750-850 per week. Student discounts available.

Lega Italiana Protezione Uccelli, Lazio Regional Office, V. Aldrovandi 2, Rome 00197 (☎06 32 11 07 52; www.lipuostia.it). Works to preserve the natural habitat of birds and teach environmental awareness. Locations throughout Italy, including on the coast near Rome. Welcomes volunteers to their many projects; also organizes bird-watching excursions and courses.

Parco Nazionale d'Abruzzo, Lazio e Molise, V. Roma S.N.C., Villetta Barrea 67030, AQ (☎08 64 89 102; www.parcoabruzzo.it). Hosts over 100 summer volunteers for 1-3 weeks. Responsibilities range from park maintenance to visitor assistance. 18+. Program fee 1 week €110, 2 weeks €170, 3 weeks €230.

Torre Argentina Cat Shelter, V. Marco Papio 15, Rome 00175 (☎6 45 42 52 40; www.romancats.com, torreargentina@tiscali.it). Roman city ordinances dictate that no cat can be evicted from the place it was born. Thankfully, at Torre Argentina they care for these stray kitties. Manned 24hr. by volunteers and supported by donations. For more information contact Silvia Vivarini.

World-Wide Opportunities on Organic Farms (WWOOF Italia), V. Casavecchia 109, Castagneto Carducci 57022, Livorno (www.wwoof.it). Provides a list of organic farms that introduce volunteers to tasks like harvesting olives, grapes, and even bamboo. Knowledge of farming not necessary, although volunteers should be physically capable and willing to work hard. Membership fee €25.

YOUTH AND THE COMMUNITY

Community-based projects are among the most rewarding volunteer experiences. Programs listed below promote interactive humanitarian work through English language programs and projects aimed at assisting the disadvantaged. Due to their one-on-one nature, knowledge of Italian is often necessary. Large international volunteer organizations, such as Habitat for Humanity, Amnesty International, and the Red Cross may also have volunteer opportunities in and around Rome.

Association for Intercultural Exchanges and Activities (AFSAI), Vle. dei Colli Portuensi 345 B2, Rome 00151 (☎06 53 70 332; www.afsai.it). Founded independently in 1958, AFSAI collaborates with the **European Voluntary Service (EVS)** and **Youth for Europe** (a work exchange program) to arrange cultural exchange and volunteer programs with homestays for Italians and non-Italians aged 16-30. Small fee for some programs.

iBO Italia, V. Montebello 46A, Ferrara 44101 (☎05 32 24 32 79; www.iboitalia.org). Italian organization that places volunteers in 2-4 week work camps throughout Italy. Volunteers aid families, communities, and youth associations. Provides simple accommodations and board. 18+.

International Internship and Volunteer Network, P.O. Box 574, Largo, FL 33779, USA (☎+1-727-252-8480; www.iivnetwork.org). Volunteer and internship placements in social work, among other areas. 18+. US$1550 fee.

Service Civil International, 5505 Walnut Level Rd., Crozet, VA 22932, USA (☎+1-434-823-9003; www.sci-ivs.org). Places volunteers in small, 2- to 4-week work camps that range from festival assistance to social work to environmental or historical restoration. Long-term opportunities are also available. 18+. Program fee €50-150.

VIDES, 5630 W. Commerce st., San Antonio, TX 78237, USA (☎+1-210-435-1919; www.vides.us). Catholic organization, but accepts non-Catholics open to living with a religious family. Placements in educational, developmental, and outreach services in Italian communities. Some religiously-oriented; youth ministry, for example. Free.

Volunteers for Peace, 1034 Tiffany R., Belmont, VT 05730, USA (☎+1-802-259-2759; www.vfp.org). Provides info on volunteer programs. Most programs 18+. Program fee US$300.

BEYOND TOURISM

ART, CULTURE, AND RESTORATION

Italy's rich cultural heritage, which dates back to ancient Rome, is increasingly in danger of crumbling or being overrun by modern life. Volunteers looking for a labor-intensive way to engage with Italy's historical past should research groups that specialize in landmark preservation. Contact **Museums** (see p. 193) directly for volunteer docent openings. Local colleges and universities in your home country are excellent sources of information on archeological digs and other projects. Check with the departments of the Classics, archaeology, anthropology, fine arts, or other relevant area studies; many excavations send information and applications directly to individual professors or departments rather than to the general public.

The Archeological Institute of America, 656 Beacon St., Boston, MA 02215, USA (☎+1-617-353-9361; www.archeological.org), lists over 250 field sites throughout the world on their website, many in or around Rome or with a focus on Roman ruins elsewhere in the Mediterranean.

ArchaeoSpain, PO Box 1331, Farmington, CT 06034, USA (☎+1-866-932-003; www.archaeospain.com). Archaeology buffs help out in Rome at Monte Testaccio. Once an ancient pottery dump, the site is now the best record of ancient Roman commerce. English speakers and all ages welcome. University credit on individual arrangement. 2-week program US$2915, housing and meals included.

Capitoline Museums, P. del Campidoglio 1, Rome 00186 (☎06 671 024 75). Interested volunteers should send a resume and letter of introduction to the address above.

Gruppo Archeologico Romano, V. Baldo degli Ubaldi 168, Rome 00165 (☎06 39 37 67 11; www.gruppoarcheologico.org). Holds lectures and field trips for members and organizes summer excavation programs. 15+. Membership fee €37. National organization, **Gruppi Archeologici d'Italia** (www.gruppiarcheologici.org) provides updated listings on upcoming and ongoing volunteer archeological digs throughout Italy.

STUDYING

It's completely natural to want to play hookey on the first day of school when it's raining and first period Trigonometry is meeting in the old cafeteria, but when your campus is Trastevere and your meal plan revolves around *pasta cacio e pepe*, what could be better than the student life?

A growing number of students report that studying abroad is the highlight of their learning careers. If you've never studied abroad, you don't know what you're missing—and, if you have studied abroad, you do know what you're missing. Study-abroad programs range from basic language and culture courses to university-level classes, often for college credit (sweet, right?). In order to choose a program that best fits your needs, research as much as you can before making your decision—determine costs and duration as well as what kinds of students participate in the program and what sorts of accommodations are provided.

In programs that have large groups of students who speak English, there is a trade-off. You may feel more comfortable in the community, but you will not have the same opportunity to practice a foreign language or to befriend other international students. For accommodations, dorm life provides a better opportunity to mingle with fellow students, but there is less of a chance to experience the local scene. If you live with a family, you could potentially build lifelong friendships with natives and experience day-to-day life in more depth, but you might also get stuck sharing a room with their pet iguana. Conditions can vary greatly from family to family.

VISA INFORMATION. Italian bureaucracy often gives international visitors the run-around, but there are ways to minimize paperwork confusion. Just remember that all **non-EU citizens** are required to obtain a visa for any stay longer than three months. For info and applications, contact the Italian embassy or consulate in your country (see **Essentials, p. 11**). Before applying for a student visa, however, be sure to obtain the following documentation: valid passport, visa application form (available from most embassy websites), four passport-size photographs, proof of residency, and complete documentation on the course or program in which you are participating. If you are under the age of 18, you will also need an affidavit of financial support from parents, and your parents' most recent bank statement. All **non-EU citizens** are also required to register with the *Ufficio degli Stranieri* (Foreigners' Bureau) at the *questura* (local police headquarters) to receive a *permesso di soggiorno* (permit to stay) within eight days of arrival. The kit required to complete the *permesso di soggiorno* can be obtained and submitted at most major post offices. The same documentation is necessary for the *permesso di soggiorno* as for the visa; additionally, applicants must have the required *permesso di soggiorno* form and a *Marco da Bollo*, which costs €15 and is available at most Italian *tabaccherie*. **EU citizens** must apply for a *permesso di soggiorno* within three months, but they do not need a visa to study in Italy. Once you find a place to live, bring your *permesso di soggiorno* (it must have at least one year's validity) to a records office. This certificate will both confirm your registered address and expedite travel into and out of Italy. Make sure to check with your local Italian embassy or consulate in case visa requirements have changed recently.

UNIVERSITIES

Most university-level study-abroad programs are conducted in Italian, although many programs offer classes in English as well as lower-level language courses. Savvy linguists may find it cheaper to enroll directly in a university abroad, although getting college credit may be more difficult. You can search **www. studyabroad.com** for various semester-abroad programs that meet your criteria, including your desired location and focus. If you're a college student, your friendly neighborhood study-abroad office is often the best place to start.

AMERICAN PROGRAMS

American Institute for Foreign Study (AIFS), River Plaza, 9 W. Broad St., Stamford, CT 06902, USA (☎+1-866-906-2437; www.aifs.com). Organizes programs for high-school and college study in universities in Italy.

Council on International Educational Exchange (CIEE), 300 Fore St., Portland, ME 04101, USA (☎+1-207-553-4000 or +1-800-407-8839; www.ciee.org). A comprehensive resource for work, academic, and internship programs in Italy. Places high school students in Italian schools for study abroad semesters.

BEYOND TOURISM

Institute for the International Education of Studets (iES), 33 N. LaSalle St., 15th fl., Chicago, IL 60602, USA (☎+1-800-995-2300; www.iesabroad.org). Year-long, semester, summer, and internship placement programs for college study in Rome. Some classes taught (in English) in conjunction with the Italian universities Roma Tre and La Sapienza. Summer US$6295, semester $18,215; includes housing.

School for International Training (SIT) Study Abroad, 1 Kipling Rd., P.O. Box 676, Brattleboro, VT 05302, USA (☎+1-888-272-7881 or 802-258-3212; www.sit.edu/studyabroad) runs **The Experiment in International Living** (☎+1-800-345-2929; www.experimentinternational.org). 3- to 5-week summer programs offer high-school students cross-cultural homestays, community service, cooking classes, ecological adventure, and language training in Italy. Programs begin in Rome and general include travel to other parts of Italy. US$6800, including airfare.

Temple University, International Programs, 200 Tuttleman Learning Center, 1809 N. 13th St., Philadelphia, PA 19122, USA (☎+1-215-204-0720; www.temple.edu/studyabroad). Rome branch offers programs in topics ranging from art history to business management. Summer US$6000, semester $15,000; includes housing.

ITALIAN PROGRAMS

Universities in Rome are generally very crowded, but if you apply early, your chances of finding an open class or two are significantly increased. **The Ufficio Centrale Studenti Esteri in Italy,** Lungotevere Vallati 14 (☎06 88 04 062; www.ucsei.org), is a national organization that can also provide assistance for foreign students who have already started their course of study in Italy. For EU students, the **ERASMUS** program can also provide a channel for studying abroad in Italian universities.

La Sapienza, Piazzale Aldo Moro 5, Rome 00185 (switchboard ☎06 49 911; www.uniroma1.it). Among Rome's main universities. Non-EU students must apply to the Italian consulate in their home country; if accepted, their study visa will be issued and once they arrive they will take an Italian test and, if required, an admissions test. EU students should apply to the Foreign Qualifications secretary (☎06 49 91 27 07) to begin the administrative procedures.

John Cabot University, V. della Lungara 233, Rome 00165 (☎06 68 19 121; www.johncabot.edu), and 14100 Walshingham Rd., Suite 36 #10, Largo, FL 33774, USA (☎+1-866-457-6160). This American international university in Trastevere offers undergraduate degrees in art history, business, English literature, and international affairs. Foreign students can enroll for summer (US$5300), semester (US$13,600), and year-long sessions. Helps students find internships in their fields of study.

LANGUAGE SCHOOLS

Old lady making snarky comments to you in the *piazza?* Imprudent cashier at the *trattoria?* Cute moped girl that is totally into you? To communicate is to be human, and without the local language in your toolbelt, you're up a creek without a *pala.* Fear not! Language school here to help.

While language school courses rarely count for college credit, they do offer a unique way to get acquainted with the culture and language of Rome. Schools can be independently run or university affiliated, local or international, youth-oriented or full of old people—the opportunities are endless. And there are hundreds of them in the city; shop around to make sure you are getting what you want. Some worthwhile organizations include:

Ciao Italia, V. delle Frasche 5 (☎06 48 14 084; www.ciao-italia.it). Offers standard (from 2 weeks at €360), intensive (from 2 weeks at €885), and individual (from €34 per hr.)

courses. Also teaches cooking classes on Sundays. Can help with finding accommodation, either in homestay or hotel.

Istituto Dante Alighieri, V. Aurelia 137 (☎06 39 37 59 66; www.languageinitaly.com). School located near the Vatican with standard, summer, evening, and long-term classes. Staff organizes events and cultural activities. 2-week standard program €300.

Italiaidea, 1st fl., V. dei Due Macelli 47, Rome 00187 (☎06 60 94 13 14; www.italiaidea.com). 1-week to 6-month Italian language and culture courses near the Spanish Steps for individuals and groups of 10 or fewer. Courses qualify for credit at many American universities. Students can request to live in private homes, homestays, or apartments; reserve ahead. Courses from €165 per week, plus €50 registration fee.

Scuola di Italiano Appia Vecchia (☎06 96 25 752; francesca.valentini@btinternet.com, www.scuolaappiavecchia.com), in the Castelli Romani. Residential school where visitors live in Professor Valentini's home, take classes, and go on excursions in and around Rome. 5- to 14-day courses available at all levels; thematically-focused courses (on a particular facet of Italian culture, for example) available for advanced students.

CULINARY SCHOOLS

Cook Italy, (☎34 90 07 82 98; www.cookitaly.com). Region- or dish-specific cooking classes. Venues include Bologna, Cortona, Florence, Lucca, Rome, and Sicily. Courses 3- to 6- nights from €1250. Housing, meals, and recipes included.

Cooking Classes in Rome, at the Le Fate Restaurant, Vle. Trastevere 134 (☎347 13 96 84; www.cookingclassesinrome.webs.com). Chef Andrea Consoli teaches 1-day classes for only €35 per person. Student discount available. Reservation necessary.

Diane Seed's Roman Kitchen, V. del Plebiscito 112 (☎06 67 85 759; www.italiangourmet.com/cookingschool.php). Classes from 1 day (€200) to a week (€1000); include market visits to get the fresh, seasonal produce used in class recipes.

The International Kitchen, 330. N. Wabash #2613, Chicago, IL 60611, USA (☎+1-800-945-8606; www.theinternationalkitchen.com). A leading provider of cooking school vacations to Italy. Traditional cooking instruction in beautiful settings for individuals and groups. Program locations include the Amalfi Coast, Liguria, Tuscany, and Venice. Courses 2-10 nights; 1-day classes also available. Programs start at US$220.

LEARNING LATIN

Aestiva Romae Latinitatis (Summer Latin in Rome), P. Reginald Foster OCD, Tersianum, P. San Pancrazio 5A, Rome I-00152. Free 6-week summer Latin program in Rome with legendary Father Reginald Foster, an American priest who works in the "Latin Letters" section of the Vatican's Secretariat of State. Foster has taught this program for nearly 25 years. Lessons in written and conversational Latin for intermediate and advanced students. Optional lesson "sub arboribus" (under the trees in the monastery garden) given in the evenings. Write for info and application materials. For an account of a student's experience in the program, see p. 45.

WORKING

We haven't yet found money growing on trees, but we do have a team of dedicated Researchers looking high and low. In the meantime, Rome is filled with great opportunities to earn a living and travel at the same time. As with volunteering, work opportunities tend to fall into two categories. Some travelers want long-term jobs that allow them to integrate into a community, while others seek out short-term jobs to finance the next leg of their travels. In Italy, short-term work in agriculture, the service sector, and tourism is the easiest to come by. Though job hunters must navigate the inevitable challenge of Italy's soaring unemployment rates and the premium that Italian employers place on both practical experience and advanced degrees, take heart: with a little research in advance, long-term opportunities are not outside the realm of possibility. **Transitions Abroad** (www.transitionsabroad.com) and **Jobs Abroad** (www.jobsabroad.com) offer far more updated online listings for work over any time span than we could possibly list here.

Check out weekly job listings in *Corriere della Sera*'s **Corriere Lavoro** (online at trovolavoro.it) or *Il Sole 24 Ore*'s **Cercolavoro Giovani,** which specializes in listings for recent university graduates. **GoAbroad.com** (www.internabroad.com/Italy.cfm) has a user-friendly online database of internship listings in Italy. **Youth Info Centers Informagiovani** (www.informagiovani-italia.com) in each region target both Italians and visitors and offer free information on work regulations, employment trends, volunteer programs, and study opportunities. Note that working abroad often requires a special work visa.

MORE VISA INFORMATION. Working legally in Italy as a foreigner is a bureaucratic challenge regardless of your nationality. **EU passport holders** do not require a special visa to live or work in Italy. They do require a permit to stay *(permesso di soggiorno per lavoro),* which grants permission to remain in Italy for the duration of employment. To obtain a *permesso di soggiorno,* EU citizens must register at the local police headquarters *(questura)* within eight days of arrival for a permit to search for work *(ricevuta di segnalazione di siggiorno).* **Non-EU citizens** seeking work in Italy must possess an Italian work permit *(autorizzazione al lavoro in Italia)* before entering the country. Only a prospective employer can begin the process, guaranteeing that the individual has been offered a position. Permits are authorized by the Provincial Employment Office and approved by the police headquarters before being forwarded to the employer and prospective employee. The prospective employee must then present the document, along with a valid passport, in order to obtain a work visa. **Non-EU citizens** must also obtain both the *permesso di soggiorno* and a workers' registration card *(libretto di lavoro),* which will function as an employment record for up to 10 years. Visit the **Italian Ministry of Foreign Afffairs** website (www.esteri.it) or the **US Embassy** site (http://italy.usembassy.gov) for more information.

LONG-TERM WORK

If you're planning on spending a substantial amount of time (more than three months) working in Rome, search for a job well in advance. Newcomers to Italy may be disgruntled to learn how important contacts are in finding a job. International placement agencies are often the easiest way to find employment abroad, especially for those interested in teaching. Although they are often only available to college students, **internships** are a good way to ease into working abroad. Many students say the interning experience is well worth it, despite low pay (if you're lucky enough to get paid at all). Be wary of advertisements for companies offering to get you a job abroad for a fee—often times, these same listings are available online or in newspapers.

Unemployment is high in central and southern Italy, making job searches in Rome difficult and sometimes fruitless. Italian law requires employers to pay substantial sums of money for pensions and benefits even for short-term employees, making new hires very substantial investments. The ability to speak Italian can be immensely useful both in being hired and developing networks of contacts. If you have the time and resources before heading off to Rome, acquiring at least a basic knowledge of conversational Italian could give you a distinct advantage. However, lack of Italian will not necessarily bar you from obtaining English specialty work (such as ESL and work in the tourist industry). Again, your best resource for these jobs is community bulletin boards and magazines, such as **Wanted in Rome** (below), or placement organizations. Some reputable organizations include:

English Yellow Pages, V. Belisario 4/B, Rome 00187 (☎06 474 0861 OR 97 61 75 28; www.englishyellowpages.it). Resources for English-speaking expats in Italy run by an American who relocated to Italy in 1982 to teach English. Includes job listings, classifieds, photos, blogs, and more.

Global Experiences, 168 West St., Annapolis, MD 21401, USA (☎+1-877-432-27623; www.globalexperiences.com). Arranges internships with companies in Rome. Fields include law, international business, tourism, graphic design, and fashion. 10-week programs from €4950 include intensive language training, accommodation, emergency medical travel insurance, and full-time on-site support.

Institute for the International Education of Students, 33 N. LaSalle St., 15th fl., Chicago, IL 60602, USA (☎+1-800-995-2300; www.iesabroad.org). Internships for academic credit in Rome based on availability, background, skills, and language ability. Past assignments in fashion, photography, journalism, business consulting, museum studies, and psychological research. Semester-long programs from around US$17,000. Includes tuition for up to 19 credits, orientation, housing, and medical insurance.

Wanted in Rome, V. dei Falegnami 79, Rome (☎06 68 67 967; www.wantedinrome. com). This bi-weekly magazine and website offer cultural information and a wealth of classified advertisements for jobs, housing, and more. Different ads in the print and online editions. Available at newsstands, English-language bookstores, and from their main office. For the best selection and most up-to-date information, you might want to get an early copy at **The (Almost) Corner Bookstore** or **Libreria Feltrinelli** (p. 92).

TEACHING ENGLISH

While some elite private American schools offer competitive salaries, let's just say that teaching jobs abroad pay more in personal satisfaction and emotional fulfillment than in actual cash. Perhaps this is why volunteering as a teacher instead of getting paid is a popular option. Even then, teachers often receive some sort of a daily stipend to help with living expenses. In almost all cases, you must have at least a bachelor's degree to be a full-fledged teacher, although college undergraduates can often get summer positions teaching or tutoring. Though the demand for English teachers in Italy is high, the competition is stiff. Finding a teaching job as a non-EU citizen can be especially tough. Beyond the usual difficulty of obtaining permits, many language schools require EU citizenship and most prefer British citizens to other English speakers.

Many schools require teachers to have a **Teaching English as a Foreign Language (TEFL)** certificate. You may still be able to find a teaching job without one, but certified teachers often find higher-paying jobs. Some schools within Italy that grant TEFLs will even offer both classroom instruction and practical experience or a leg up in job placement when you earn your certificate. The Italian-impaired don't have to give up their dream of teaching, either. Private schools usually hire native English speakers for English-immersion classrooms where no Italian is spoken. (Teachers in public schools will more likely work in both English and Italian.) Placement agencies or university fellowship programs are the best resources for finding teaching jobs. The alternative is to contact schools directly or to try your luck once you arrive in Italy. In the latter case, the best time to look is several weeks before the start of the school year, or as early as February or March for summer positions. The following organizations are extremely helpful in placing teachers in Italy.

Associazione Culturale Linguista Educational (ACLE), V. Roma 54, San Remo, Imperio (☎01 84 50 60 70; www.acle.org). Non-profit association working to bring theater, arts, and English language instruction to Italian schools. Employees create theater programs in schools, teach English at summer camps, and help convert a medieval home into a student art center. Knowledge of Italian useful. On-site accommodations and cooking facilities included. Ages 20-30. Camp counselor salary of €220-260 per week.

International Schools Services (ISS), 15 Roszel Rd., P.O. Box 5910, Princeton, NJ 08543, USA (☎+1-609-452-0990; www.iss.edu). Hires teachers for more than 200 overseas schools, including occasionally in Italy. Candidates should have teaching experience and a bachelor's degree. 2-year commitment is the norm.

Office of Overseas Schools, US Department of State, 2201 C St. NW, Washington, D.C. 20520, USA (☎+1-202-647-4000; www.state.gov/m/a/os). Provides an extensive list of general info about teaching overseas. See also the **Office of English Language Programs** (http://exchanges.state.gov/education/engteaching).

AU PAIR WORK

Au pairs are typically women (although sometimes men) aged 18-27 who work as live-in nannies, caring for children and doing light housework in foreign countries in exchange for room, board, and a small spending allowance or stipend. One perk of the job is that it allows you to get to know Italy without the high expenses of traveling. Drawbacks, however, can include mediocre pay and long hours. Unfortunately, with the recent adoption of laws that severely limit the availability of work visas for non-EU citizens in Italy, au pairing has become less common, especially for stays longer than three months (the maximum visa-free visiting period). The Italian government will not grant au pair-specific visas so it is imperative that au pairs take necessary steps with prospective employers to obtain work permits and visas (see **More Visa Information, p. 86**). In Italy, average weekly pay for au pair work is about €65. Much of the au pair experience depends on the family with which you are placed. The agencies below are a good starting point for looking for employment.

Euroma, Vle. B. Buozzi 19, A1 int. (☎06 80 69 21 30; www.euroma.info). Assists in au pair placement. Au pairs are required to attend 6-8hr. of language classes per week.

Childcare International, Trafalgar House, Grenville Pl., London NW7 3SA, UK (☎+44 20 8906 3116; www.childint.co.uk).

InterExchange, 161 6th Ave., New York, NY 10013, USA (☎+1-212-924-0446 or +1-800-287-2477; www.interexchange.org).

Roma Au Pair, V. Pietro Mascagni 138, Rome 00199 (☎33 97 79 41 26; www.romaaupair.it). Provides information on and listings for au pair placement throughout Italy, though generally in Rome.

SHORT-TERM WORK

Believe it or not, traveling for long periods of time can be hard on the wallet. Many travelers try their hand at odd jobs for a few weeks at a time to help pay for another month or two of touring around. Romantic images of cultivating the land in a sun-soaked vineyard may dance in your head, but in reality, casual agricultural jobs are hard to find in Italy due to the prevalence of foreign migrant workers who are often willing to work for minimal pay. Those looking for agricultural jobs will have the best luck looking in the northwest during the annual fall harvest or volunteer with **WWOOF** (p. 81). Another popular option is to work several hours a day at a hostel in exchange for free or discounted room and/or board. You can also try working on commission for one of the many pub crawls that roam the city; ads for opportunities of this nature can be found in some of the resources listed above. Most often, these short-term jobs are found by word of mouth or by expressing interest to the owner of a hostel or restaurant. Due to high turnover in the tourism industry, many places are eager for help, even if it is only temporary. *Let's Go* lists temporary jobs of this nature whenever possible.

FURTHER READING ON BEYOND TOURISM

Alternatives to the Peace Corps: A Guide of Global Volunteer Opportunities, edited by Paul Backhurst. Food First, 2005.

The Back Door Guide to Short-Term Job Adventures: Internships, Summer Jobs, Seasonal Work, Volunteer Vacations, and Transitions Abroad, by Michael Landes. Ten Speed Press, 2005.

Green Volunteers: The World Guide to Voluntary Work in Nature Conservation, by Fabio Ausenda. Universe, 2009.

How to Get a Job in Europe, by Cheryl Matherly and Robert Sanborn. Planning Communications, 2003.

How to Live Your Dream of Volunteering Overseas, by Joseph Collins, Stefano DeZerega, and Zahara Heckscher. Penguin Books, 2001.

International Job Finder: Where the Jobs Are Worldwide, by Daniel Lauber and Kraig Rice. Planning Communications, 2002.

Live and Work Abroad: A Guide for Modern Nomads, by Huw Francis and Michelyne Callan. Vacation Work Publications, 2001.

Volunteer Vacations: Short-Term Adventures That Will Benefit You and Others, by Doug Cutchins, Anne Geissinger, and Bill McMillon. Chicago Review Press, 2009.

Work Abroad: The Complete Guide to Finding a Job Overseas, edited by Clayton A. Hubbs. Transitions Abroad, 2002.

Work Your Way Around the World, by Susan Griffith. Vacation Work Publications, 2008.

BEYOND TOURISM

PRACTICAL
INFORMATION

TOURIST AND FINANCIAL SERVICES

TOURIST OFFICES

Enjoy Rome, V. Marghera 8/A (☎39 06 44 56 890; www.enjoyrome.com). From the middle concourse of the Termini between the trains and the ticket booths, exit right. Cross V. Marsala. The office is 3 blocks down V. Marghera on the left. Helpful, English-speaking staff makes reservations at museums and shows, books accommodations, orients travelers in the city, and leads walking tours of all the major areas of the city (€27, under 26 €22). Along with info on excursions and bus lines, the office also provides 2 useful publications: a free map and an *Enjoy Rome* city guide, with practical info and insider tips for making the most of a trip to Rome. Open Apr.-Oct. M-F 8:30am-7pm, Sa 8:30am-2pm; Nov.-Mar. M-F 9am-6pm, Sa 9am-2pm.

PIT Info Points (☎06 48 90 63 00). Run by the city, these round green kiosks have multilingual staff and provide limited info on events, hotels, restaurants, and transportation, as well as brochures and a basic map of sights. Most open daily 9:30am-7pm. **Branches:** Ciampino and Fiumicino airports (in international arrivals; open 9am-6:30pm), Castel Sant'Angelo (P. Pia), V. Marco Minghetti, P. Sidney Sonnino, Trevi Fountain, Fori Imperiali, P. di Spagna, P. Navona, Trastevere, Santa Maria Maggiore, P. San Giovanni in Laterano, V. del Corso, V. Nazionale, and Termini (open 8am-8:30pm). The same info is available by phone from the **Call Center Comune di Roma** (☎06 06 08; http://060608.it). Open daily 9am-9pm.

CURRENCY EXCHANGE AND BANKS

Banca di Roma and **BNP Paribas** have good rates. **ATMs** are readily available all over town; they are especially concentrated in Termini and P. Venezia. BNP branches open daily 8:30am-1:30pm and 2:45-4:15pm.

American Express: P. di Spagna 38 (☎06 67 641; for lost or stolen cards and checks, 80 19 64 66 65 outside the US, 06 72 90 03 47 in Italy). Open M-F 9am-5:30pm, Sa 9am-12:30pm.

LOCAL SERVICES

LUGGAGE STORAGE

Splashnet, V. Varese 33 (☎06 49 38 04 50; www.splashnetrome.com). €2 per day. Open daily in summer 8:30am-1am, in winter 8:30am-11pm. In **Termini** (☎06 47 44 777), below track 24. 1st 5hr. €4, €0.60 per hr. up to 12hr., €0.20 per hr. thereafter. Open daily 6am-midnight.

LOST PROPERTY

Oggetti Smarriti, Comune di Roma: Circonvallazione Ostiense 191 (☎06 67 69 32 14). Open M-F 8am-6:30pm. **On bus:** ☎06 58 16 040. **On Metro A:** P. dei Cinquecento (☎06 48 74 309). Open M, W, and F 9am-12:30pm. **On Metro B:** Circonvallazione Ostiense 191 (☎06 67 69 32 14). Open M-F 8am-6:30pm. **ATAC:** (☎06 57 003; www. atac.roma.it). Open M-Sa 8am-8pm. **Credit cards:** American Express (☎06 72 90 03 47), MasterCard (☎80 08 70 866), Visa (☎80 08 19 014).

BOOKSTORES

🖎 **The Lion Bookshop and Café,** V. dei Greci 33-36 (☎06 32 65 40 07 or 65 04 37; www. thelionbookshop.com), off V. del Corso. Open M 3:30-7:30pm, Tu-Su 10am-7:30pm.

Libreria Feltrinelli International, V. Emanuele Orlando 84/86 (☎06 48 27 878 or 06 48 70 999; www.lafeltrinelli.it), near P. della Repubblica. Open Sept.-July M-Sa 9am-8pm, Su 10:30am-1:30pm and 4-8pm; Aug. M-Sa 9am-8pm.

Anglo-American Bookshop, V. della Vite 102 (☎06 67 95 222; www.aab.it), off V. del Corso, near the Spanish Steps. Open Sept.-Jun. M-F 10am-7:30pm, Sa 10am-2pm; July M-F 10am-7:30pm, Sa 10am-2pm. Scientific and technical section at V. della Vite 27 (☎06 67 89 657). Open Sept.-Jun. M-F 9am-1pm and 2-6pm, Sa 9am-1pm; in Jul. and most of Aug. open M-F 9am-1pm. AmEx/D/MC/V.

Mel Bookstore, V. Nazionale 252-255 (☎06 48 85 405; www.melbookstore.it). Open in summer M-Sa 9am-8pm, Su 10am-1:30pm and 4:30-8:30pm; in winter M-Sa 9am-8pm, Su 10am-1:30pm and 4-8pm.

LIBRARIES

Biblioteca Nazionale Centrale di Roma, Vle Castro Pretorio 105 (☎06 49 891; www. bncrm.librari.beniculturali.it). The national library in Rome; extensive selection of books in Italian, English, and other languages. Open M-F 8:30am-7pm, Sa 8:30am-1:30pm; in summer, limited hours; closed mid-Aug.

Santa Susanna Lending Library, 2nd fl., V. XX Settembre 15 (☎06 48 27 510; santasusanna.org). Run by the Catholic church of Santa Susanna. Over 20,000 volumes, mostly in English. English-speaking staff. Annual membership €35 with refundable €25 deposit. Open Tu 10am-1pm, W 3-6pm, F 1-4pm, Sa-Su 10am-12:30pm. Reduced hours in summer.

Universita degli Studi La Sapienza, V. del Castro 9 (☎06 49 14 58; www.uniroma1.it). Library of the La Sapienza university. Open to public M-F 9am-6:45pm, Sa 9am-1pm.

HEALTH CLUBS AND GYMS

CMS105, V. di Monteverde 105 (☎06 58 20 05 03; www.cms105.it), in Monteverde, near the Gianicolo and Trastevere. Aerobic and weight rooms, plus classes taught in everything from pilates to Krav Maga. 1-day pass €10, monthly €60. Open June-July and Sept. M-F 8am-10:30pm, Sa 9am-6pm; open Oct.-May M-F 8am-10:30pm, Sa 9am-6pm, Su 10am-2pm.

Dabliu, V. Santa Nicola da Tolentino 30 (☎06 42 01 25 15; www.dabliu.com), near P. Barberini. Additional locations throughout the city. Swanky gym offers fitness rooms and classes. Open M-F 9am-8pm.

Roman Sport Center, V. del Galoppatoio 33 (☎06 32 01 667; www.romansportcenter. com). Ⓜ A-Spagna, near the Villa Borghese. Massive fitness complex with fitness rooms, classes, spa, and more. 1-day membership €27. Open M-F 7am-10:30pm, Sa 7am-8:30pm, Su 9am-3pm.

GLBT RESOURCES

ARCI-GAY, V. Zabaglia 14 (☎06 64 50 11 02, helpline 800 713 713; www.arcigayroma. it). ⓜB-Piramide. Holds discussions, dances, and special events. Provides psychological and legal counseling, and information on HIV testing, and other services. Welcome group W 7-9pm. Open M-F 4-8pm.

Circolo Mario Mieli di Cultura Omosessuale, V. Efeso 2/A (☎06 54 13 985; www. mariomieli.org). ⓜB-San Paolo. From the stop, walk to Largo Beato Placido Riccardi, turn right on V. Corinto. Promotes GLBT rights and holds cultural activities. AIDS activists offer psychological and legal assistance. Welcome group Su 3pm. Open M-Th 10am-7pm, F 10am-6pm.

Libreria Babele, V. dei Banchi Vecchi 116 (☎06 68 76 628; www.libreriababeleroma. it), across from Castel Sant'Angelo. Library focusing on gay literature. Open M 3-7pm, Tu-Sa 11am-7pm.

LAUNDROMATS

▨ **Splashnet,** V. Varese 33 (☎06 49 38 04 50; www.splashnetrome.com), 3 blocks from Termini. Internet €1.50 per hr. Free maps. Helpful, English-speaking staff. Wash €3 per 6kg. Dry €3 per 7kg. Ask for the *Let's Go* discount. Open daily in summer 8:30am-1am, in winter 8:30am-11pm.

Bolle Blu, Via Palestro 59/61 (☎06 44 65 804), V. Principe Amedeo 116 (☎06 44 70 30 98), V. Montebello 11 (☎06 47 82 59 77); near Termini. Wash and dry €10. Luggage storage €2. Open daily 8am-midnight.

OndaBlu, V. Principe Amedeo 70/B (☎05 16 25 68 98; www.ondablu.com). 29 locations throughout the city. Wash €3.50 per 7kg. Dry €3.50 per 7kg. Detergent €1. Internet €2 per hr. Wi-Fi available. Open daily 8am-10pm.

SUPERMARKETS

Standa: V. Cola di Rienzo 173, ⓜA-Lepanto or Ottaviano, inside the COIN department store. Open daily 9am-8pm. Also at V. di Trastevere 60, Tram 8 from Largo Argentina, inside the Oviesse department store. Open M-Sa 9am-8pm, Su 8:30am-1:30pm and 4-8pm. Primarily within department stores.

DìperDì: V. del Gesù 58/59 (☎06 69 38 08 75; www.diperdi.it), in the *centro storico*. Open M-Sa 8am-9pm, Su 9am-8pm.

Despar: V. del Pozzetto 119, in P. di Spagna. Slightly more expensive than DìperDì and Standa, but with more gourmet products. Open M-Sa 8am-9pm, Su 9am-9pm. Also at V. Nazionale 211/213. Open daily 9am-9pm.

Supermercato Sma, P. Santa Maria Maggiore 3 (www.smasupermercati.it). Large selection at low prices. Open M-Sa 8am-9pm, Su 8:30am-8:30pm.

Conad, P. dei Cinquecento (www.conad.it), lower level of Termini. Open daily 6am-midnight.

EMERGENCY AND COMMUNICATIONS

EMERGENCY PHONE NUMBERS

Pan-European Emergency Line (Police, Fire, Medical): ☎112.
General Emergency: ☎113.
Fire: ☎115.
Medical: ☎118.
Red Cross Ambulance Service: ☎5510.

Car Breakdown Assistance: ☎116.

Poison Control: ☎06 49 06 63.

Veterinary Emergency: ☎06 66 21 686.

Directory Assistance: ☎12. International operator (English-speaking) ☎170.

Police: Central police station (☎06 46 86). Rome city police (☎06 67 691). Highway police (☎06 22 101).

CRISIS AND COUNSELING LINES

Rape Crisis Line: Centro Anti-Violenza, V. di Torre Spaccata 157 (☎06 23 26 90 49; www.differenzadonna.it) and V. di Villa Pamphili 100 (☎06 58 10 926). Open 24hr.

Samaritans, V. San Giovanni 250 (☎80 08 60 022; www.samaritansonlus.org), in Laterano. English spoken. Counseling available; call ahead. Open daily 1-10pm. For additional resources consult www.controviolenzadonne.org.

Alcoholics Anonymous: ☎06 47 42 913; www.aarome.info.

Narcotics Anonymous: ☎06 86 04 788; www.na-italia.org.

Joel Nafuma Refugee Center, V. Napoli 58 (☎06 48 83 339; www.stpaulsrome.it), inside St. Paul's. English spoken.

PHARMACIES

Farmacia Internazionale, P. Barberini 49 (☎06 48 25 456 or 71 195; www.farmint.it). ⓂA-Barberini. Open 24hr.

Farmacia Piram, V. Nazionale 228 (☎06 48 80 754; www.piram.it). Open daily 8:30am-11:30pm. AmEx/MC/V.

HOSPITALS

Italy's medical system is socialized, so all public hospitals offer free emergency care (including ambulance service) and may only charge a minimal amount for non-emergency treatment, regardless of citizenship. However, this also means that they tend to be crowded, slow, often without English-speaking doctors, and may require extended waits for appropriate treatment. They also do not allow choice of physician or facilities. Consult your insurance company for accepted private hospitals. two private clinics and one public hospital are listed below.

International Medical Center, V. Firenze 47 (24hr. ☎06 48 82 371; www.imc84.com). Private hospital and clinic. Prescriptions filled. Paramedic crew on call. Referral service to English-speaking doctors. General visit €110, house visits at night and on weekends €150. Call ahead. Open M-F 9am-8pm; house calls after hours and on weekends.

Policlinico Umberto I, Vle. del Policlinico 155 (emergency ☎06 49 97 70 25, first aid and appointments 06 49 971; www.policlinicoumberto1.it), north of Termini. ⓂB-Policlinico or bus #649. English spoken. Largest public hospital in Rome. No cost for emergency treatment; approximately €25 for treatment of non-emergencies. Open 24hr.

Rome-American Hospital, V. Emilio Longoni 69 (24hr. ☎06 22 551, appointments 06 22 55 290; www.rah.it). English spoken. Private emergency and laboratory services, HIV tests, and pregnancy tests. Visits average €100-200, but prices vary based on required treatment. Reception and appointments open 9am-2pm. Doctors on call 24hr.

THE BLOOD OF THE ROMANS. When it is hot and humid outside, mosquitoes swarm Rome. While the nasty little buggers love feasting upon foreign blood, Romans seem to avoid the pestilent attacks. Consequently, insect repellents are extremely overpriced in the city. If you are prone to allergic reactions, bring antihistamine cream and bug spray.

INTERNET ACCESS

Internet Cafe, V. Cavour 213 (☎06 47 82 30 51). Internet €0.50 1st 5min., €0.10-0.20 per min. thereafter. Printing €0.20 per page. €0.50 for CDs/DVDs. Open M-F 11am-1am, Sa-Su 3pm-1am. Cash only.

Yex Internet Points, www.yex.it. 3 locations between P. Navona and Campo dei Fiori at C. V. Emanuele 106 (☎06 47 45 98 18; open daily 10am-7pm), P. Sant'Andrea della Valle 3 (☎06 97 84 42 46; open daily 10am-10pm), and V. dei Pastini 22 (☎06 67 94 423; open daily 10am-10:30pm). About €6 per hr. Also offer wire transfer and currency exchange.

POST OFFICES

V. Giolitti 14, in Termini, and **P. San Silvestro 19** (☎06 69 73 72 13). Both open M-F 8am-7pm, Sa 8am-1:15pm. Additional locations throughout the city, each with different hours; see www.poste.it/online/cercaup (in Italian) for a full listing. Stamps available at more numerous *tabacchi*. Postcards cost between €0.40-0.80 to send internationally; all mail can be dropped in red post boxes mounted on walls throughout Rome.

Postal Codes: 00100 to 00200; V. Giolotti 00185; P. San Silvestro 00187. **Code finder**: www.poste.it/en/postali/cap/index.shtml.

PRACTICAL INFORMATION

ACCOMMODATIONS

BY PRICE

UNDER €20 (❶)

Alessandro Downtown (109)	T
Casa Olmata (110)	T
Chianti Hostel (110)	T
Eurorooms (108)	T
Fiesta Terrace Hostel (111)	T
Freedom Traveller (107)	T
Hostel Funny (105)	T
Hostel Pink Floyd (111)	T
Hotel and Hostel Des Artistes (108)	T
Legends Hostel (107)	T
M&J Place Hostel (107)	T
Mosaic Hostel (110)	T
Pop Inn Hotel (107)	T
Stargate Hotel and Hostel Termini (105)	T
The Yellow (105)	T

€21-35 (❷)

⚜Alessandro Palace (105)	T
⚜Colors (103)	VC
Fawlty Towers Hotel and Hostel (105)	T
Hostel Beautiful (107)	T
Hostel Happy Days (104)	VC
Hostel Roma Inn 2000 (111)	T
Hotel Beautiful 2 (107)	T
Hotel Cervia (108)	T
Hotel Galli (108)	T
Hotel Giamaica (107)	T
⚜Hotel Papa Germano (108)	T
Hotel Positano (108)	T
Ivanhoe Hostel (110)	T
Rome Student House (98)	AC
Sandy Hostel (98)	AC

€36-50 (❸)

Affittacamere Aries (109)	T
Hotel Boccaccio (102)	PDS
Hotel Bolognese (109)	T
Hotel Lella (109)	T
Hotel San Pietrino (103)	VC
Pensione di Rienzo (110)	T
Pensione Rosetta (98)	AC

€51-65 (❹)

Blues B&B (111)	T
Hotel Cortorillo (110)	T
Hotel Giù Giù (110)	T
Hotel Julia (102)	PDS
Hotel Lady (104)	VC
⚜Hotel Scott House (109)	T
Pensione Panda (102)	PDS
Pensione Paradise (104)	VC
Rosetta Hotel (101)	CS
Welrome Hotel (109)	T
Yes Hotel (105)	T

OVER €65 (❺)

Albergo del Sole (101)	CS
Albergo Pomezia (101)	CS
Casa Banzo (101)	CS
Cesare Balbo Inn (98)	AC
Daphne Inn Veneto (97)	PDS
Due Torri (100)	CS
Hotel Amalia (104)	VC
Hotel Anahi (102)	PDS
Hotel Bolivar (100)	AC
Hotel Borromeo (100)	AC
Hotel dei Quiriti (104)	VC
Hotel DePetris (102)	PDS
Hotel Elite (97)	PDS
Hotel Fiori (100)	AC
Hotel Florida (103)	VC
Hotel Fontanella Borghese (101)	CS
Hotel Hiberia (100)	AC
Hotel Isa (103)	VC
Hotel Madrid (102)	PDS
Hotel Navona (101)	CS
Hotel Pincio (103)	PDS
Hotel Rinascimento (101)	CS
Hotel Smeraldo (100)	CS
Hotel Suisse (102)	PDS
Hotel Valle (100)	AC
Orange Hotel (103)	VC
Relais Palazzo Taverna (100)	CS
San Carlo Hotel (103)	PDS
TeatroPace33 (100)	CS
Trevi Hotel (102)	PDS

AC = Ancient City
CS = Centro Storico
PDS = Piazza della Signoria

VC = Vatican City
T = Termini

Rome swells with tourists around Easter, from May to July, and in September; be sure to book well in advance for those times. Most establishments also raise their prices during long weekends and holidays, and also through-out the high season. In general, prices vary widely with the time of year, and a proprietor's willingness to negotiate increases with length of stay, number of vacancies, and group size. Some hotels and hostels list such discounts on their websites, but the best way to get a price that's tailored to your stay is to call or email proprietors directly. As a general rule, independent establishments are more flexible than chains. Also be sure you're booking into a reputable place, and be careful about who you get advice from. Termini is swarming with hotel scouts. Many are legitimate and have IDs issued by tourist offices. However, some impostors have fake badges and direct travelers to run-down locations with exorbitant rates, especially at night. It's better to book a stay by going to a tourist office yourself. Better still, book in advance and know what you're getting. It may be necessary just to find a bed: some hostels, for instance, require 48 hours notice.

As Borgo/Prati and Trastevere tend to be somewhat more residential neighborhoods, they're also good places to search for an apartment rental, although they can be a bit pricey. Apartments many also become available in the *centro;* there's nothing like waking up among 17th century *palazzi* every morning, but it may cost you. Traveler seeking cheap long-term accommodations may find themselves on the city periphery. **Your Flat in Rome,** Borgo Pio 160, also rents spacious, short-term apartments near St. Peter's Square to individuals or groups for as little as €24 per person per night. (☎338 95 60 061; www.yourflatinrome. com.) **Hotel Trastevere,** V. Luciano Manara 24a (☎06 58 14 713; www.hoteltrastevere.net), in P. San Cosimato, also has short-term apartments available. **Short Lets Assistance,** V. Zucchelli 26 (☎06 48 90 58 97; www.shortletsassistance.com), by P. Barberini, oversees 120 apartments.

ANCIENT CITY

Due to their proximity to the major sights, these small hotels come at a price.

Pensione Rosetta, V. Cavour 295 (☎06 47 82 30 69; www.rosettahotel.com), past the Fori Imperiali. Buzz at the large, wooden front doors and walk through the Vespa and palm-filled courtyard. Affordable for the location. Spacious rooms have baths, TVs, phones, and fans. A/C €5-10. Free Wi-Fi in lounge. Singles €50-60; doubles €85; triples €95; quads €120. AmEx/MC/V. ❸

Rome Student House, V. Merulana 117. From the Colosseum, walk down V. Labicana and make a left at V. Merulana. Buzz at the front and take Scala II to the 3rd floor. Make reservations beforehand so the owner, who occasionally cooks guests dinner, is not out when you arrive. Colorful rooms with fans, linens, and Wi-Fi. Check-out 10:30am. Reserve online (www.hostelworld.com). 4- to 6-person dorms €20-25. Cash only. ❷

Sandy Hostel, V. Cavour 136 (☎06 48 84 585; www.sandyhostel.com). Near the main ancient sights. Try to ignore the key-operated elevator as you hike up 6 flights of stairs—low prices, attentive staff, and close proximity to the Ancient City will be your reward. Bare-bones backpacker accommodations. Computer with internet in lounge. Linens free. Lock-out 11:30am-2:30pm. Online reservations required. 6-person dorms €15-25; quads with private bath €20-30. Cash only. ❷

Cesare Balbo Inn, V. Cesare Balbo 43 (☎06 98 38 60 81 or 32 72 06 25 59; www. cesarebalbosuite.com). From V. Cavour, make a right on V. Panisperna; walk 2 blocks and make a right on V. Cesare Balbo. The owner, Glenn, lives on site and caters to your every need. Neat, spacious rooms with private bath. A/C and cable TV. Breakfast in room. Free Wi-Fi. Doubles €80; triples €90. AmEx/D/MC/V. ❺

Hotel Hiberia, V. 24 Maggio 8 (☎39 06 67 826 62; www.hotelhiberia.it). From V. Nazionale, make a right on V. Mazzarino; walk to the end and it will be facing you. Large rooms with relief sculptures and lit paintings hanging on the walls. Book ahead and ask for a room with views of P. Venezia at no extra cost. Restaurant open for lunch and dinner; bar open until midnight. Breakfast included. Free safes. Free Wi-Fi. Singles €90; doubles €110; triples €150; quads €180. AmEx/D/MC/V. ●

Hotel Fiori, V. Nazionale 163 (☎06 67 97 212; www.hotel-fiori.com). At the end of V. Nazionale, right before it intersects with V. 24 Maggio. Begrudgingly helpful concierge caters to visitors occupying small but well-kept rooms with ceiling fans and A/C. Breakfast included; served by the bar (open 24hr.), overlooking the *piazza* below. Free Wi-Fi and 1 computer in the bar. Check-out 11am. Singles €80; doubles €100; triples €140; quads €170. AmEx/D/MC/V. ●

Hotel Borromeo, V. Cavour 117 (☎39 06 48 84 915; www.hotelborromeo.com), directly after the intersection with V. Quattro Cantoni. Rooms in this 4-star hotel are kept quiet from the traffic of V. Cavour by double-pane glass. Breakfast included; served in top-floor lounge with stunning views. A/C. 24hr bar. Wi-Fi €1 per 30min. Singles €100; doubles €120; triples €150; quads €200. AmEx/D/MC/V. ●

Hotel Bolivar, V. della Cordonata 6 (☎39 06 67 91 025; www.bolivarhotel.it). From V. Nazionale, make a right on V. Mazzarino. Walk to the end, make a left, and look for a large sign directing you right onto V. della Cordonata. Ceiling frescoes, oil paintings, and chandeliers adorn the stately rooms, complete with marble baths. Breakfast included; enjoy it on the rooftop. Bar open 24hr. Wi-Fi €2 per hour, €15 per day. Singles €150; doubles €180; triples €210; quads €240. AmEx/D/MC/V. ●

Hotel Valle, V. Cavour 134 (☎00 64 81 57 36; www.hotelvalle.it), directly after the intersection with V. Quattro Cantoni. Sizeable rooms with safes, large showers, and A/C. Breakfast served in a lounge with a large flatscreen TV. Wi-Fi €5 per 30min., €10 per 2hr. Doubles €150; triples €170; quads €190. AmEx/D/MC/V. ●

CENTRO STORICO

Due to their proximity to the major sights, these small hotels come at a price. You'll still get value for your money, but hostelers and those with limited budgets ought to try other neighborhoods.

TeatroPace33, V. Teatro della Pace 33 (☎06 68 61 371; www.hotelteatropace.com), off V. dei Giubbonari. Tucked away in a quiet corner near P. Navona, this hotel in a converted 17th-century *palazzo* is a great value. All rooms come with A/C, TVs, internet, minibars, and safes. Be prepared to carry your bags up the dramatic central staircase. Breakfast included. Singles €100-120; doubles €150-210. AmEx/MC/V. ●

Relais Palazzo Taverna, V. dei Gabrielli 92 (☎06 20 39 80 64; www.relaispalazzotaverna. com). From P. Navona, take V. Agonale north and make a left onto V. dei Coppelle/V. dei Coronari and another left onto V. dei Gabrielli. Renovated 15th-century building with lots of charm. Each spacious room with A/C, TV, and safe. Wi-Fi. Singles €100-140; doubles €140-210; triples €160-240. AmEx/MC/V. ●

Due Torri, V. del Leonetto 23 (☎06 68 80 69 56; www.hotelduetorriroma.com). Make a right onto V. della Campana from V. di Monte Brianzo and take the first right onto V. del Leonetto. Difficult to find, but worth the effort. Renaissance-era building with clean, comfortable rooms. Each room with A/C, TV, and internet. Breakfast included. Wheelchair-accessible. Book well in advance. Singles €110-130; doubles €150-195; apartment-style quad €220-260. AmEx/MC/V. ●

Hotel Smeraldo, V. dei Chiodaroli 9 (☎06 47 82 30 69). From Campo dei Fiori, take V. dei Giubbonari and make a left. What this hotel lacks in decor, it makes up for with amenities and reasonable rates. Immaculate rooms all have private baths, TVs, and A/C. Breakfast included. Internet. Singles €75-115; doubles €115-145; triples €135-175. AmEx/MC/V. ❺

Casa Banzo, P. del Monte di Pieta 30 (☎06 68 33 909; www.casabanzo.it). From Campo dei Fiori, take V. dei Giubbonari and make a right onto V. Arco d. Monte; it's is on your left. Stunning, richly furnished hotel in a former *palazzo*. Comfortable rooms with A/C and TVs, great for families and anyone looking for a bit of glamour. Internet access. Doubles €90-140; triples €160-180; quads €180-200. AmEx/MC/V. ❺

Hotel Navona, V. dei Sediari 8, 1st fl. (☎06 68 21 13 92; www.hotelnavona.com). Bus #64 to C. V. Emanuele II or #70 to C. del Rinascimento. Take V. de Canestrari from P. Navona and cross C. del Rinascimento. A favorite of both Keats and Shelley. A/C, TV, and luggage storage. Breakfast included. Internet. 1st night deposit required with reservation. Singles €100-125; doubles €135-155; triples €180-210. Occasional online discounts. Cash discount for stays longer than 5 days. MC/V. ❺

Albergo del Sole, V. del Biscione 76 (☎06 68 80 68 73; www.solealbiscione.it), off Campo dei Fiori. One of the best deals in the *centro storico*. Comfy rooms with antique furniture and TVs. A/C in some rooms. Internet. Wheelchair-accessible. Reserve ahead in high season. Singles €75, with private bath €100-130; doubles €100-110/125-145; triples €200; quads €240. Discount for larger groups. Cash only. ❺

Hotel Fontanella Borghese, Largo Fontanella Borghese 84, 2nd fl. (☎06 68 80 96 24; www.fontanellaborghese.com). Heading north from P. Venezia, take a left on Largo Fontanella Borghese. Once owned by the Borghese princes, this centrally located hotel has lots of character. Rooms with A/C, minibars, phones, and satellite TVs. Breakfast included. Internet access. Wheelchair-accessible. Singles €110-160; doubles €180-250; triples €220-260; quads €240-275. Frequent online discounts. AmEx/MC/V. ❺

Rosetta Hotel, V. Cavour 295, 1st fl. (☎06 47 82 30 69; www.rosettahotel.com), past the Fori Imperiali. Buzz at the large front doors and walk through the courtyard. Small, affordable *pensione*. Spacious rooms come with TVs, phones, and fans. A/C €10. Reservations recommended in high season. Singles €60; doubles €85; triples €95; quads €110. AmEx/MC/V. ❹

Hotel Rinascimento, V. del Pellegrino 122 (☎06 68 47 813; www.hotelrinascimento. com). A straight shot from Campo dei Fiori. Popular hotel on a quiet street with convenient access to sights. Clean rooms with A/C, TVs, and minibars. Breakfast included. Internet €5 per 3hr. Wheelchair-accessible. Singles €95-110; doubles €115-190; triples €185-230; quads €195-260. AmEx/MC/V. ❺

Albergo Pomezia, V. dei Chiavari 13 (☎06 68 61 371), off V. dei Giubbonari. Comfortable rooms with A/C and TVs. Breakfast included. Internet access and Wi-Fi. Reservations recommended in high season. Singles from €70; doubles from €100; triples from €130. AmEx/MC/V. ❺

PIAZZA DI SPAGNA

Accommodations in this area might run you a few more euros per day, but they offer the convenience of being closer to the Metro and are often newer than those found in the *centro storico*. Besides, can you really put a price tag on living a few steps from Prada? John Keats wouldn't.

Daphne Inn Veneto, V. di San Basilio 55 (☎06 47 82 35 29; www.daphne-rome.com). ⓂA-Barberini. Daphne has just what a top-notch, urban B&B ought to have: spotless rooms with A/C and comfortable beds in an unbeatable location minutes away from the Trevi Fountain. Brand-new furniture, mini-fridges, tea service, and safes. Internet access.

A 2nd location at V. degli Avignonesi 20. Singles €100-160; doubles €140-220; triples €210-300. AmEx/MC/V. ❺

Hotel Suisse, V. Gregoriana 54, 3rd fl. (☎06 67 83 649 or 67 86 172; www.hotelsuisserome.com). ⓂA-Spagna/Barberini. From the Spanish Steps, veer right facing away from P. di Spagna. Close to the Steps, but away from the hubbub; at night you'll think you're in another city. This small hotel with impeccable service, sleek, old-fashioned furniture, and an inviting lounge extends over the 3rd floor of a former *palazzo*. All 12 rooms come with comfortable beds, phones, fans, and baths. English-speaking staff. Continental breakfast included. A/C €10. Free Wi-Fi; computer available. Singles €90-110; doubles €140-170; triples €190-220; quads €200-250. MC/V. ❺

Pensione Panda, V. della Croce 35, 2nd fl. (☎06 67 80 179; www.hotelpanda.it). ⓂA-Spagna. Between P. di Spagna and V. del Corso. Situated in a 19th-century building, Hotel Panda is one of the oldest hotels in the historical center of Rome. Immaculate, elegantly-furnished rooms with arched ceilings (some with Italian frescoes). A/C €6. Free Wi-Fi. Reservations recommended. Singles €65-68, with bath €75-80; doubles €75-78/98-108; triples €130-140; quads €180. Rooms sleep a flexible number of occupants; ask for details when booking. AmEx/MC/V. ❹

Hotel Boccaccio, V. del Boccaccio 25, 1st fl. (☎06 48 85 962; www.hotelboccaccio. com). ⓂA-Barberini. Off V. del Tritone near P. Barberini. This quiet, eco-friendly hotel is a renovated 1937 flat in the Trevi area, offering 8 elegant rooms with high ceilings and a breezy terrace. Each room has a fan, but no A/C. Singles €45; doubles €80, with bath €100. Ask about low-season discounts. AmEx/MC/V. ❸

Hotel Elite, V. Francesco Crispi 49 (☎06 67 83 083, www.elitehotel.eu). ⓂA-Spagna/ Barberini. Modern, spotless rooms with first-rate amenities, a stylish restaurant, and wine bar in a restored ancient building. Rooms have baths, phones, A/C, and TVs. Wi-Fi and computer in lounge area. Breakfast included. Reception 24hr. Singles €70-110; doubles €90-150; triples €120-185; quads €160-210. AmEx/MC/V. ❺

Hotel Madrid, V. Mario de Fiori 93-5 (☎06 67 84 548; www.hotelmadridroma.com). ⓂA-Spagna. Appropriately named for its proximity to the Spanish Steps, the hotel occupies a renovated 19th-century building with lots of character. Clean rooms with striking views over the Eternal City. A/C, TV, Wi-Fi, safe, and minibar. Parking and laundry service available. Breakfast included; served on a romantic terrace. Doubles €150-240; triples €170-280; quads €280-350. AmEx/MC/V. ❺

Hotel Anahi, V. della Penna 64 (☎06 47 82 35 29; www.hotellocarno.com). ⓂA-Barberini. This gorgeous Art Noveau hotel is just a stone's throw from the splendid P. del Popolo. Romantic and intimate, Anahi is ideal for anyone seeking comfort in the heart of Rome. Consists of 2 buildings joined by a garden smelling of wisteria where guests can take their breakfast. Clean, bright rooms with A/C, TVs, and minibars. Internet access. Free bike rental. Singles €90-140; doubles €110-200. AmEx/MC/V. ❺

Trevi Hotel, V. del Babuccio 20 (☎06 67 89 563; www.hoteltrevirome.com). ⓂA-Barberini. As the name suggests, this hotel is blocks away from the mesmerizing Trevi Fountain; turn right off V. Scanderbeg. A comfortable hotel with a refined ambience on a quiet street. Spotless rooms with warm colors, cherry furniture, and soft lighting. A/C, TV, minibar, and safe. Reading room and other common areas. Breakfast included. Singles €99-139; doubles €129-199. Suites and junior suites also available. AmEx/MC/V. ❺

Hotel DePetris, V. Rasella 142 (☎06 48 19 626; www.hoteldepetris.com). ⓂA-Barberini. A tasteful hotel with 53 large rooms offering all imaginable modern comforts: private bath, hairdryer, radio, satellite TV, phone, internet access, safe, minibar, and A/C. Breakfast may be taken on the leafy patio. Singles €210; doubles €330; each additional bed €60. AmEx/MC/V. ❺

Hotel Julia, V. Rasella 29 (☎06 48 81 637; www.hoteljulia.it).ⓂA-Barberini. This small 19th-century palace in the historic V. Rasella has a facade on a quiet street adjoining the presidential palace of Rome (Ciao, Silvio!). All 33 rooms comfortable, though somewhat dark. A/C, TV, internet access, minibar, and safe. Continental breakfast included. Hotel welcomes small pets and can provide dog-sitting service for a fee. Singles €60-150, with external private shower €40-90; doubles €99-220, with queen bed €88-190; triples €115-250; quads €120-270. The same owners have an apartment-style setup for longer stays. AmEx/D/MC/V. ❹

San Carlo Hotel, V. delle Carrozze 92-3 (☎06 67 84 548; www.hotelsancarloroma. com). ⓜA-Spagna. A 17th-century mansion on a quiet side street adjacent to the V. Condotti and its world-renowned luxury boutiques. Huge rooms in an elegant contemporary style each include bathtub or spacious shower stall, flatscreen TV, A/C, minibar, and free Wi-Fi. Continental breakfast included. Singles €80-125; doubles €115-188; triples €135-220; quads €200-370. AmEx/MC/V. ❺

Hotel Pincio, V. Capo le Case 50 (☎06 67 90 758; www.hotelpincio.com). From ⓜA-Spagna, make a right off V. Sistina onto V. Francesco Crispi, then veer right. A family-run hotel tucked away in the heart of Rome. Continental breakfast served on a lovely roof garden. Overlooks the Church of Sant'Andrea delle Fratte with its magnificent bell tower, designed by Bernini in the 1600's. Internet access. A/C. Doubles €110-195; triples €125-230. AmEx/MC/V. ❺

VATICAN CITY

Pensioni near the Vatican offer better deals than many areas in Rome's city center. But hardcore party-fiends beware: as you might imagine, most of your nightlife options lie outside this quiet, affluent area.

▨ Colors, V. Boezio 31 (☎06 68 74 030; www.colorshotel.com). ⓜA-Ottaviano. Take a right on V. Terenzio, off V. Cola di Rienzo, then left on V. Boezio. True to its name, Colors offers 18 beds in rooms painted with a verve that would put Raphael to shame. 2 hostel floors and a 3rd floor with private rooms. A/C. Kitchens and tranquil terraces on all floors. Breakfast included. Internet access €2 per hr. Reserve dorms by 9pm the night before; wise to book earlier. Dorms €27; singles €90, with bath €105; doubles €100/130; triples €120. Low season discount up to 30%. Cash only. ❷

Orange Hotel, 86 Via Crescenzio (☎06 68 68 969; www.orangehotelrome.com). Stylish, eco-friendly boutique hotel offers a lovely terrace with a solarium and a panoramic view over the cupola of San Pietro. Points for guessing the color scheme. Delightful amenities include a rooftop restaurant, parking garage, terrace hot tub, and in-hotel laundromat. All rooms with bathtubs, A/C, TVs, internet, safes, and minibars. Breakfast included. Doubles €93-174, junior suites €154-214; triples €158-218; extra beds available. AmEx/MC/V. ❺

Hotel San Pietrino, V. Giovanni Bettolo 43, 3rd fl. (☎06 37 00 132; www.sanpietrino.it). ⓜA-Ottaviano. Exit on V. Barletta and turn left on V. Bettolo. A quirky amphibian motif manifests itself in frog paintings, frog statues, and stuffed frogs in the hallways. Spacious rooms are comfortable and clean with A/C, TVs, and (sometimes) DVD players. Laundry €8. Internet access. In high season, reserve months ahead. Singles €32-92; doubles €48-118; triples €72-148; family quad €92-168. Discounts negotiable for longer stays or larger groups. MC/V. ❸

Hotel Isa, V. Cicerone 39, 2nd fl. (☎06 32 12 610; www.hotelisa.net). A straight shot from ⓜA-Flaminio, down V. Colonna/V. Cicerone. An elegant hotel with spacious rooms. High ceilings, marble trim, and all the necessary amenities for your *dolce vita*: TV, Wi-Fi, minibar, and A/C. Singles €85-155; doubles €130-190; triples €170-230; quads €190-250. Fancier rooms also available. AmEx/MC/V. ❺

Hotel Florida, V. Cola de Rienzo 243, 2nd fl. (☎06 32 41 872 or 32 41 608; www.hotelfloridaroma.it). ⓜA-Ottaviano. 18 comfortable rooms, recently redone with chic new furniture, in a fantastic location on Prati's main street. A/C. TV. Some rooms have safes and minibars. Singles €70-105; doubles €85-125; triples €95-150; quads €100-185. Fancier rooms approximately €20 more. AmEx/MC/V. ❺

Pensione Paradise, V. Giulio Cesare 47, 3rd fl. (☎06 36 00 43 31; www.pensioneparadise.com). Clean, minimalist, great-value *pensione* with Ⓜ️A-Lepanto just outside the door. English-speaking staff always ready to help with hints and suggestions to make your stay in Rome memorable. A/C. Internet access. Singles €52-62, with shared bath €42-52; doubles €65-98; triples €110-125; quads (with a twin bunk and a double) €135-150. AmEx/MC/V. ❹

Hotel Lady, V. Germanico 198, 4th fl. (☎06 32 42 112; www.hotelladyroma.it), between V. Fabbio Massimo and V. Paolo Emilio. The old-fashioned Hotel Lady has the romantic charm of Audrey Hepburn on a Roman Holiday. Originally a 19th-century monastery built over the ancient ruins of Hadrian's Circus, the hotel will delight you with its dimly-lit halls and rich wooden beams. Rooms have antique furniture, desks, phones, and fans. Internet access. Singles €50-70; doubles €80-100, with bath €90-130; triples €100-135. Prices vary seasonally. AmEx/MC/V. ❹

Hotel dei Quiriti, V. Germanico 198, 4th fl. (☎06 36 00 53 89; www.hoteldeiquiriti. com). Ⓜ️A-Ottaviano/Lepanto. No-frills, comfortable rooms in a small hotel on a leafy convenient street. TV, minibar, A/C, and internet. Breakfast included. Shares a reception with Hotel Giuggioli on the 1st floor. Singles €89-109; doubles €99-129; triples €119-159. AmEx/MC/V. ❺

Hotel Amalia, V. Germanico 66 (☎06 39 72 33 56; www.hotelamalia.com), on a quiet side street right off of V. Ottaviano. Delightful and comfortable hotel, halfway between the Vatican and Ⓜ️A-Ottaviano, with large rooms. TV, minibar, A/C, safe, and Wi-Fi. Parking available. Breakfast included. Standard singles €80-130; doubles €135-200; triples €180-280; quads €220-320. 10% discount when paying in cash; free upgrade to a fancier room when paying cash in the low season. AmEx/MC/V. ❺

Hostel Happy Days, V. Cola de Rienzo 217 (☎06 39 72 33 56; www.happydayshostel. com). Spotless, apartment-style hostel with kitchen and living room, in an excellent location (5min. from the Pope's crib). 4, 6, and 8 bed dorms available. Be careful with your valuables: guests can let people in the door without management seeing. Free internet. TV in common room. Dorms €20-35. Rates vary nightly. Cash only. ❷

MO' MONEY, NO PROBLEMS. Most independently-run hostels and hotels will offer discounts if you pay in cash in order to avoid a 10% tax from credit companies. Put your credit card away and hit up the ATMs.

TERMINI AND SAN LORENZO

LET'S NOT GO. Don't have so much fun in Termini that you completely let your guard down—Termini can be a sketchy area, especially at night, and you can't rely only on your kung fu skills to deter pickpockets.

Welcome to budget traveler central. The accommodations around the **Termini station** are some of the least expensive and most centrally located in Rome. They also play host to the most backpackers and students, so look no further if a fun atmosphere is what you crave.

ACCOMMODATIONS

SAN LORENZO AND NORTHEAST OF TERMINI

Alessandro Palace, V. Vicenza 42 (☎06 44 61 958; www.hostelalessandropalace. com). From Termini's track 1, turn left on V. Marsala and right on V. Vicenza. Renovated dorms with baths and A/C. Fun bar with flatscreen TV and cheap drinks (happy hour; €3 beers daily 10-11pm). Fantastic English-speaking staff. Breakfast and pizza dinners included. Lockers free; supply your own lock. Towels €2; included with doubles, triples, and quads. Internet (computer lounge and Wi-Fi) free 30min. per day; €1 per hr. thereafter. Check-in 3pm. Check-out 10am. 4- to 8-person dorms €25-35; doubles €110; triples and quads €44 per person. MC/V. ❷

The Yellow, V. Palestro 44 (☎06 49 38 26 82; www.the-yellow.com). From Termini, exit on V. Marsala, head down V. Marghera, and take the 4th left. Look no farther if you want to party hearty with people from all over the world. Huge rooms with stenciled *Blues Brothers* and *Pussy Wagon* logos accent this modern, chic youth hostel. Rocking hostel bar next door (see p. 238) caters to guests. Lockers, linens, luggage storage, and fans included. A/C in rooms with bath. Breakfast €2. Free Wi-Fi in lounge; rent a laptop for 30min. for free or €1 per hr. Check-in 1:30pm. Check-out 10am. 4- to 12- person dorms with shared bath €10-30; 4- and 6-person dorms with private bath €10-34. €5 cash discount. AmEx/D/MC/V. ❶

Fawlty Towers Hotel and Hostel, V. Magenta 39, 5th fl. (☎06 44 50 374; www.fawltytowers.org). From Termini, cross V. Marsala onto V. Marghera and turn right on V. Magenta. Relaxed, bohemian feel. Brightly colored rooms. Comfortable common room with stained glass, TV, A/C, DVD player, book exchange, and free internet on 1 computer. Most rooms have A/C—ask for it when reserving, at no extra cost. Free lockers, linens, and towels. Kitchen with stocked fridge available for snacking. Free BBQs 2-3 Fridays per month in summer on the sweet outdoor terrace. Check-out 10:30am for dorms, 11am for private rooms. Reception 24hr. 3-bed dorms €25-30; 4-bed dorms €18-25; singles €30-55, with shower or full bath €35-60; doubles €45-70/50-85; triples €70-95/75-99; quads €80-100/80-110. Cash only; pay in advance. ❷

Yes Hotel, V. Magenta 15 (☎06 44 36 38 29; www.yeshotelrome.com). From Termini, cross V. Marsala onto V. Marghera and turn left on V. Magenta. Brand-new hotel with ultra-modern facilities, including a shockingly spacious elevator, lounge covered in black leather and metal, and flatscreen TVs in every room. All rooms have baths, A/C, minifridges, phones, hair dryers, and safes. Breakfast included. Doubles €50-150; triples €70-170; quads €90-190. Check for discounts online. AmEx/MC/V. ❹

Hostel Funny, V. Varese 31/33 (☎06 44 70 35 23, cell 39 34 07 88 00 60; www.hostelfunny.com). From Termini's track 1, turn right on V. Marsala, left on V. Milazzo, and right on V. Varese. Owner Mabri will leave you laughing with his welcoming nature. He also owns **Splashnet** laundromat-internet cafe (p. 93; reception in same location), where you can kill 3 birds with 1 stone by using the free internet while washing and drying your clothes for €5. Breakfast included; any time of day. Free bottle of wine upon arrival. Free pasta party M-F nights. Dining room, sitting room with TV, and new kitchen. TVs and lockers in rooms. Free fans for rooms without A/C. Check-out 10am. Reception 8:30am-midnight. 4-bed dorms €15-30; doubles €50-90, with bath and A/C €50-100; triples €60-110/60-120. Ask about the *Let's Go* discount. Cash only. ❶

Stargate Hotel and Hostel Termini, V. Palestro 88 (☎06 44 57 164; www.stargatehotels. com). From Termini, exit on V. Marsala, head down V. Marghera, and take the 4th right. Exposed brick ceilings and reliefs of Rome's famed sights decorate the interior of this recently renovated hotel. Rooms with free Wi-Fi, TVs, fridges, A/C, safes, and baths with hairdryers. Bright lounge with fresh flowers. Breakfast included. Free luggage storage. Kitchen available. Check-in 2pm. Check-out 10am. Lockout 11am-2pm. 4- and 6-bed dorms €13-25; singles €35-50; doubles €50-100; triples €60-120. Cash only. ❶

Legends Hostel, V. Curtatone 12 (☎06 44 70 32 17; www.legendshostel.com). From Termini's track 1, turn right on V. Marsala, continue on V. Volturno, turn right on V. Gaeta, and then right on V. Curtatone. Pop in a DVD from the hostel's extensive collection and enjoy complimentary hot chocolate and coffee. Full kitchen open 7:30am-10pm. Breakfast included. Free pasta party daily. Write them a blog or thank-you letter and they'll post it on the wall next to all the others. Free lockers. Towels €2. Free Wi-Fi and internet. Reception 24hr. Check-out 10am. 4- and 8-bed dorms have communal bath, others private. 4-bed dorms €14-37; 5-bed mixed and female dorms €14-35; 6-bed dorms €12-32; 8-bed dorms €10-30. AmEx/D/MC/V. ❶

Freedom Traveller, V. Gaeta 23 (☎06 47 82 38 62; www.freedom-traveller.it). From Termini's track 1, turn left on V. Marsala, continue on V. Volturno, and turn right on V. Gaeta. Grab the Texas Hold 'Em chips set and win back the handful of change you paid for your room on one of the covered tables in the outdoor courtyard or in front of the TV in the air-conditioned lounge. Big private rooms with frescoed ceilings. Full kitchen open 8am-11pm. Free luggage storage. Breakfast included. Free nightly pasta dinners with wine Nov.-Mar.; free pizza and beer parties Tu nights Apr.-Oct. Free Wi-Fi and 2 computers in lounge. Reception 24hr. Check-in 2pm. Check-out 10:30am. 4-bed mixed or female dorms €15-23, with bath €18-25; doubles €50-65/60-75; triples €70-85/75-95; quads €80-100/90-110. MC/V. ❶

M&J Place Hostel, V. Solferino 9 (☎06 44 62 802; www.mejplacehostel.com). From Termini's track 1, turn left on V. Marsala and right on V. Solferino. Large party hostel is great if you can get over the dirty communal bathrooms. Luxurious private rooms. Common room, lively bar, and restaurant downstairs (p. 238). PCs with internet, TVs, and baths with waterfall-flow shower heads in private rooms. Kitchen open 3-10pm. Breakfast included; served at bar. Small lockers at reception. Free fans, linens, and luggage storage. Wi-Fi, computers, and laptop rental. Check-in 3pm. Check-out 10am. Reception 24hr. 4-, 6-, 8-, 10-bed mixed dorms and 6-bed female dorms €12-32, with bath €15-35; with bath €40-140; doubles with communal bath €40-60. Subtract €2.50-10 per person if you don't want internet and breakfast. Cash only. ❶

Hotel Beautiful 2, V. Milazzo 8/14 (☎06 44 70 39 27; www.hotelbeautiful.com). From Termini's track 1, turn right on V. Marsala and left on V. Milazzo. Sister hotel of Hostel Beautiful is another favorite of young travelers. Lounge around on a sofa in the comfy common area or in your modern room. Breakfast in room and weekly dinners included. Towels and linens included. Internet free 30min. per day in cafe, €1.50 per hr. after. Reception 24hr., with safe. Ask for a room with A/C at no extra cost. Check-in 2pm. Check-out 10am. 4-bed dorms €15-20, with bath €20-35; 6-bed dorms with bath €18-30; doubles with bath €60-100; quads with bath €100-120. Discounts for groups of 15+. Cash only. ❷

Pop Inn Hotel, V. Marsala 80 (☎06 49 59 887; www.popinnhostel.com). Disney characters and gleeful stick figures smile at you from the wallpaper and behind frames. Some rooms have round beds and shared bathrooms with whirlpool tubs. Festive common room filled with guests listening to music, reading, or watching TV on the big screen. Free Italian breakfast all day at nearby bar, 15min. of internet per day at a cafe, small lockers, and ceiling fans. Private rooms have bath and A/C. Check-in 3:30pm. Check-out 10:30am. Lock-out 10:30am-3:30pm. 4- to 7-bed mixed dorms with shared bath €16-31; singles €40-85, with bath €46-105; doubles €42-104/52-120; triples €57-135; quads €68-152; quints €80-165. Cash only, in advance. ❶

Hotel Giamaica, V. Magenta 13 (☎06 49 01 21; md0991@mclink.it). From Termini, turn left on V. Marsala, right on V. Vicenza, and left on V. Magenta. Check out the top of your head in the mirror ceiling as you walk through the green hall, off of which are large rooms with double doors, flower-print sheets, shared baths, and fans. Breakfast (€5) is served in a bright room with turquoise accents and greenery. Common fridge. Free luggage storage. Reception 6am-1:30am. Check-out 11am. Singles €33; doubles €56; triples €69. Cash only.

Eurorooms, V. Palestro 87 (☎06 44 57 164; www.stargatehotels.com). From Termini, exit on V. Marsala, head down V. Marghera, and take the 4th right. Homey hostel provides a small-town feel in the middle of Rome. Each room with bath, A/C (€10 extra in dorms), TV, fridge, and free Wi-Fi. Breakfast included. Wheelchair-accessible. Check-in 2pm. Check out noon. 4- and 6-bed dorms €18-22; singles €40-55; doubles €50-80; triples €60-110; quads €90-140. AmEx/D/MC/V. ❶

Hotel and Hostel Des Artistes, V. Villafranca 20, 5th fl. (☎06 44 54 365; www.hoteldesartistes.com). From Termini's middle concourse, exit right, turn left on V. Marsala, right on V. Vicenza, and take 5th left. Hang out on the large rooftop terrace (with heated section for winter) to meet other travelers. English spoken. Free movies in English and Italian. Wi-Fi €1 per hr., €5 per day. Check-out 10:30am. Hotel: each room with bath, A/C, TV, safe, fan, and hair dryer. Breakfast included. Doubles €50-150; triples €70-170; quads €90-190. Hostel: pastel-colored common room with TV. Breakfast €1.50. Lockers and linens included. Private rooms have TV, safe and fan. Luggage storage. All rooms have communal bath. 4-bed dorms €12-30; 6-bed dorms €10-28; doubles €40-100; triples €55-115; quads €70-130; 5-bed dorms €100-140, 6-bed dorms €120-150. AmEx/MC/V. Hotel ❹/hostel ❶.

Hotel Cervia, V. Palestro 55, 1st fl. (☎06 49 10 57; www.hotelcerviaroma.it). From Termini, exit on V. Marsala, head down V. Marghera, and take the 4th left. Clean rooms with fans in this *albergo historico* (50+ years of service). Multilingual staff. Recently renovated sister hotel, **Restivo** (www.hotelrestivo.com) in the same building, has only private rooms with bath and caters more to families, but at same prices. Private rooms in both have TVs; all rooms have safes. Continental breakfast €5. Check-out 11am. 2- to 5-person dorms €20; singles €30-40, with bath €35-55; doubles €40-70/50-80; triples €60-80/75-120; quads €80-110/100-140. 5% *Let's Go* discount when paying in cash; discounts negotiable for longer stays and check online. AmEx/D/MC/V. ❷

Hotel Galli, V. Milazzo 20 (☎06 44 56 859; www.albergogalli.com). From Termini's middle concourse, exit right. Turn right on V. Marsala and left on V. Milazzo. Reception on 2nd fl. Clean, new rooms with baths, mini-fridges, phones, TVs, and safes. A/C €5. Breakfast €5. Check-in 11am. Check-out 10am. Singles €25-75; doubles €40-110; triples €65-120; quads €80-160. Check for discounts online. 2-day cancellation policy. AmEx/D/MC/V. ❷

Hotel Positano, V. Palestro 49 (☎06 49 03 60; www.hotelpositano.it). From Termini, turn left on V. Marsala, right on V. Vicenza, and left on V. Palestro. Straight-up accommodations with breakfast (€5), towels (€1), and little-to-no decorations save plaster and white paint. Safe at reception. Free luggage storage. Linens included. Reception 24hr. Request a room with a balcony and great view at same price. 5- to 6-bed mixed dorms with shared bath €15-28; doubles €40-60, with bath €50-100; triples €75-105/90-140; quads with shared bath €72-120. AmEx/MC/V. ❷

> **TIP**
> **I SAY TOMATO, YOU SAY TOMAHTO.** In Italy, the 1st floor is actually floor 0 (known as *pianterreno*). Consequently, every floor thereafter is numbered 1 less than you might expect.

VIA XX SETTEMBRE AND NORTHWEST OF TERMINI

Dominated by government ministries and private apartments, this area is less noisy and touristy than nearby Termini.

🌟 **Hotel Papa Germano,** V. Calatafimi 14/A (☎39 06 48 69 19; www.hotelpapagermano.com). From Termini, turn left on V. Marsala, which becomes V. Volturno, and take

4th right on V. Calatafimi. Clean, simple rooms with TVs. Helpful, English-speaking staff. Continental breakfast included. A/C €5; free fans. Free internet on 3 computers. Reception 24hr. Check-in noon. Check-out 10am. 4-bed dorms €21-28; singles €35-50; doubles €50-80, with bath €60-105; triples €60-90/80-120; quads €85-120/95-140. AmEx/D/MC/V. ❷

Affittacamere Aries, V. XX Settembre 58/A (☎06 42 02 71 61; www.affittacamerearies.com). From Termini, turn left onto V. Marsala, which becomes V. Volturno, and right onto V. Cernia. Make a left on V. Goito and follow it to V. XX Settembre. Comfy rooms with fridges, TVs, towels, free Wi-Fi, and A/C. English spoken. Breakfast €3. Check-in noon. Check-out 11am. Singles €35-80; doubles €45-100, with bath €50-120; triples €70-150. Ask about the *Let's Go* discount; make sure to have your book with you. D/MC/V. ❸

Hotel Bolognese, V. Palestro 15, 2nd fl. (☎/fax 06 49 00 45; www.hotelbologneseinrome.com). From Termini, exit right; walk down V. Marghera and take the 4th left onto V. Palestro. The proud artist-owner's impressive paintings and the cleanliness and comfort of the newly renovated rooms set this hotel apart. Private baths and TVs. Rooms with A/C cost extra. Request a room with a balcony at no extra cost. Breakfast included. Free fans and luggage storage. Check-out 11am. Singles €35-60; doubles €60-100; triples €80-120. AmEx/MC/V. ❸

Hotel Lella, V. Palestro 9. (☎06 48 49 40; www.hotellella.com). From Termini, exit right; walk down V. Marghera and take the 4th left onto V. Palestro. Full-service hotel whose low rates, convenient location, and knowledgeable staff cater to backpackers looking for a bit more privacy. Private baths, A/C, TVs, and luggage storage. Some doubles and triples have balconies; request at no extra cost. Breakfast included. Check-in 2pm. Check-out 10am. Singles €40-50; doubles €70-80; triples €75-90; quads €80-120. Cash only. ❸

Welrome Hotel, V. Calatafimi 15-19. (☎06 47 82 43 43; www.welrome.it). From Termini, turn left on V. Marsala, which becomes V. Volturno, and take 4th right on V. Calatafimi. The grandmotherly owner, Mary, personalizes your stay and keeps things quiet for nappers and families. Concerned parents need not worry about their traveling children; she ensures that young guests don't bring visitors up to their rooms. Large rooms with baths, fridges, balconies, A/C, Wi-Fi, and TVs. Check-in 10am. Check-out 11am. Doubles €50-110; triples €105-148; quads €120-187. MC/V. ❹

ESQUILINO AND SOUTHWEST OF TERMINI

Esquilino, south of Termini, has tons of cheap hotels closer to the major sights. The area west of Termini is also inviting, with busy streets and shopping.

🔲 **Hotel Scott House,** V. Gioberti 30 (☎06 44 65 379; www.scotthouse.com). Exit Termini on V. Giolitti and turn left. Cross the street and take a right on V. Gioberti. Modern rooms painted in soothing colors, each with bath, A/C, phone, safe, and TV. English spoken. Breakfast included. Free luggage storage. 1 computer. Free Wi-Fi. Reception 24hr. Check-in 2pm. Check-out 11am. Singles €36-68; doubles €63-98; triples €75-122; quads €88-132. Discount for cash payments. AmEx/MC/V. ❹

Alessandro Downtown, V. Carlo Cattaneo 23 (☎06 44 34 01 47; www.hostelalessandrodowntown.com). From Termini's track #22, take a left on V. Giolitti and a right on V. C. Cattaneo. Worthwhile alternative to the Palace with the same social environment; head to the Palace to use the in-house bar. Dining room, sitting room with satellite TV, and new kitchen open 1pm-midnight. Breakfast included. Free pasta party M-F nights. Lockers, ceiling fans, and Wi-Fi in rooms. Towels €2. Internet 30min. free per day, €1 per hr. thereafter. Check-out 10am. Lockout 11am-2pm. 6- and 8-bed mixed or female dorms €17-25; doubles €70, with bath €90; quads €120/140. AmEx/MC/V. ❶

Hotel Giù Giù, V. del Viminale 8, 2nd fl. (☎06 48 27 734; www.hotelgiugiu.com). Exit Termini on V. Giolitti, turn right and walk past P. dei Cinquecento to V. Viminale; turn left. Elegant but fading *palazzo* filled with porcelain knick-knacks and Victorian furniture feels like a grandmother's house. Rooms have A/C, TVs, and safes. Breakfast €6-8 under frescoed ceiling. Check-out 10am. Singles €40-60; doubles with bath €60-95; triples €90-140; quads €120-190. Check website for low-season specials. AmEx/D/MC/V. ❹

Pensione di Rienzo, V. Principe Amedeo 79/A, 2nd fl. (☎06 44 67 131; www.hoteldirienzo.it). Exit Termini on V. Giolitti, walk down V. Gioberti, and make a left on V. Principe Amedeo. Tranquil, family-run retreat just 2 blocks from Termini. Windows overlook courtyard, offering quiet respite. Well-furnished rooms are fresh and airy. Request a room with a balcony at no extra charge. Fans available. English spoken. Breakfast in room €10. Check-out 10am. Singles €25-65, with bath €50-60; doubles €30-70/€35-80; triples with bath €90. MC/V. ❸

Mosaic Hostel, V. Carlo Cattaneo 23 (☎06 44 70 45 92; www.hostelmosaic.com). From Termini's track #22, take a left on V. Giolitti and a right on V. C. Cattaneo. Directly below Alessandro Downtown, with nearly identical facilities in a smaller hostel. Large dorms with tables. Some rooms have A/C—request it. Free fans. Breakfast included. Pasta parties M-F served in a large area with TV. Small lockers in the lounge. Kitchen available. Towels €2. Internet on 2 computers and Wi-Fi free 15min. per day. Check-in 2pm. Check-out 11am. Reception 24hr. 4-8 bed mixed dorms and 4-8 bed female dorms with shared bath €12-38. MC/V. ❶

Ivanhoe Hostel, V. Urbana 50 (☎06 48 93 05 56; www.backpackers.it/ivanhoe). ⓂB-Cavour. From the station, cross V. Cavour and go down the stairs by the Metro sign. Turn right on V. Urbana. Don't expect the music to be turned down so you can take an afternoon nap—this is a self-proclaimed party hostel that lives up to its reputation. Recently renovated, modern facilities include a large common area with spotlights and an angular geometric mural. Breakfast (€2) and bar room (open until midnight) has a kitchen for customer use, and hosts occasional open bar cocktail parties (€2). All rooms have large lockers and A/C. Towels €2. Internet on 2 computers and Wi-Fi free 15min. per day, thereafter €0.50 per 15min. Free luggage storage. Reception 24hr. Check-in before 6pm. Check-out 10am. Lock-out 11am-4pm. 6-, 8-, 12-bed mixed dorms and 8-bed female dorms with shared bath €20-30; doubles with bath €80-100. Ages 18-35 only. Cash only. ❷

Chianti Hostel, V. Carlo Alberto 53 (☎39 27 79 02 26). From Termini, turn left on V. Giovanni Giolitti and right on V. Rattazzi; follow it to the end and turn left on V. Carlo Alberto. 1-floor medium-sized hostel fosters community. Bright rooms with bunk beds. Great staff, amenities, and social environment more than make up for the cramped sleeping space. Breakfast €1.50. Free weekly dinners. 2 computers and TV in the lounge. A/C. Free lockers, linens, and kitchen use. Free Wi-Fi. Reception 24hr. Check-in 4pm. Check-out 11am. Lockout 11am-4pm. 4-bed dorms €16-31; 6-bed dorms €13-29; 10-bed dorms €10-28. Cash only. ❶

Hotel Cortorillo, V. Principe Amedeo 79/A, 6th fl. (☎06 44 66 934; www.hotelcortorillo.it). Exit Termini on V. Giolitti, walk down V. Gioberti, and make a left on V. Principe Amedeo. Reception on V. Principe Amedeo. Modern hotel with advanced surveillance system (and tons of signs to prove it). Spacious rooms with safes, baths, TVs, minifridges, and A/C. Many inexplicably lack shower curtains. Breakfast included. Check-in noon. Check-out 10am. Singles €50-100; doubles €60-130. Extra bed €15-30. Credit card required for deposit. AmEx/D/MC/V. ❹

Casa Olmata, V. dell'Olmata 36 (☎06 48 30 19; www.casaolmata.com). From Termini, walk down V. Cavour, turn left on V. Liberiana past Santa Maria Maggiore, and then right on V. dell'Olmata. Extensive renovations are currently underway in the common areas, but the rooms are clean and large, with simple accents and wooden furniture reminiscent of a countryside guest house. Gorgeous rooftop terrace with 360° view of the heart of Rome has a barbecue and kitchen, and hosts spaghetti parties every other night. The wonderful owner packs up the free continental breakfast for those who miss it in Casa, or doles out coupons for free Italian breakfast nearby. Ceiling fans, luggage storage, lockers, and TVs. Towels €1 for dorms. Free internet. Reception 8am-2pm and 4pm-midnight. Check-out 10:30am. 6- and 7-bed mixed and female dorms with private bath €16-20; singles with shared bath €36-40; doubles with shared bath €48-58; triples with shared bath €63-75. AmEx/MC/V. ❶

Fiesta Terrace Hostel, V. Cairoli 101 (☎06 97 61 20 83 or 32 41 75 70 67; www.bbfiestaterrace.com). From Termini's track 22, turn left on V. Giolitti and right on V. Cairoli. The large terrace shaded by vines is the site of numerous fiestas. Pictures of landscapes and international cityscapes in the high-ceiling rooms take you back to wherever home might be. Kitchen available 24hr. Luggage storage, lockers, and fans in dorms. Towels €1 in dorms. Free internet and Wi-Fi. Private rooms have A/C and satellite TVs. Check-out 11am. 4-6-bed mixed dorms with shared bath €13-22; doubles €40-50; triples €60-90; quads €64-100. Cash only for dorms, MC/V otherwise. ❶

Hostel Pink Floyd, V. Principe Amedeo 79A/B (☎06 49 77 31 53, 44 70 43 35, or 44 60 634; www.hotelhollywoodrome.com). From Termini's track 22, exit on V. Giolitti, walk down V. Gioberti, and make a left on V. Principe Amedeo. Enter through the beautiful courtyard filled with flowers and tropical plants into rooms whose walls are decorated with iconic imagery like the Sistine Chapel ceiling. Even Pink Floyd wouldn't tear these down. A/C €1 per person for dorms, €6 per private room. Breakfast €2 for dorms, included for private rooms. Safes at reception and in private rooms. Free Wi-Fi and internet in lounge, limited to 10min. per day. Reception 24hr. Private rooms have access to roof-top terrace with kitchen. Bar in reception lounge open until 10pm. Check-in 11am. Check-out 10am. 4-6-bed dorms with shared bath €14-25; doubles €45-94, with bath €49-114; triples €65-126/71-135; quads €80-152/88-184; quints and 6-person rooms with bath €19-29 per person. Cash only for dorms, MC/V otherwise. ❶

Blues B&B, V. Cairoli 115 (☎32 85 69 87 22; www.blues-bb.com). From Termini's track 22, turn left on V. Giolitti and right on V. Cairoli. Owners Luciana and Sabino welcome you into their home, and are very attuned to customer satisfaction. Quaint, basic B&B with quality facilities and everything included. Ideal for families and those looking for quiet privacy. Rooms have ceiling fans, TVs, fridges, and private baths with hair dryers. Breakfast included. Free internet. Check-in 11am. Check-out 10am. Doubles €40-80; triples €60-90; quads €70-110. MC/V. ❹

Hostel Beautiful, V. Napoleone III 35 (☎06 44 65 890; www.hotelbeautiful.com). From Termini, turn left on V. Giovanni Giolitti, right on V. Carlo Cattaneo, and left on V. Napoleone III. Popular backpacker hostel boasts TVs, A/C in all rooms with bath, 24hr. access to the kitchen, and no bunk beds. Safe at reception. Coffee included. Free internet at **Splashnet,** on the other side of Termini. Check-in 2pm. Check-out 10am. 4- to 6-bed dorms €20-25; doubles €60-70, with bath €68-86; triples with shared bath €75-90. Cash only. ❷

Hostel Roma Inn 2000, V. Agostino Depretis 65, 6th fl. (☎06 47 40 378; http://web.tiscalinet.it/marioromainn). From Termini, take V. Cavour, turn right at P. dell'Esquilino, and continue straight onto V. Depretis. Small hostel crowded with homey antique furniture makes you feel like owner Mario invited you to stay at his house. Good choice for young people or families. Rooms have shared baths, TVs, and fridges. Breakfast and dinner €3 each. Laundry €6. Luggage storage €3 per piece. Internet €4 per hr. Reception 6:30am-1am. Lockout 2-4pm. Curfew 1am. Check-out 10am. 7- and 9-bed dorms €23-25; doubles €50-80; quads €100-112. Cash only; pay in advance. ❷

FOOD

Romans love to eat, and eat often. Whether it's a multi-course meal or an afternoon gelato, Romans settle for nothing but the best—so should you. Don't fall into the tourist traps around major sights; you'll miss out on authentic Roman cuisine and find yourself paying high prices for mediocre food. Popular Roman dishes include *spaghetti alla carbonara* (egg and cream sauce sprinkled with bacon), *spaghetti all'amatriciana* (spicy thin tomato sauce with chili peppers and bacon), *carciofi alla giudia*(deep-fried artichokes common in the Jewish quarter), and *fiori di zucca* (stuffed, fried zucchini flowers). Pizza—eaten with fork and knife, of course—is unsurprisingly popular in Rome. Rome's proximity to the sea makes *pesce* (fish) popular as well. Expect to pay an extra €1-1.50 for *coperto* (service) and bread—whether or not you eat it.

BY PRICE

UNDER €6 (❶)	
Antico Caffe Greco (118)	PDS
Biscottificio Artigiano Innocenti (122)	TR
Blue Ice (128)	AVE
Caffe della Pace (117)	CS
Caffe Demacri (126)	T
Caffe Palombini (129)	EUR
Caffe Stella Ruschena (124)	VB
Caffe Tazza d'Oro (116)	CS
Caffe Trombetta (126)	T
Cambi (118)	PDS
Castroni (120)	VC
Da Felice e Silvana (127)	AVE
🍽 Da Simone (121)	TR
Dolce Maniera (121)	VC
Franchi (121)	VC
Gelarmony (128)	EUR
Gelateria La Dolce Vita (116)	AC
🍽 Giacomini (127)	AVE
Giolitti (118)	CS
🍽 Giorgagel (121)	TR
Hostaria Romana da Dino (125)	T
Il Cornettone (128)	EUR
Il Fornaio (119)	Campo
Il Gelatone (115)	AC
L'Angolo dell'Artista (119)	Campo
Makasar (121)	VC
Miscellanea (117)	CS
Mr. Kebab (128)	EUR
Panella (126)	T
Panifico Arnese (122)	TR
Parinando (128)	AVE
Pasta Fresca Mea (128)	AVE
🍽 Pasticceria Ebraico Boccione (119)	JG

UNDER €6 CON'T	
Pizza & Mortadella (115)	AC
Pizza Art (116)	CS
Pizzarium (120)	VC
Pizzeria da Baffetto (116)	CS
Pizzeria da Secolo (125)	T
Portico (120)	JG
Sant'Eustachio il Caffe (116)	CS
Sapori ai Parioli (124)	VB
Siven (122)	TR
The Old Bridge (120)	VC
Zi' Fenizia da Michele (117)	PDS
€6-12 (❷)	
Ai Spaghettari (123)	TR
Al Ponticello (129)	EUR
Andrea (125)	T
Arancia Blu (125)	T
🍽 Babette (117)	PDS
Cacio e Pepe (120)	VC
Carrot's Cafe (124)	VB
Columbus (129)	EUR
🍽 Cul de Sac (116)	CS
Da Enzo (122)	TR
Da Paolo (123)	TR
Da Vittorio (129)	EUR
Enoteca Cavour 313 (116)	CS
EUR Caffe Casini (129)	EUR
Fagianetto (126)	T
Fusion Food (119)	PDS
Gusto (118)	PDS
Hostaria da Bruno (125)	T
Hostaria Nerone (115)	AC
🍽 I Buoni Amici (114)	AC
I Mattarelli (128)	AVE

AC = Ancient City	JG = Jewish Ghetto
AVE = Aventine & Testaccio	PDS = Piazza della Signoria
Campo = Campo de' Fiori	T = Termini
CS = Centro Storico	TR = Trastevere
EUR = EUR & Marconi	VB = Villa Borghese, Parioli, Flaminio
	VC = Vatican City

€6-12 CON'T

La Fraschetta di Mastro Giorgio (127)	AVE
La Pollarola (119)	Campo
La Torre (123)	TR
La Tradizione (120)	VC
▓ L'Antica Birreria Peroni (115)	AC
L'Insalata Ricca (119)	Campo
Luzzi (115)	AC
Mo' Sto (123)	TR
Ombralonga Vinerie (129)	EUR
Paninoteca da Guido e Patrizia (121)	VC
Pastarito (125)	T
Pizza Roma (123)	TR
Pizzeria Corallo (117)	CS
Ristorante da Angelo (126)	T
Ristorante da Nazzareno (125)	T
Ristorante Grappolo d'Oro (119)	Campo
Ristorante Wanted & Birreria Moretti (115)	AC
Roma Sparita (123)	TR
Salsamentaria Croce (119)	PDS
Shanti (121)	VC
Taverna dei Fori Imperiali (115)	AC
Taverna dei Quaranta (115)	AC
Trattoria dal Cav. Gino (116)	CS
Trattoria San Teodoro (115)	AC
Tree Bar (124)	VB
Vini e Buffet (118)	PDS
▓ Vladimiro Ristorante Marcello (117)	PDS
Volpetti Salumeria-Gastronomia (128)	AVE
Il Campidano (129)	EUR
Il Cantinone (127)	AVE
Il Capriccio (123)	TR
Il Gelato di San Crispino (117)	CS

€6-12 CON'T

▓ Il Volpetti Piu (126)	AVE
La Creperie di Testaccio (127)	AVE
La Famiglia (125)	T

€13-19 (❸)

Africa (126)	T
Allo Specchio (124)	VB
Bla Kongo (124)	VB
Caffe Canova-Tadolini (118)	PDS
Corsetti Il Galeone (123)	TR
Da Oio a Casa Mia (127)	AVE
Felice a Testaccio (127)	AVE
Fiaschetteria Beltramme (117)	PDS
I Leoni d'Abruzzo (126)	T
Il Brillo Parlante (118)	PDS
▓ La Taverna del Ghetto (120)	JG
Le Tavernelle (115)	AC
Naturist Club (118)	PDS
Osteria degli Amici (127)	AVE
Palatium Enoteca Regionale (118)	PDS
Pecorino (128)	AVE
Ripa 12 (122)	TR
Taverna Ponziani (122)	TR
Trattoria da Giggetto (120)	JG
Trattoria da Settimio All'Arancio (118)	PDS

€20-25 (❹)

Da Velando (121)	VC
Peccato Divino (121)	VC

OVER €25 (❺)

Casina Valadier (124)	VB

FOOD

ANCIENT CITY

The area around the Fora and the Colosseum is home to some of Italy's finest tourist traps. Head to side streets where cheap and delicious culinary outposts are oases in a desert of color-photograph menus.

▓ **I Buoni Amici,** V. Aleardo Aleardi 4 (☎06 70 49 19 93). ⓜB-Colosseo. From the Colosseum, take V. Labicana, then take a right on V. Merulana and a left on V. Aleardo Aleardi. Look for a blue *osteria* sign. You'll hear the languages of Italian and mathematics spoken in this local favorite near an engineering school. Try the popular *linguine alle vongole* (pasta with clams; €8). Self-serve *antipasto* bar €12. *Primi* and *secondi* €7-14. Wine €8-35 per bottle. Dessert €4. Cover €1. Open M-Sa 12:30-3pm and 7:30-11pm. AmEx/D/MC/V. ❷

🔳 **L'Antica Birreria Peroni,** V. San Marcello 19 (☎06 67 95 310; www.anticabirreriap-eroni.it). From the Vittorio Emanuele monument, turn right on V. Cesare Battisti and left into P. dei Santissimi Apostoli. 2 blocks down on the left. Energetic *enoteca* with a German twist and backlit beers tempting you from a ledge on the wall. Wash down a *wurstel* (€6-7) with 1 of 4 delicious Peroni beers on tap (€2-5). Fantastic *fiori di zucca* €1. *Primi* €6-7. Cover €1. Open M-Sa noon-midnight. AmEx/D/MC/V. ❷

Hostaria Nerone, V. delle Terme di Tito 96 (☎06 48 17 952), between the Colosseum and the Domus Aurea. Ⓜ️B-Colosseo. Take V. Nicola Salvi and turn right on V. delle Terme di Tito. Built on the ruins of Nero's Golden House, offering spectacular views of the Col-osseum and the Trajan Forum. Traditional Roman menu, featuring homemade gnocchi and ox tail. House wine €2 per ¼ L. *Primi* €9-10. *Secondi* €9-15. Cover €1.50. Open Sept.-July M-Sa noon-3pm and 7-11pm. AmEx/MC/V. ❷

Luzzi, V. San Giovanni in Laterano 88 (☎06 70 96 332), just down V. dei Fori Imperiali from the Colosseum. No-fuss *osteria* packed with locals. Specials like *pennette al sal-mone* (€7) will leave you wanting more. Enjoy inexpensive seafood (shrimp and prawns €10) and enough cheap wine to scuttle a liner (€4 per L). *Primi* €5-7. *Secondi* €7-11. Dessert €4. Open M-Tu and Th-Su noon-3pm and 7pm-midnight. AmEx/MC/V. ❷

Taverna dei Quaranta, V. Claudia 24 (☎06 70 00 550). Ⓜ️B-Colosseo. Up the hill past P. del Colosseo. Enjoy delicious dishes in the quiet shade ascending the Caelian Hill while watching Italian news on the huge projection screen inside. Try the *oliva ascolane* (fried olives stuffed with meat; €4). 20 types of pizza available only at dinner. House wine €11 per L. *Primi* €8-10. *Secondi* €8-13. Dessert €4-6. Cover €1. Open daily noon-3:30pm and 7pm-midnight. AmEx/D/MC/V. ❷

Taverna dei Fori Imperiali, V. della Madonna dei Monti 16 (☎06 67 98 643). Ⓜ️B-Colosseo. Walk up V. dei Fori Imperiali and turn right through the park at the beginning of V. Cavour. V. della Madonna dei Monti runs parallel to V. Cavour on the left. Steps away from Trajan's Forum. Quiet, outdoor seating and creative twists on traditional Roman favorites like *tagliolini cacio e pepe e zafferano* (thin noodles in a pecorino cheese and pepper saffron sauce; €8). *Primi* €8-10. *Secondi* €11-14. Cover €1.50. Open M and W-Su 12:30-3pm and 7-10:30pm. Reservations recommended for dinner. AmEx/D/MC/V. ❷

Ristorante Wanted & Birreria Moretti, V. dei Serpenti 166-168. From V. Cavour, turn onto V. dei Serpenti and it's on the right. Large portions of Roman and Tirolean special-ties are served alongside draft Moretti beers (€3). Enjoy 1 of more than 30 types of pizza (€6-10), *calzoni* (€8-9), and home made desserts (€5) as you peruse the exten-sive wine list. Open M and W-Su noon-midnight. MC/V. ❷

Le Tavernelle, V. Panisperna 48 (☎06 47 40 724; www.tavernelle.com) From V. dei Ser-penti, turn right onto V. Panisperna. Enjoy the A/C or covered patio as the solicitous staff serves you tasty dishes. Try the *ravioli alla Zarina* ("Empress" ravioli), an homage to the late Pope John Paul II. Extensive *antipasti* buffet €12. *Primi* €8-12. *Secondi* €8-22. Open Tu-Su 12:30-3pm and 5:30-11:30pm. AmEx/D/MC/V. ❸

Pizza & Mortadella, V. Cavour 283, on the left up V. Cavour from V. dei Fori Imperiali. Market and take-away pizza and sandwich shop with a wide assortment of prepared foods, deli meats, cheeses, wine, and beer. Open daily 7:30am-9pm. Cash only. ❶

Trattoria San Teodoro, P. della Consolazione 54 (☎06 67 80 933; www.st-teodoro.it). From P. Bocca della Verità, take V. San Giovanni Decollato 2 blocks uphill to the P. della Consolazione. Peacefully situated next to the Church of Consolation and the Capitoline Hill. A full cafe as well as pastries and sandwiches (€3) to take away. Sit comfort-ably outdoors and enjoy a margherita pizza and beer (€12.50). *Primi* €9.50. *Secondi* €14.50. Cover €2. Open daily 7:00am-10:30pm. AmEx/D/MC/V. ❷

Il Gelatone, V. dei Serpenti 28 (☎06 48 20 187). From V. dei Fori Imperiali, take a left on V. Cavour, then left on V. dei Serpenti. Neon-colored *gelateria* with creamy, smooth

FOOD

gelato. Try the specialty *gelatone,* a blend of chocolate and vanilla with chocolate chips, or the unique *pinolo* (pine nut) combination flavors. The cool and refreshing *pompelmo rosa* (pink grapefruit) complements *limoncello* nicely. Over 65 flavors, including soy-based gelato. Cones €2-3.50, 4-flavor cone-bowls €4. Open daily 10am-1am. Cash only. ❶

Gelateria La Dolce Vita, V. Cavour 306. From V. dei Fori Imperiali, turn onto V. Cavour. Signed photos of Italian celebrities grace the walls next to diplomas from gelato schools. You'll question your choice of major when you try the house specialty pistachio, the creators of which were too well trained to have added any artificial green coloring. Cones €1.50-3, 4-flavor cone-bowls €4. Open daily 11am-midnight. Cash only. ❶

CENTRO STORICO

Dining in the touristy *centro* can be pricey, but it doesn't have to be. Stick to *pizzerie, enoteche,* and cafes for filling meals and excellent deals on some of the best food in the city.

▨ **Cul de Sac,** P. Pasquino 73 (☎06 68 80 10 94), off P. Navona. One of Rome's 1st wine bars. Substantial list of reasonably priced wines by the glass (from €2.50). At aperitif time, pair your pick with a snack like tuna, tomato and green bean salad, or the tasty *baba ghanoush. Primi* €7-8. *Secondi* €7-9. Open daily noon-4pm and 6pm-12:30am. AmEx/MC/V. ❷

Pizzeria da Baffetto, V. del Governo Vecchio 114. Street runs parallel to Corso V. Emanuele II. This neighborhood *trattoria* quickly fills up with a local crowd. Thin crust pizzas €4.50-10. Open daily 6:30pm-1am. ❶

Pizza Art, V. Arenula 76 (☎06 68 73 16 03 78). From C. V. Emanuele II, cut through Largo di Torre Argentina and walk toward the river. Counter seating only. Thick focaccia pizza topped with arugula, goat cheese, and fried treats including *supplì* (fried rice balls) and *crochette.* Most pizza €11-13 per kg; average slice €2.50. Open daily 8am-10pm. Cash only. ❶

Sant'Eustachio Il Caffè, P. de Sant'Eustachio 82 (☎06 68 80 20 48). Turn right on V. Palombella behind the Pantheon. Muscle your way to the front of the line for the *gran caffè speciale* (double espresso with sugar; €2.20 standing, €4.20 table service). Ground coffee €22 per kg. Open M-Th and Su 8:30am-1am, F 8:30am-1:30am, Sa 8:30am-2am. Cash only. ❶

Enoteca Cavour 313, V. Cavour 313 (☎06 67 85 496). ⓜB-Cavour. Sip a glass of *grappa* in one of this French-style bar's intimate booths. Organic and locally produced ingredients. *Misto di formaggi* (mixed cheese plate) €8-12. Organic mixed vegetables in oil €10. Mixed plate of meat €7-14. Wine €3-8 per glass; bottles from €13. Open Sept.-July M-Sa 12:30am-2:45pm and 7:30pm-12:30am, Su 7:30pm-12:30am. Closed Aug. AmEx/MC/V. ❷

Trattoria dal Cav. Gino, V. Rosini 4 (☎06 68 73 434), across from P. del Parlamente. Make a left from V. di Campo Marzio. Affable owner Gino greets guests himself. Dine under the blue sky, grapevines, and birds painted on the ceiling. Home-style Italian menu includes pasta dishes as well as Northern fare like *ossobuco* (braised veal shanks). *Primi* €6-8. *Secondi* €7-12. Open Sept.-July M-Sa 1-2:30pm and 8-10:30pm. Reservations recommended. Cash only. ❷

Caffè Tazza d'Oro, V. degli Orfani 84 (☎06 67 89 792; www.tazzadorocoffeeshop.com). Boasts *"il migliore caffè al mondo"* (the best coffee in the world) and an extensive tea selection. The *granita di caffè con panna* (with fresh whipped cream; €2.50) is to die for. Coffee from €0.80. Open M-Sa 7am-10pm. ❶

FOOD

Miscellanea, V. della Palombella 34/35 (☎06 67 80 983), around the corner from the Pantheon. This cavernous *ristorante* lures hungry students with gigantic portions and low prices. Friendly staff and fast service make this an ideal place for a quick bite. Sweet *fragoli*, a free "sexy wine" (as the owner calls it), included with every meal. Salads €6. *Panini* €4. Desserts €2-3. Open daily 11am-2am. AmEx/MC/V. ●

Caffè della Pace, V. della Pace 3-7 (☎06 68 61 216; www.caffedellapace.it), off P. Navona. This old-school, swanky *enoteca* is a perfect spot for aperitifs and late-night snacks. Espresso €3. Prosecco €8. Mixed drinks €10. Open daily 9am-3pm and 4pm-3am. Cash only. ●

Il Gelato di San Crispino, P. della Maddalena 3 (☎06 97 60 11 90; www.ilgelatodisancrispino.it), steps away from the Pantheon. This world-renowned gelato maker churns out fabulous ice cream in flavors like meringue and chocolate. But fame has a price, and you'll be paying it: a tiny cup will cost you a cool €2.30. Gelato €2.30-8.50. Open in spring and summer M-Th and Su noon-12:30am, F-Sa noon-1:30am; in fall and winter M, W-Th, and Su noon-12:30am, F-Sa noon-1:30am. Check website for other locations around the city. AmEx/MC/V. ❷

Pizzeria Corallo, V. del Corallo 11 (☎06 68 30 77 03). Head north from V. del Governo Vecchio. Regulars claim this local hangout serves the best pizza in the city. At night big crowds can mean long waits for a table, but most of the time the pies are well worth it. Pizza €8-9. *Secondi* €16-17. Open daily noon-4pm and 6:30pm-1am. Cash only. ❷

Giolitti, V. degli Uffici del Vicario 40 (☎06 69 91 243; www.giolitti.it). From the Pantheon, follow V. del Pantheon, take V. della Maddalena to its end, and turn right on V. degli Uffici del Vicario. More than 50 unique flavors of gelato like *limoncello*, champagne, and *crema*. Top off your cone with homemade *panna* (whipped cream). Cups or cones from €2.20. Wi-Fi. Open daily 7am-1:30am. AmEx/MC/V. ●

PIAZZA DI SPAGNA

▨ **Babette,** V. Angelo Brunetti 6 (☎06 32 00 407; www.babetteristorante.it). ⓜA-Flaminio. Dining a la carte can be expensive at this stylish, French-Italian brasserie, but the weekday lunch buffet (daily 1-3pm €10 for the 1st plate, €3.50 for subsequent) is one of the best deals in the area. The price spikes on weekends and holidays (€25 per person; €15 for children), but "Babette's feast" includes wine, coffee, and sweets. Restaurant open daily 1-3pm and 8-11pm. Bar open daily 9am-8pm. AmEx/MC/V. ❷

▨ **Vladimiro Ristorante Marcello,** V. Aurora 37 (☎06 48 19 467; www.vladimiroristorante.com). ⓜA-Barberini. From V. Veneto, take V. Liguria and make a left onto V. Aurora. Yes, you're surrounded by Americans, but they're onto something. Vladimiro serves some of the best *antipasti* in the city. €10 sounds pricey, but ordering the *antipasti misti* gets you a big-boy portion of fresh cheese, meats, and vegetables. *Primi* €8-12. *Secondi* €8-16. Open M-Sa noon-3pm and 7:30-11pm. AmEx/MC/V. ❷

Zi' Fenizia da Michele, V. dell' Umiltà 31 (☎349 25 25 347). ⓜA-Barberini. From the Trevi Fountain, walk 1 block down V. San Vincenzo and make a right. Michele's kosher pizza is some of the best in Rome and certainly better than the other options around the Fontana. A substantial slice from this storefront—topped with eggplant, potatoes, zucchini, or other goodies—will run you about €2.50. Open M-Th and Su 8am-8pm, F 8am-3:30pm. Closed Jewish holidays. Cash only. ●

Fiaschetteria Beltramme, V. della Croce 39 (www.fiaschetteriabeltramme.com). ⓜA-Spagna. This magnetic little oasis (open since 1886) hosts a mixed crowd of Romans and foreigners who've fled the tourist hordes. Short menu of well-prepared pasta, fish, and meat dishes in a cozy setting. *Primi* €10. *Secondi* €15-18. Open M-Sa noon-2:30pm and 7-10:30pm. MC/V. ❸

F O O D

Gusto, P. Augusto Imperatore 9 (☎06 32 26 273; www.gusto.it). ⓂA-Spagna. After a day of shopping on V. Condotti, skip the overpriced full restaurant at this multi-space dining complex and go for a tasty pizza (€6-9.50) or bruschetta (€2-5) on the ground-floor terrace. Fantastic spot for people-watching young, energetic, Roman diners. Open daily 12:45-3pm and 7:45-midnight. AmEx/MC/V. ❷

Il Brillo Parlante, V. della Fontanella 12 (☎06 32 43 334; www.ilbrilloparlante.com). ⓂA-Flaminio. Take V. del Corso away from P. del Popolo and turn left on V. Fontanella. This is where Pinocchio's Talking Cricket *(Il Grillo Parlante)* comes to get *brillo* (tipsy)—thus the cricket on the facade. Heed the pun and be prepared. While the wood-burning oven cooks great pizza (€4.50-10), be sure to also try the handmade pasta and smaller dishes like *pecorino* cheese with honey and walnuts (€8.50). *Primi* €8-9.50. *Secondi* €9.50-30. Open M 5pm-1am, T-Su 12:30pm-1am. Bar open 5-7:30pm. Reservations recommended. MC/V. ❸

Vini e Buffet, V. della Torretta 60 (☎06 68 71 445), near P. di Spagna. From V. del Corso, turn on P. di San Lorenzo in Lucina. Turn left on V. Campo Marzio and right on V. della Torretta. A favorite among local venophiles. *Antipasti* €4-9. Salads €7.50-11. Regional wines €10-24 per bottle. Wine by the glass also available. Open M-Sa 12:30-3pm and 7:30-11pm. Reservations recommended. Cash only. ❷

Caffè Canova-Tadolini, V. del Babuino 150/A-B (☎06 32 11 07 02; www.museoateliercanovatadolini.it). Once upon a time, this bohemian cafe was a studio that belonged to such famous 19th-century sculptors as Antonio Canova and his student, Adamo Tadolini. Take a quick coffee break at the counter or dine on cheesy *cacio e pepe* (cheese and pepper) amid the larger-than-life sculptures. *Primi* €11-14. *Secondi* €16-26. Open M-Sa 8am-noon, Su 10am-8pm. Cash only. ❸

Palatium Enoteca Regionale, V. Frattina 94 (☎06 69 20 21 32; www.enotecapalatium. it). ⓂA-Spagna. Run by the Lazio government's Agricultural Authority, this sleek restaurant and wine bar offers traditional dishes made with the finest and freshest produce of the region, such as the *cacio e pepe* (pasta dish with pecorino romano sheep cheese and black pepper). Also stocks locally made wines, oils, and other products. *Primi* €9.50-11. *Secondi* €10-18.50. Open M-Sa 11am-midnight. AmEx/MC/V. ❸

Antico Caffè Greco, V. dei Condotti 86 (☎06 67 91 700; www.gusto.it). ⓂA-Spagna. When it opened in 1760, this plush, luxurious cafe served Casanova and Goethe. Now it serves French tourists. It is worth a visit, if only for the glorious red walls and impressive Romantic decor. A *caffè* at the bar is a reasonable €0.90, but for once it might be worth putting up for the more expensive table service. Open M and Su 10:30am-7pm, Tu-Sa 9am-7:30pm. Cash only. ❶

Trattoria da Settimio all'Arancio, V. dell'Arancio 50 (☎06 68 76 119). Take V. dei Condotti from P. di Spagna; after V. del Corso bear right on V. Tomacelli and take the 1st left. Generous portions of hearty classics at this family-friendly neighborhood restaurant. Appetizers include the elusive *burrata* (€6), mozzarella's sexier cousin. *Primi* €8-18. *Secondi* €8-35. Open M-Sa 12:30-3:30pm and 7:30pm-midnight. Reservations recommended. AmEx/MC/V. ❸

Naturist Club, V. della Vite 14, 4th fl. (☎06 67 92 509). Heading toward P. del Popolo on V. del Corso, take a right on V. della Vite. Wonderful for health-conscious travelers. Macrobiotic menu is 90% organic and features Italian specialties for vegetarians, vegans, and pescatarians. "Natural snacks" €8-10. Vegetarian dinner *menù* €14; a la carte options also available. Open for lunch M-F 12:30-3pm and tea 3-5:30pm. Open for dinner M-Sa 7:30-11pm. Reservations required for dinner. MC/V. ❸

Cambi, V. del Leoncino 30 (☎06 68 78 081). ⓂA-Spagna. Take V. Condotti past the Corso; make a left. Right across from Fendi, this gourmet store sells breads (under €1), wine, meats, and sweets like *crostate* (a fruit pie; €11). A small but reasonably priced selection. Avoid the pricey tourist traps on the Corso and make yourself a picnic on the steps of the Basilica dei Santi Ambrogio e Carlo. Open M-Sa 8am-8pm. Cash only. ❶

Salsamenteria Croce, V. della Croce 78 (☎06 67 83 153). Ⓜ A-Flaminio. A stylish, modern option for a midday snack or quick lunch. Serves salads (€9-13) and basic Italian sandwiches like prosciutto, mozzarella, and tomato (€6.50) in a cool, white setting. Also sells some specialty groceries and bread from the excellent Roscioli bakery. Open daily 11am-9pm. MC/V. ❷

Fusion Food, V. Angelo Brunetti 6 (☎06 32 00 407; www.sushifusionfood.com). Ⓜ A-Flaminio. This tiny, bare-bones storefront, a block from Piazza del Popolo, has a limited but high-quality selection of sushi, salads, and other healthy snacks. Prepackaged meals make for the perfect takeout, but a quiet table or counter seat may also seem appealing after the frenzy on the Corso. Free delivery to anywhere in Rome with minimum order; call for details. Most sushi meals €9-15. Open Tu-Su 12:30-9:30pm. Cash only. ❷

CAMPO DEI FIORI

The area near the Campo has some exquisite, inexpensive options for sit-down meals. Rejoice!

Ristorante Grappolo d'Oro Zampanò, P. della Cancelleria 83 (☎06 68 97 080), between C. V. Emanuele II and the Campo. Enjoy delicious homemade pasta to the soothing sound of the *piazza's* fountain. Appetizers include *burrata* and a fine *panzanella* (tomato and bread soup). *Primi* €8.50-12. *Secondi* €13-18. Cover €1.50. Open M and W-Sa noon-4:30pm and 7:30-11pm, Su noon-3pm and 7:30-11pm. MC/V. ❷

L'Angolo dell'Artista, Largo dei Librari 86 (☎34 72 623 817). Take V. dei Giubbonari from Campo dei Fiori; Largo dei Librari is on the left. This popular crepe joint is great for a quick lunch or a late-night snack. The tangy, creamy plain frozen yogurt (€2) will make you forget about gelato. Sweet crepes €4-4.50, savory crepes €5. Open M-Sa 1pm-1am. ❶

La Pollarola, P. Pollarola 25/27 (☎06 68 80 16 54), just behind the Campo dei Fiori. Traditional dishes done well. Try the *cannelloni specialista* (pasta filled with meat, tomato, and mozzarella; €8) or the satisfying *antipasto rustico* (€6). *Primi* €6-10. *Secondi* €7.50-20. Desserts €5. Cover €1. Open M-Sa 12:30-3pm and 5:30-11pm. AmEx/D/MC/V. ❷

L'Insalata Ricca, Largo dei Chiavari 85-6 (☎06 68 80 36 56; www.linsalataricca.it), off C. V. Emanuele II near P. Santa Andrea della Valle. Casual takeout joint meets full-service restaurant. Serious selection of Parma ham and cheeses. The real stars are the mammoth salads (€6.50-11). Bruschetta €1.30-4. Cover €1.10. Open daily noon-midnight. 12 locations throughout Rome. AmEx/D/MC/V. ❷

Il Fornaio, V. dei Baullari 5 (☎06 68 80 39 47). Take V. dei Baullari from Campo de Fiori. Oodles of savory sweets, some by the kg, some by the piece. Extensive selection of *biscotti* and *crostatine*. Airy, giant meringues €1.50. Pizza from €7 per kg. Open M-Sa 7am-8:30pm, Su 9:30am-9pm. Cash only. ❶

JEWISH GHETTO

The Jewish Ghetto, about 10min. south of Campo dei Fiori and near the Tiber, serves tempting kosher and traditional Jewish specialties with an Italian twist—which can be a welcome break from pasta and pizza. The best Roman-Jewish dishes are the mouth-watering *carciofi alla giudia* (Jewish artichoke, crisp-fried and salted). Keep in mind that much of the Ghetto is closed on Saturdays for the Sabbath.

▨ Pasticceria Ebraico Boccione, V. del Portico d'Ottavia 1 (☎06 68 78 637), on the corner of P. Costaguti. The unmarked storefront is difficult to find; keep an eye on the street numbers. Tiny, family-run bakery serves only about 8 specialties, including delicious custard-filled *challah* (€0.60) and sugar-dusted *ciambelle* (doughnuts; €0.80). Open in summer M-Th 8am-7:30pm, F 8am-3:30 pm, Su 8am-2pm and 4-7:30pm; in winter M-Th and Su 8am-7:30pm, F 8am-3:30pm. ❶

🏴 **La Taverna del Ghetto,** V. del Portico d'Ottavia 8 (☎06 68 80 97 71; www.latavern-adelghetto.com). Popular kosher *taverna* prides itself on homemade pasta and delicacies like *lingua all'ebraica* (veal tongue). The *carciofo* (artichoke; €5) is exceptionally well-prepared. *Primi* €11.50. *Secondi* €13.50-25. Desserts €5.50-6.50. Cover €1.50. Open M-Th and Sa-Su noon-3pm and 6:30-11pm, F noon-3pm. Reservations recommended. AmEx/MC/V. ❸

Portico, V. del Portico d'Ottavia 1/D (☎06 68 64 642). Great patio for people-watching. Filling pizza with plentiful toppings from €4. *Primi* €5.50-9. *Secondi* €6-16. Open daily noon-3:30pm and 7pm-midnight. MC/V. ❶

Trattoria da Giggetto, V. del Portico d'Ottavia 21-22 (☎06 68 61 105; www.giggettoalportico.it), next to the Portico d'Ottavia ruins. Traditional Roman fare like *fritto misto* (mixed fried vegetables; €12) and Jewish delicacies. *Primi* €9-18. *Secondi* €9-22. Cover €1.50. Open Tu-Su 12:30-3pm and 7:30-11pm. Closed last 2 weeks of July. Reservations required for dinner. AmEx/MC/V. ❸

VATICAN CITY

Don't even think about eating in Vatican City itself, unless you're into overpriced, mediocre sandwiches, touristy bars, or communion wafers. Instead, venture down V. Cola di Rienzo toward P. Cavour and explore the residential side streets. The area west of P. Risorgimento and north of the City is also full of delicious family-run eateries.

Cacio e Pepe, V. Giuseppe Avezzana 11 (☎06 32 17 268). From Ⓜ A-Ottaviano, take the V. Barletta exit; right onto V. de Milizie, then left onto V. Avezzana. Worth the walk. In summer, rub elbows with locals at the close-packed tables outside. Namesake specialty is perfectly *al dente,* topped with olive oil, grated cheese, and fresh-ground pepper (€6). Open M-F 12:30-3pm and 7:30-11pm, Sa 12:30-3pm. Cash only. ❷

La Tradizione, V. Cipro 8/e (☎06 39 72 03 49; www.latradizione.it). This gourmet store, steps from Ⓜ A-Cipro, has been educating palates for nearly 3 decades with a broad selection of fine meats, wines, and over 300 cheeses. Beautifully-prepared foods (including regional specialties) sold by the kg. A large meal €15. Open M 3-8:15pm, Tu-Sa 8am-2pm and 4:30-8:15pm. AmEx/MC/V. ❷

Pizzarium, V. della Meloria 43 (☎06 39 74 54 16). Just down the street from Ⓜ A-Cipro, this unpretentious, charming storefront serves one of the best pizzas in the city, made with seasonal gourmet toppings. Pizza is priced by the kg, with your basic *pizza bianca* €11 per kg and an average slice €2.50-3. Also sells pastries, liquor, and high-quality kitchen basics. Counter, but no seating. Open M-Sa 9:30am-10pm. Cash only. ❶

The Old Bridge, V. le dei Bastioni di Michelangelo 5 (☎06 39 72 30 26). Off P. del Risorgimento, across from the bend in the Vatican Museum's outer wall. Your wait in the Vatican museum lines will seem much shorter (and sweeter) with a heaping, melty cone—if you make it past the lines at this beloved local gelato shop. 20 homemade flavors. Cup or cone €1.30-4. Open M-Sa 10am-2am and Su 3pm-2am. Cash only. ❶

Castroni, V. Cola de Rienzo 206 (☎06 32 17 268; www.castroni.com). The original 1932 store is part of a family-owned Roman chain of gourmet groceries, offering a traditional, strong *caffè* (€0.80). Grab some specialty candies while you're at it. There's a 2nd location with both counter and table service on V. Ottaviano, just steps away from the Metro. Be warned: you'll pay double or more for a sit-down coffee. Both branches open M-Sa 8am-8pm. Cash only. ❶

Makasar, V. Plauto 33 (☎06 68 74 602; www.makasar.it), off V. Crescenzio. Relax with a pot of exotic tea (€4.50-5.50) from the broad selection at this quirky cafe after battling the crowds at the Vatican. Offers Turkish and Lebanese coffee (€3.50), a small selection of sweets, and stacks of magazines for visitors to peruse. Open Tu-Su 10am-1pm and 4-8pm. Cash only. ❶

Shanti, V. Fabio Massimo 68-70 (☎06 32 44 922; www.ristoranteshanti.com). ⓂA-Ottaviano. Travelers waving the white flag after their 12th Italian meal may want to try this popular Indian and Pakistani place off V. Cola de Rienzo. The standard *tandooris, tikkas,* and *curries* at affordable prices. *Antipasti* €1.50-6.50. Entrees €5-20. Open daily 12:30-3pm and 7-12pm. AmEx/MC/V. ❷

Da Velando, Borgo Vittorio 26 (☎06 68 80 99 55; www.ristorantevelando.com), on a street parallel to V. Crecenzio. This minimalist restaurant is a best-kept local secret, featuring the cuisine of the Lombardy region (soups, risotto, the veal dish *ossobuco,* etc.). The tasting menus, though pricey (from €35), are worth a look. Open M-Sa 12:30-2:30pm and 8-11pm. Reservations recommended. AmEx/MC/V. ❹

Dolce Maniera, V. Barletta 27 (☎06 37 51 75 18). ⓂA-Ottaviano. Tired of the stale *cornetti* in your hotel's breakfast buffet? Go straight to the source—this tiny 24hr. bakery supplies many of the area's restaurants with pastries and cakes. Carries a variety of cookies and savories like flatbread (€1.50-3) as well as several tasty varieties of the flaky croissant (€0.60). Open 24hr. Cash only. ❶

Paninoteca da Guido e Patrizia, Borgo Pio 13 (☎06 68 75 491), near Castel Sant'Angelo. A charming, casual local favorite. Grab a quick bite in this little sandwich shop and watch the owners chat with friends and pontificate behind a *tavola calda* (snackbar), stocked with fresh meats, cheeses, and produce. Full meal (*primo, secondo,* and drink) around €11. Open M-Sa 8am-6pm. Cash only. ❷

Franchi, V. Cola di Rienzo 200-204 (☎06 68 74 651; www.franchi.it). Luxurious picnic supplier for nearly 50 years. Cheaper and better of a quality than most Vatican-area snack bars. Try the delicious *fritti misti* (deep-fried zucchini flowers and artichoke hearts) or the house ravioli. Don't let the listed prices freak you out—most goods are sold by kg. Stuff yourself for around €8. Open M-Sa 9am-8:30pm. AmEx/MC/V. ❶

Peccato Divino, V. Properzio 30 (☎06 45 42 31 68; www.enotecapeccatodivino.it). ⓂA-Ottaviano. Steps from P. Risorgimento. Sinfully-delectable cuisine to match this romantic enoteca's name—"divine sin." Pair exquisite wine with gourmet cheeses (€12) and indulge in a chocolate dessert. *Secondi* €20-25. Open M-Sa noon-3:30pm and 7pm-2am for meals, 6:30pm-2am for aperitifs. AmEx/MC/V. ❹

TRASTEVERE

🔲 **Giorgiagel,** V. di San Francesco a Ripa 130 (☎32 01 65 02 66 or 33 32 70 59 18). Turn right on V. de San Francesco a Ripa from Vle. Trastevere. Large portions of amazing Sicilian pastries and gelato that is right up there with the best in Rome. Unbelievably decadent *cioccolato fondente* (dark chocolate) and intense *frutti di bosco* (forest fruit) make a great pair. Ingredients listed. Gelato €1.50-3. *Frappè* €2.50. Open daily 1pm-9pm. Cash only. ❶

🔲 **Da Simone,** V. Giacinto Carini 50 (☎06 58 14 980). From Acqua Paola on the Gianicolo hill, walk behind the fountain and down V. Giacomo Medici to the end of the street. Turn right, walk under the arches to V. Carini; it's behind the bus stop to the left. Treats you to fantastic pizza and prepared foods with only the best ingredients—fine extra virgin olive oil, buffalo mozzarella, and no animal fat. The pizza with *'nduja* (spicy Calabrian sau-

ON THE MENU
LITTLE RED BOOK

Foodies looking for an exhaustive gourmet guide may want to check out the publications of Gambero Rosso. This Italian food and wine guidebook empire started life over two decades ago as an eight-page supplement to the left-wing daily Il Manifesto. Rather un-left-winglishly, the Gambero—its full name means "the red prawn"—was devoted to showcasing Italian gourmet cooking, including the best restaurants and enoteche. Due to high demand for gastronomic tips, the guide soon developed into a publication in its own right.

Today, Gambero Rosso publishes a range of guidebooks and listings in English as well as Italian. Unfortunately for Anglophones, the Italian-language versions are more helpful: they contain more budget and local-friendly listings. Still, a good meal translates pretty well into any language, and you'll be able to use the handy rating system (zero to three forks, beans, or wineglasses) to locate promising addresses.

Large Roman bookstores like MEL and Feltrinelli carry major titles like Bar d'Italia and Ristorante d'Italia, all updated yearly. Those who don't want to pay up will find abbreviated listings on www.gamberorosso.it.

sage) is especially great. Reasonably priced by weight (a large slice of margherita around €2-3). Open M-Sa 7:30am-8:15pm. Cash only. ❶

Siven, V. di San Francesco a Ripa 137 (☎06 58 97 110). Northwest on V. de San Francesco a Ripa from Vle. Trastevere. A hole in the wall that sells tasty pizza and prepared pastas and meats (priced by weight) to a constant stream of locals, all of whom treat the chefs like old friends. When you taste their concoctions, you'll understand why. Amazing spicy chicken and lasagna. Cod filets on F. Take your sizeable portion (around €4) and eat in the scenic *piazza* next door—there's no seating. Open M-Sa 9am-10pm. Cash only. ❶

Biscottificio Artigiano Innocenti, V. della Luce 21 (☎06 58 03 926). From P. Sonnino, take V. Giulio Cesare Santini and turn left on V. della Luce. This haven of baked goodness sells a dizzying variety of cookies and biscuits featured in countless international culinary magazines. Stock up on hazelnut, almond, chocolate, and jam cookies (€10-15 per kg; about €2.50 for 10). Open M-Sa 8am-8pm, Su 9:30am-2pm. Cash only. ❶

Taverna Ponziani, P. dei Ponziani 7A (☎06 58 30 33 03, reservations 36 08 99 766). East of Vle. Trastevere, near the river. Turn right on V. dei Vascellari from Lungotevere Ripa to reach P. de Ponziani. The intimate, vibrant interior displays modern art, while the outdoor patio in the peaceful *piazza* surrounds diners with flowers as they feast on typical Roman dishes. Try the pasta with zucchini, smoked provolone and mint (€12), or the salmon in an orange brandy sauce (€10). *Primi* €7-12. *Secondi* €10-20. Open M-Tu and Th-Sa 7-11pm, Su noon-3pm. MC/V. ❸

Da Enzo, V. dei Vascellari 29 (☎06 58 18 355 or 32 72 09 25 90). East of Vle. Trastevere, near the river. Turn right on V. dei Vascellari from Lungotevere Ripa. Children's drawings of animals cover the canary yellow walls of this local Roman *trattoria,* where every dish is made with family love. *Primi* €6.80-9.80. *Secondi* €7.80-14. House wine €6.50-7.50 per L. Open M-Sa 1-3:30pm and 7-10pm. AmEx/D/MC/V. ❷

Panificio Arnese, V. del Politeama 27 and V. del Moro 15 (☎06 58 17 265). From Ponte Sisto, cross the street to P. Trilussa and go left. Local postings and pictures are the only wall coverings of the flour-drenched kitchen, which houses a wood oven that spits out delicious bread and pastries (priced by weight). The best, cheapest pizza in the area about €8-13 per kg. Open daily 7am-2am. Cash only. ❶

Ripa 12, V. di San Francesco a Ripa 12 (☎06 58 09 093; www.ripa12.com). Go west on V. di San Francesco a Ripa from Vle. Trastevere. The perfect way to prepare seafood has been passed down through the generations, and you get the full benefit of the family's fishy history. All dishes include seafood. Served in the elegant, modern glass and metal interior or on the *via* terrace. Try Ripa's acclaimed tuna steak (€15). *Primi* €11-15. *Secondi* €14-20. Open M-Sa noon-3pm and 7:30pm-midnight. AmEx/MC/V. ❸

Ai Spaghettari, P. di San Cosimato 57/60 (☎06 58 00 450; www.aispaghettari.it). Go west on V. di Fratte di Trastevere from Vle. Trastevere, and turn left into P. San Cosimato. The century-old tradition of making scrumptious Roman cuisine is reflected in its popularity among locals, who pack it every day. Pictures of customers and wrestlers adorn the interior, while the flower shop across the street in the scenic *piazza* perfumes the large terrace. Pizza €6.50-9.50. *Primi* €8.70-10.50. *Secondi* €13.50-18.50. Open daily noon-1am. AmEx/D/MC/V. ❷

Roma Sparita, P. di Santa Cecilia 24 (☎06 58 00 757; www.romasparita.com). Next to the Church of Santa Maria in Trastevere, down V. dei Vascellari from Lungotevere Ripa. Small selection of carefully prepared traditional Roman pasta dishes and pizza, served in the miniscule, simple interior or comparatively huge exterior patio. Great *tagliolini cacio e pepe* (pecorino cheese and pepper; €10). Pizza (dinner only) €5-10. *Primi* €10-12. *Secondi* €10-18. Open Tu-Sa 12:30-2:30pm and 7:30-11:30pm, Su 12:30-2:30pm. AmEx/D/MC/V. ❷

Da Paolo, V. di San Francesco a Ripa 92 (☎06 58 12 393). Go east on V. di San Francesco a Ripa from Vle. Trastevere. Jovial family-run *trattoria* specializes in cuisine from the Abruzzo region, served under 1 large brick arch. *Primi* €8-9. *Secondi* €8-10. 0.75L beer €3. Open M-Sa 12:30-3:30pm and 7pm-midnight. Cash only. ❷

La Torre, V. Natale del Grande 10 (☎06 58 12 048). Go west on V. di San Francesco a Ripa from Vle. Trastevere, and left on V. Natale del Grande. Warm colors abound and fruit provides eye candy for diners, who have enjoyed the classic Roman cuisine and wood-oven pizza here since 1933. Pizza €5-8.50. *Primi* €6.50-9. *Secondi* €7-15. Open Tu-Su noon-3pm and 7pm-midnight. AmEx/D/MC/V. ❷

Corsetti Il Galeone, P. di San Cosimato 27 (☎06 58 09 009 or 06 58 16 311; www.corsettiilgaleone.it). Go west on V. de Fratte di Trastevere from Vle. Trastevere and turn left into P. San Cosimato. Step inside and you'll feel like you just boarded a galleon, but this one has a lobster tank, fresh fish on ice, and not a single case of scurvy to be found. Enjoy some fresh sea creature before you hunt for booty or snag Moby Dick at the waterfront bars. *Primi* €8-10. Seafood pasta €12-14. Fish €10-23. Meat €13-18. *Menú* €20. Open Th-Tu noon-3pm and 7:30pm-midnight. AmEx/D/MC/V. ❸

Mo' Stò, V. della Pelliccia 24 (☎06 64 56 22 99; www.tavernamosto.com). Near P. Trilussa, at the intersection with V. del Moro. Burnt orange highlighted by leafy green plants and stone walls define the tasteful interior, where Roman cuisine with a twist (like the addition of artichoke to the classic *cacio e pepe;* €9) is served. *Primi* €7-12. *Secondi* €11-18. Open M-Tu and Th-Su 12:30-2:30pm and 8pm-2am. AmEx/D/MC/V. ❷

Il Capriccio, V. Roma Libera 19 (☎06 58 16 469; www.ilcapriccio.biz). Go west on V. de Fratte di Trastevere from Vle. Trastevere and turn left into P. San Cosimato; it's at the far right corner. Exposed copper pipes and stone form the backdrop to Sicilian cuisine. Stuff yourself with the stuffed swordfish (€12). Pizza €5-8. *Primi* €7-12. *Secondi* €12-18. Open daily noon-3pm and 6:30pm-1am. AmEx/D/MC/V. ❷

Pizza Roma, P. di San Cosimato 48/49 (☎06 83 60 10 44; www.pizzaromanw.com). Go west on V. de Fratte di Trastevere from Vle. Trastevere and turn left into P. San Cosimato. Generous portions for very low prices, served by attentive, humorous staff. Pasta €6-10. Grilled meat €7.50-14. Pizza €5.50-8. Calzoni €6-7. House wine €6 per L. Cover €1. Open daily 10am-2am. Delivery available, min. €10. D/MC/V. ❷

FOOD

VILLA BORGHESE, PARIOLI, AND FLAMINIO

The area around Villa Borghese and Villa Ada is mostly upscale and residential. Accordingly, budget dining options are limited and widely-spaced. Still, travelers willing to dig around a bit can eat very well and spend little. Look for neighborhood *trattorie*, gourmet stores, and wine bars serving light snacks.

Tree Bar, V. Flaminia 226 (☎06 32 65 27 54).◉A-Flaminio. Tram 2 runs up V. Flaminia; otherwise, prepare for a substantial walk from the Metro. This mod wooden restaurant looks like it's been kidnapped from California and plopped in Roman park. Wraparound windows give patrons a view of the neighborhood—when the glass is opened, it feels like you're dining outside. Fills up with a neighborhood crowd ordering pastas (€9) and salads (€5-8) from the short but appealing daily menu. Bar kicks up at night. *Secondi* €7-13. Open M-Sa. Cash only. ❷

Bla Kongo, V. Ofanto 6/8 (☎06 85 46 705). This sunny little bistro off V. Po serves delicious Swedish and Swedish-ish food to a crowd of Parioli locals and professionals from the neighborhood's many office buildings. The baked potatoes (€7), topped with treats like yogurt and smoked salmon, make for a great light lunch. Appetizers €3-7. Salads €3-6. *Secondi* €8.50-18. Open in summer Tu-Sa 12:30-4pm and 7:30pm-midnight., Su 7:30-midnight; in winter Tu-Su 12:30-4pm and 7:30pm-midnight. Cash only. ❸

Allo Specchio, V. Ofanto 35 (☎06 96 03 77 42; www.allospecchio.it). From Corso d'Italia, make a left onto V. Po and then a right. This little *trattoria* just opened May 2009. For now, at least, it charges eminently reasonable prices for modern Italian fare. The lunch *menùs* (around €10-12), which include a main dish, a side or dessert, water, and bread, are especially good deals. The light, flavorful apple cake is a winner. *Primi* €7-11. *Secondi* €11-15. Open M-Sa noon-3pm and 8pm-1am. Cash only. ❸

Sapori ai Parioli, V. V. Locchi 19D (☎06 807 38 08). This little storefront is a hit with neighborhood cheese fans: it gets its different varieties of *mozzarella di buffala* straight from the province of Caserta. Also stocks baked items, preserved goods, and spreads. Cheeses from around €8 per kg; most run about €15-20 per kg. Open M-Sa 9:30am-2:30pm and 5-7:30pm. Occasionally closes Sa afternoon. Cash only. ❶

Caffè Stella Ruschena, V. Flaminia 231 (☎06 32 27 492). ◉A-Flaminio. Take Tram 2 or prepare to schlep. This old-school neighborhood cafe serves an above-average breakfast to a local clientele. The sweet and frothy *caffè con panna* (€1.30) is a must-have any time of the day. Open M-F and Su 6:30am-8pm. MC/V. ❶

Casina Valadier, Vle. del Belvedere (☎06 69 92 20 90; www.casinavaladier.it). ◉A-Flaminio. Climb the hill to Villa Borghese from the Metro; this place is right off P. Bucarest. Consider splashing out on a meal here for a special occasion. An upscale clientele comes here for mixed drinks and solid takes on Italian fare. The real star, however, is the setting: you'll be dining under frescoes in a restored Neoclassical building right in the Villa Borghese itself. Be prepared to spend upwards of €30 per person even if you cast a frugal eye on the menu. Open daily 12:30-3pm and 8-11pm. Reservations required. AmEx/MC/V. ❺

Carrot's Cafe, P. Euclide 1 (☎06 80 74 594; www.carrotscafe.it), at the top of Parioli, right by ◉Euclide. A stylish orange and silver interior and shaded outdoor seating make this a comfortable place for lunch or a coffee. Attracts a young, local crowd. Stays open until late night for *aperitivi* and more. *Primi* €7-8. *Secondi* €8. Open M-F 9:30am-2am, Sa-Su 6pm-2am. MC/V. ❷

TERMINI AND SAN LORENZO

San Lorenzo offers inexpensive food with local character to the budget-conscious student with a discriminating palate. There's a **Conad** supermarket on the lower floor of Termini Station (open daily 6am-midnight).

LET'S NOT GO. Termini and the surrounding areas are unsafe at night. Stay alert and avoid walking alone in the neighborhood after dark.

Hostaria da Bruno, V. Varese 29 (☎06 49 04 03). Take V. Milazzo from V. Marsala and turn right on V. Varese. A bastion of authenticity in a sea of tourist traps. Try *tortellini al sugo* (meat tortellini) or *fettucine alla gricia* (white amatriciana; €7) as you check out the pictures of founder Bruno with Pope John Paul II hanging on the wall. Open M-F noon-3pm and 7-10pm, Sa 7-10pm. AmEx/MC/V. ❷

Hostaria Romana da Dino, V. dei Mille 10 (☎06 49 14 25). From Termini's track 1, turn left on V. Marsala, right on V. Vicenza, and left on V. dei Mille. Delicious dishes for dirt-cheap prices. Loyal local following. Delectable pizza €5-7. Pasta €5-5.50. House wine €1.50 per ¼L. Open M-Tu and Th-Su 11:30am-3pm and 6:30-11pm. MC/V. ❶

Arancia Blu, V. Prenestina 396 (☎34 91 21 51 80), in San Lorenzo, southeast of Termini. Popular restaurant and *enoteca* surrounds diners with wine and makes vegetarian cuisine exciting with adventurous dishes like mint and potato tortellini with pecorino cheese (€8.50). Ask chef-owner Fabio for the refreshing *Moscato Giallo*, a tasty, unlisted Tirolean white wine (€15 per bottle). *Piatti* €8.50-10. Wine €4.50 per glass. Open Sept.-July daily noon-3pm and 8pm-midnight; Aug. 8pm-midnight. AmEx/MC/V. ❷

La Famiglia, V. Calatafimi 11 (☎06 47 28 24). From Termini's track 1, turn left on V. Marsala, continue on V. Volturno, and make a right on V. Calatafimi. 40+ year history of elegant dining on the cheap will make you feel like part of the family. Suited waiters bring the homemade *tortellini famiglia* (meat tortellini in a mushroom, ham, and pea cream sauce; €7) to you indoors or out. Pizza €5-7. Large *antipasto* buffet €6-8. House wine €6 per L. *Primi* €5-8. *Secondi* €6-12. Cover €1.30. Open daily 12:15pm--3:30pm and 6-10:45pm. AmEx/MC/V. ❷

Andrea, V. Castelfidardo 30 (☎06 48 68 48). From Termini's track 1, turn left on V. Marsala, continue on V. Volturno, make a right on V. Cernaia, and a left on V. Castelfidardo. Dine among the blinking holiday lights in the interior or the secluded patio, surrounded by flowers and vines. Try the grilled fish (€8.50-13) or house specialty *Farinata Genovese* (Genovese porridge; €15 for 2 people). *Primi* €7-8. *Secondi* €7.50-16.50. Open M-Th and Sa-Su 12pm-3pm and 6pm-midnight. AmEx/D/MC/V. ❷

Ristorante da Nazzareno, V. Magenta 35-37 (☎06 49 59 211). From Termini's track 1, turn right on V. Marsala, left on V. Marghera, and walk to the intersection with V. Magenta. Caters to both the traditional and the adventurous diner on a budget, serving up grilled sirloin (€8) and *fritto di cervello con carciofi* (fried brain with artichokes; €9) alike. *Antipasto* buffet €7. Wine €5-7 per glass. *Primi* €4-9. *Secondi* €6-14. Open M-Tu and Th-Su noon-3pm and 6-11pm. AmEx/D/MC/V. ❷

Pizzeria del Secolo, V. Palestro 62 (☎06 44 57 606). From Termini's track 1, turn left on V. Marsala, right on V. Vicenza, and walk to the intersection with V. Palestro. Constant stream of locals go through this favorite with a wide selection of pizzas with serious toppings and inexpensive, fresh *piatti*. Most pizzas priced by weight; full pizza with drink €5. *Primi* €5-6. *Secondi* €7-8. 66cl Peroni €3. Delivery available. Open daily 8am-midnight or 1am. Cash only. ❶

Pastarito, V. Gioberti 25 (☎06 48 82 252). From Termini's track 22, take a left on V. Giolitti and a right on V. Gioberti. Painted caricatures of chefs laugh from the walls as you choose from several types of homemade pasta, combined with fragrant concoctions like the *profumo d'autunno* (fondue, pumpkin cream, porcini mushrooms, and chestnuts; €9). Pasta, pizza, and calzone €5-11. Open daily noon-midnight. MC/V. ❷

Faglanetto, V. Filippo Turati 21 (☎06 44 67 306). From Termini's track 22, turn left on V. Giolitti, right on V. Gioberti, and left on V. Filippo Turati. Gruff waiters serve oversized portions of classic Roman fare to patrons seated inside at French-style long tables, or outside on the shady patio. Pizza €5-8. *Menú* €13. *Primi* €6-11. *Secondi* €6-16. Open daily 10am-3pm and 6pm-11pm. AmEx/MC/V. ❷

Africa, V. Gaeta 26-28 (☎06 49 41 077), near P. Indipendenza. An over 30-year tradition of affordable Eritrean and Ethiopian cuisine. Vegetarian menu available. Lounge around in the red-hued, velvety interior as you try the house specialty *Zighini* dishes (€10-12). *Secondi* €9-13. Cover €1. Open Tu-Su 8am-1am. AmEx/D/MC/V. ❸

Panella, L. Leopardi 2 (☎06 48 72 344), Ⓜ A-Vittorio. Just southwest of P. Vittorio. Gourmet shop serving delicious pastries, bread, coffee, and more. Wide selection of deluxe jams, teas, honey, and mousse cakes. Try the lemon and champagne mousse, a house specialty. Caters to those with specific food allergies (nuts, gluten, etc.). Rome's famous monuments are sculpted in decorative confections. Most things priced by the kg. Pastries €1-4, jams and honeys €4-6. Open M-W and F 8am-2pm and 5-8pm, Th 8am-2pm, Sa 8am-2pm and 4:30-8pm, Su 8:30am-2pm. AmEx/D/MC/V. ❶

Caffè Demacri, V. Goito 31-33 (☎34 77 59 67 90). From Termini's track 1, turn left on V. Marsala, continue on V. Volturno, turn right on V. Montebello sul Sangro, and then left on V. Goito. The barista hustles like Rudy in this bustling snack bar where you can grab tasty, cheap coffee-house beverages (€1), pastries (€1), and *panini* (€2-3). Down a draft beer for a cool €1.60. M-F 5:30am-7:30pm, Sa 5:30am-2:30pm. Cash only. ❶

Caffè Trombetta, V. Marsala 46 (☎06 49 14 78; www.caffetrombetta.com). Exit from Termini's track 1 onto V. Marsala. Several stations around this busy cafe and shop serve up quality gelato (€2-3), pastries and cakes (€1-3), panini (€1.50-3), bottled drinks, and coffee (beverages and beans). Open daily 6am-11:30pm. AmEx/MC/V. ❶

I Leoni d'Abruzzo, V. Vicenza 44 (☎06 44 70 02 72). From Termini's track 1, turn left on V. Marsala and right on V. Vicenza. Step down onto the marbled tile floor of this small basement restaurant and dine under the watchful gaze of painted lions. Try the *rigatoni alla contadina* ("country girl style" rigatoni with mushrooms and prosciutto in tomato sauce; €8.50). Fresh gnocchi served Th. *Primi* €7-10. *Secondi* €7-14. Cover €2. Open M-Sa noon-3pm and 6:30-11pm. AmEx/D/MC/V. ❸

Ristorante da Angelo, V. Gioberti 35/a (☎06 47 40 244). From Termini's track #22, take a left on V. Giolitti and a right on V. Gioberti. Surround yourself with wood paneling and wine at this simple *pizzeria* and restaurant. The *carciofi alla Romana* (Roman-style artichokes; €6) and white pizza with salmon (€9) set it apart from the rest. *Primi, secondi,* and pizza €6-10. Grilled fish €9-14. Open daily 10am-midnight. MC/V. ❷

AVENTINE AND TESTACCIO

P. Testaccio is just past V. Luca della Robbia. In the *piazza*, you will find **Testaccio Market,** a small market set up in metal huts. Numerous vendors offer fresh fruit, vegetables, meat, fish, pasta, candy, nuts, and a variety of prepared foods. (Prices vary, most by weight. Open M-Sa 6am-2pm. Cash only.)

▨ **Il Volpetti Più,** V. Alessandro Volta 8 (☎06 57 44 306; www.volpetti.com). Turn left on V. A. Volta, off V. Marmorata. Relive high school as you slide down the lunch line at this *tavola calda* (cafeteria)—but replace day-old sloppy joes with authentic Italian fare. *Primi* €6-7.50. *Secondi* €4-7.50. Fresh fish F €6-8. Desserts €4. Open M-Sa 10:30am-3:30pm and 5:30-9:30pm. AmEx/D/MC/V. ❷

▨ **Giacomini,** V. Aventino 104-106 (☎06 57 43 645). ⓂB-Circo Massimo. South on V. Aventino from the Metro stop, past V. Licinia. Inside this *alimentari*, owner Claudio, certified *Maestro Salumiere Gastronomio*, prepares indescribably wonderful *panini* to order (€4-8) with the highest quality ingredients, as he has done for over 50 years. Wide selection of hand-picked meats and cheeses from only the best producers, priced by weight. Next door, his wife and daughter create similarly wonderful pizza. Open M-Sa 7:30am-2pm and 4:45-6:30pm. AmEx/MC/V. ❶

Felice a Testaccio, V. Mastro Giorgio 29 (☎06 57 46 800; www.feliceatestaccio.com). ⓂB-Piramide. Turn left on V. Galvani off V. Marmorata and right on V. M. Giorgio. Black squares of foam hang just below the ceiling in the dining room, probably to dampen the cheers of patrons who have just tasted their food. Feast on *spaghetti alla Felice* (cherry tomatoes, basil, mint, oregano, thyme, marjoram, and ricotta; €10) in front of post-Impressionist paintings strung up in a line on the wall. Special *menú* for each day of the week. Famed *tonnarelli cacio e pepe* (pasta with cheese and pepper) €10. *Primi* €8-10. *Secondi* €13-22. Cover €1. Open M-Sa 12:30-2:45pm and 8-11:15pm. AmEx/MC/V. ❸

Il Cantinone, P. Testaccio 31/32 (☎06 57 46 253). ⓂB-Piramide. Turn left on V. Giovanni Battista Bodoni off V. Marmorata; P. Testaccio is past V. Luca della Robbia. Patrons slurp down pappardelle with wild boar sauce (€8) and hearty meat-and-gravy dishes (€12-22). Enormous brick oven pumps out delicious pizza (€4-8) from 7pm. Terrific house white wine €7 per L. Open M and W-Su noon-3pm and 7pm-midnight. AmEx/D/MC/V. ❷

La Fraschetta di Mastro Giorgio, V. Mastro Giorgio 19 (☎06 57 41 369; www.lafra-schettadimastrogiorgio.com). ⓂB-Piramide. Turn left on V. Galvani off V. Marmorata and then right on V. M. Giorgio. Exposed ducts and casks balanced between rafters give this large restaurant the feel of a converted barn (in a good way). Start your meal with the special meats and cheeses from the counter, including pig head sausage and ewe's ricotta (€3-8). *Primi* €8-9. *Secondi* €8-14. Open M-F noon-3pm and 7:30pm-1am, Sa 7:30pm-1am. AmEx/D/MC/V. ❷

Da Oio a Casa Mia, V. Galvani 43/45 (☎06 57 82 680). ⓂB-Piramide. Turn left on V. Galvani off V. Marmorata. Pictures of family and friends line the walls of the dining room, where red-and-white checkered tables play host to traditional Roman plebe food, like the *coratella* (heart, liver, spleen, lung with artichoke; €14). *Primi* €8-12. *Secondi* €9-18. Gnocchi Th €8. Open M-Sa 12:30-3pm and 7:30-11:30pm. MC/V. ❸

Osteria degli Amici, V. Nicola Zabaglia 25 (☎06 57 81 466; www.osteriadegliamici.info). ⓂB-Piramide. Turn left on V. Galvani off V. Marmorata and walk to the intersection with V. Nicola Zabaglia. Lamps hang from chains and keep the interior dim in this elegant eatery, even in the light of day. Original pasta dishes include *strozzapreti* with sausage, pumpkin, and wild fennel (€7). Curious spicy chocolate soufflé €5. *Primi* €7-9. *Secondi* €10-18. Open M and W-Su 12:30-2:30pm and 7:30pm-midnight. AmEx/D/MC/V. ❸

Da Felice e Silvana, P. Testaccio 28-29 (☎06 57 46 342). ⓂB-Piramide. Turn left on V. Giovanni Battista Bodoni off V. Marmorata; P. Testaccio is just past V. Luca della Robbia. Ink prints and photographs of Testaccio and Piramide decorate the walls around the counter, from which customers ferry prepared foods (pasta and meat €4-5) to small tables or home. *Pizze tonde* (full pizzas) €3.50-5.50. Calzones €2. Open M-Sa 9am--3pm and 6-9pm. Cash only. ❶

La Crêperie di Testaccio, V. Galvani 11 (☎06 57 43 814; www.lacreperieditestaccio. it). ⓂB-Piramide. Turn left on V. Galvani off V. Marmorata. Specializes in (spoiler alert) crepes and Mediterranean cuisine, plus featured dishes from around the world. Extensive daily organic and gluten-free menus. Traditional *primi* €4-7. Crepes €4-8. Foreign cuisine €8-14. Open Tu-F-12:30-3:30pm and 4:30pm-12:45am, Sa-Su 4:30pm-12:45am. AmEx/D/MC/V. ❷

F O O D

I Mattarelli, V. Giovanni Battista Bodoni 58/62 (☎06 57 30 28 17). ⓂB-Piramide. Turn left on Via Giovanni Battista Bodoni off V. Marmorata and walk to the intersection with V. E. Torricelli. Typical Roman cuisine, wood-oven pizza, and succulent meats are the specialties in this austere restaurant. Modern paintings of red-lipped women gaze out on dark wooden tables. Lunch buffet features meat and homemade pasta (€5) with side dishes (€3). Pizza €5-9. Meat priced by kg. *Primi* €9. *Secondi* €13-15. Open daily noon-3pm and 7-11pm. AmEx/MC/V. ❷

Pecorino, V. Galvani 64 (☎06 57 25 05 39; www.ristorantepecorino.it). ⓂB-Piramide. Turn left on V. Galvani off V. Marmorata. Cloves of garlic hang from the ceiling and classic Moretti beer posters blasphemously grace the walls in this restaurant, which stands next to the location of the original Peroni brewery. Forgive them after you taste the *maltagliati con carciofi* (fresh pasta with artichoke; €10). Pizza €7-12. Moretti draft €4.50-6. *Primi* €9-13. *Secondi* €12-18. Open Tu-Su 12:30-3pm and 7:30pm-midnight. AmEx/D/MC/V. ❸

Volpetti Salumeria-Gastronomia, V. Marmorata 47 (☎06 57 42 352; www.volpetti. com), around the corner from its sister restaurant, Il Volpetti Più. Duck to avoid hanging meat shanks at this spiffy shop and wander among shelves lined with fresh gourmet cheeses, homemade pasta, and baked goods priced per kg. Open M-Sa 8am-2pm and 5-8:15pm. AmEx/D/MC/V. ❷

Pasta Fresca Mea, P. Testaccio 3 (☎06 57 50 843). ⓂB-Piramide. Turn left on V. Aldo Manuzio off V. Marmorata; P. Testaccio is just past V. Luca della Robbia. Watch the master fresh pasta artisans at work in the back, as they have been in this shop since 1947, as you select from a variety of their creations and marinated vegetables (priced per kg). Open M-W and F-Su 7:30am-1:30pm and 4:30-7:30pm. MC/V. ❶

Blue Ice, P. Santa Maria Liberatrice 30 (☎06 61 77 42 89; www.blueiceitalia.com). ⓂB-Piramide. Turn left on V. Luigi Vanvitelli off V. Marmorata; P. Santa Maria Liberatrice is just past V. Mastro Giorgio. Brightly colored gelateria appears like a low-quality chain, but has surprisingly delicious gelato at non-tourist-trap prices. Choices include soy-based gelato and excellent pistacchio. Gelato €1.50-3. Open daily 9am-1am. Cash only. ❶

Parinando, V. della Robbia 30 (☎06 57 50 674). ⓂB-Piramide. Turn left on V. Alessandro Volta off V. Marmorata and walk to the intersection with V. della Robbia. A variety of breads, pizzas, *crostini,* and *ripiene* (priced per kg) are prepared and baked in the large oven in the back. Calzones €3. Pastries €1-2. Open M-Th 7:30am-2:10pm and 4:30-8:30pm, F 7:30am-2:10pm and 4:30-9pm, Sa 7:30am-2:10pm and 5-9pm. AmEx/D/MC/V. ❶

EUR AND MARCONI

Mr. Kebab, V. Oderisi da Gubbio 231 (☎33 87 68 52 14). Steaming-hot storefront serves one of the best kebabs (€3.50-5) in town, over rice or in a sandwich. The falafel wrap (€3) is stellar. All ingredients are fresh, and the friendly servers cook them right in front of your eyes—hence the high temperatures. Good-looking sides, pizza, *supplì,* and sweet Middle Eastern desserts. Open Tu-Su. Cash only. ❶

Il Cornettone, V. Oderisi da Gubbio 219 (☎06 55 87 922). Romans rave about this *cornetto* joint, which serves over 50 varieties of the city's favorite coffee accompaniments. But these babies aren't just for breakfast—the shop doesn't even open some mornings, but it's open late every night, when it becomes a neighborhood hangout. Open M-Th 6am-1pm and 6pm-3am, F-Sa 7pm-5am, Su 6pm-3am. Cash only. ❶

Gelarmony, V. Oderisi da Gubbio 201-5 (☎06 55 66 808). You'll get a serious sugar surge from the brightly colored gelato at the Marconi branch of this Sicilian-style chain. Generous chunks of meringue, chocolate, and other tooth-killers are whipped up fresh and elaborately presented. Also sells what it proudly proclaims "real Sicilian cannoli"

(€2)–they're filled with sweet and creamy ricotta as you wait. Cones and cups from €1.50. Open daily 9am-2am. MC/V. ❶

Ombralonga Vinerie, V. Oderisi da Gubbio 41/43 (☎06 55 94 212). Relaxed neighborhood wine bar with white brick walls stocks nearly 200 different bottles on a mammoth row of shelves. Popular with locals at aperitif time for a relaxing glass of wine (most around €4) and some cheese and *charcuterie*. Also serves a light lunch and dinner. Open M-Sa 10:30am-11:30pm. MC/V. ❷

Da Vittorio, V. Mario Musco 29/31 (☎06 54 08 272). Ⓜ B-Marconi or bus #761/671 from EUR to V. di Grotta Perfetta. Local families include the chefs and staff in their epicurean revelry, under the watchful eyes of Italian movie stars hanging on wall tacks. Summer special *polenta spuntature e salsiccia* (polenta with spare ribs and sausage, €13, available W). *Primi* €5-10. *Secondi* €6-14. Wine from €12 per bottle. Open M-F noon-2:30pm and 7:30-10pm, Sa noon-2:30pm. AmEx/D/MC/V. ❷

EUR Caffè Casini, Vle. della Civiltà del Lavoro 14/34 (☎06 54 21 81 10; www.eur-caffecasini.it). Ⓜ B-EUR Palasport or EUR Magliana, west of P. Marconi. Fresh fish is the specialty at one of the only bastions of affordability in the heart of EUR, served outdoors under a permanent metal awning and modern oil paintings. Snack bar delivers drinks, pastries, and sandwiches from 1 long counter. Self-service lunch. *Primi* €8-12. Fish and meat *secondi* priced by weight. Snack bar open daily 6am-1am. Restaurant open daily noon-3pm and 7pm-1am. D/MC/V. ❷

Caffè Palombini, P. Konrad Adenauer 12 (☎06 59 11 700), west of P. Marconi. Ⓜ B-EUR Palasport or EUR Magliana. Huge, flowering bushes fill the air with a pleasant fragrance around this classy cafe's softly glowing tables. Delicious gelato (€1.80-3.10); the passion fruit will leave you refreshed and all tingly. Pastries (€1-3), *panini*, and calzones (€1-3) feed your appetite in between rounds of coffee and drinks. Open M-Th 7am-midnight, F-Sa 7am-1am, Su 8am-midnight. AmEx/D/MC/V. ❶

Columbus, V. Civiltà del Lavoro 96 (☎06 59 26 150), in P. Marconi. 50 ft. from the epicenter of Mussolini-town, the plant-shielded patio is a quiet oasis of shockingly affordable fare in an elegant setting. Self-service lunch (daily noon-3pm) allows a choice of *primi* (€3.90), *secondi* (€4.70), fish (€5.70), and fresh fruit (€2.80), along with a selection of gelato and pastries. Pizza €6-9. *Primi* €7.50-10. *Secondi* €12-23. Dinner served daily 7:30pm-midnight. AmEx/D/MC/V. ❷

Il Campidano, V. Fonte Buono 7/9 (☎06 54 00 698). Ⓜ B-Marconi or bus #761/671 to V. Vedana. Landlubbers need not apply in this nautically-themed restaurant (number of dishes without suckers or gills: 1), but the seafood might make you shiver your timbers. Waiters ferry dishes filled with tentacles and spuds (poached octopus with potatoes €15) to tables encircled by beach paintings and wallpaper. *Primi* €10-20. Fish €15-25. Drown your crustacean (paradox?) with a L of house wine (€7). Open M-Sa 12:30-3pm and 8-11pm, Su 12:30-3pm. AmEx/D/MC/V. ❸

Al Ponticello, V. Ostiense 415/419 (☎06 54 10 118). Ⓜ B-Marconi. Cheap, sumptuous pasta and wood-oven pizza melts in your mouth as you're transported away from the concrete-and-graffiti jungle outside by skilled murals depicting the countryside. Specializes in grilled meat, especially *fiorentina alla brace* (T-bone steak; €4 per 100g). *Primi* €6-9. Pizza €4-8. Desserts €4. Beer €4. House wine €7 per L. Open daily 7pm-midnight. AmEx/D/MC/V. ❷

SIGHTS

ANCIENT CITY

In the midst of the countless scattered stones, walls, and columns of the Roman Forum and the Palatine stands a truncated, brick pillar. Despite its seeming insignificance, this spot is the **Umbilicus Urbis,** the "navel of the city," marking the geographical center of the ancient city. More than any other monument in Rome, it symbolizes the city's past status as the *ombelico del mondo*, the center of the West's political, economic, social, and religious life. Despite the ravages of time, the glory of Rome's history is still palpable. In a relatively small area, one can see the venues of Roman government, religion, entertainment, privilege, and even sanitation. Over the millennia, much of Rome's ancient heritage has been built upon, built over, reused, and modified. As a result, the ancient city presents visitors with an organic whole, where residences and churches rest on ancient theaters and ancient temples, while ceaseless excavations continue discovering more Roman wonders. Exploring the ancient city is time-consuming and involves a great deal of walking; give yourself a full day to visit the Forum, the Palatine, and the Colosseum thoroughly.

PALATINE HILL

South of the Roman Forum, this hill was home to the Roman emperors. Open daily from last Su of Mar. to Aug. 8:30am-6:15pm; Sept. 8:30am-6pm; from Oct. 1 to last Sa of Oct. 8:30am-5:30pm; from last Su of Oct. to Dec. 8:30am-3:30pm; from Jan. 2 to Feb. 15 8:30am-4pm; from Feb. 16 to Mar. 15 8:30am-4pm; from Mar. 16 to last Sa of Mar. 8:30am-4:30pm. Last entry 1hr. before closing. Only combination tickets for the Colosseum, Palatine Hill, and Roman Forum can be purchased; the Forum and the Hill are treated as one. Purchase tickets at any entrance to any sight, though the biglietteria 100m down V. di San Gregorio from the Colosseum (behind the Arch of Constantine) tends to be the least crowded. €12, EU citizens ages 18-24 €7.50, EU citizens over 65 free or under 18. Ticket requires you to see both sights in 2 days, with only 1 entrance to each. Audio tours for the Palatine Hill (€4) available in English, Italian, French, German, Spanish, Russian, Chinese, Arabic, and Japanese. Combined audio tour with the Roman Forum €6. Italian-only tours on weekends at 10am (Forum) and noon (Palatine Hill). Cash only.

One legend has it that prior to the founding of Rome, the Vestal Virgin Rhea Silvia, niece of King Amulius, was impregnated by Mars, the Greek god of war. The king, fearing that Rhea's progeny would overthrow him, imprisoned her until she gave birth to Romulus and Remus. He became enraged by the sight of the remarkable twins and ordered them killed. Fearing the wrath of Mars, Amulius' servant furtively placed them in a basket on the banks of the Tiber River. When the banks flooded, the twins were carried down stream to the Palatine Hill, a plateau between the Tiber River and what would become the Roman Forum. This plateau was home to *la lupa*, the she-wolf that then nourished and cared for Romulus and Remus. However, in Latin, *la lupa* was also a term for the lowest class of prostitutes, known to frequent the Palatine Hill. Romulus and Remus: raised by wolves, prostitutes, or neither? You decide.

During the Republic, the Palatine was the city's most fashionable residential quarter, where aristocrats and statesmen—including Cicero and Marc Antony—built their homes. In 36 BC, with the construction of his relatively modest house, Octavian Augustus transformed the hill into the official residence

131

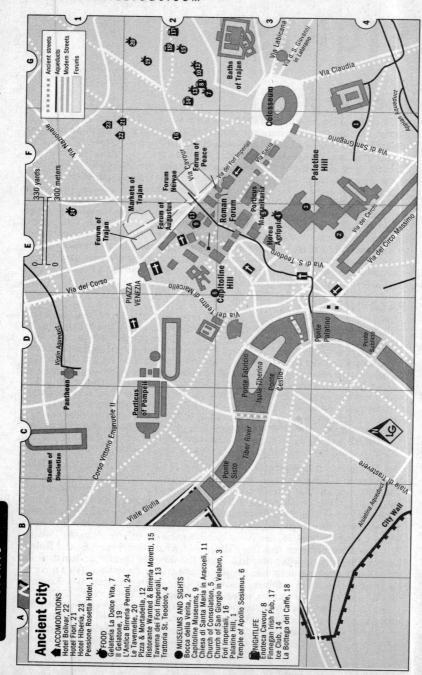

SIGHTS

Ancient City

▲ ACCOMODATIONS
Hotel Bolívar, 22
Hotel Fiori, 21
Hotel Hiberia, 23
Pensione Rosetta Hotel, 10

● FOOD
Gelateria La Dolce Vita, 7
Il Gelatone, 19
L'Antica Birreria Peroni, 24
Le Tavernelle, 20
Pizza & Mortadella, 12
Ristorante Wanted & Birreria Moretti, 15
Taverna dei Fori Imperiali, 13
Trattoria St. Teodoro, 4

● MUSEUMS AND SIGHTS
Bocca della Verità, 2
Capitoline Museums, 9
Chiesa di Santa Maria in Aracoeli, 11
Church of Consolation, 5
Church of San Giorgio in Velabro, 3
Fori Imperiali, 16
Palatine Hill, 1
Temple of Apollo Sosianus, 6

● NIGHTLIFE
Enoteca Cavour, 8
Finnegan Irish Pub, 17
Ice Club, 14
La Bottega del Caffè, 18

of emperors. Later emperors, beginning with Nero, built progressively more luxurious palaces illustrative of their absolute power. By the middle of the first century AD, the Palatine was transformed into a gargantuan palace complex. Indeed, the hill's Latin name, *Palatium*, became synonymous with the palace that dominated it. After the fall of Rome, the hill suffered the same fate as the Forum, although Byzantine ambassadors and even popes sometimes set up house in the crumbling palace.

ORTI FARNESIANI. Built on the foundations of Augustus's imperial palace, the Orti Farnesiani opened in 1625 as the first botanical gardens in the world. Views of the Roman Forum make the gardens perfect for a picnic; *"Affacciata sul Foro"* (Facing the Forum) signs point to a lookout over reflecting pools at the **House of Vestal Virgins.** On the southwest side of the hill directly below the Farnese Gardens, the remains of an ancient village feature the **Temple of Cybele,** constructed in 204 BC on the orders of a prophecy from a Sibylline book. Immediately to its left are the remains of a ninth-century BC village, the **Casa di Romulo,** alleged home of Romulus. These remains can be dated to roughly the same period as the Forum's archaic necropolis, which supports the theory that Rome was founded in the eighth century BC. The Iron Age inhabitants (who may well have included the legendary twins) built their oval huts out of wood; all that remains are the holes they sunk into the tufa bedrock for their roofposts.

To the left of Casa di Romulo is the **Casa di Livia.** Livia was Augustus's wife, the first Roman empress, and according to Robert Graves's *I, Claudius,* an "abominable grandmother." She had the house—with its vestibule, courtyard, and three vaulted living rooms—connected to the **Casa di Augusto** (not to be confused with Domus Augustana) next door. Along the pathways between the House of Livia and the House of Augustus, excavations and restorations are carried out on rooms once lined with marble and gold. *(Take your first right as you start up the hill from the Arch of Titus.)*

IMPERIAL COMPLEX

CRYPTOPORTICUS. Descending the stairs from the terrace to the Domitian's (AD 81-96) imperial complex, you cross the long, spooky Cryptoporticus, a tunnel that connected Tiberius's palace with the buildings nearby. Used by slaves and imperial couriers as a secret passage, it was built by Nero in one of his more paranoid moments. The mosaic tiles lining the tunnel remain in excellent condition, one of the few surviving remnants of Nero's famed "Golden House." Domitian, equally paranoid about the threat of assassination, incorporated the secret passageway into his own palace as a potential escape route. Unfortunately, the tunnel was unable to prevent his eventual murder at the hands of his wife and bodyguard.

DOMUS FLAVIA. To the left of the Casa di Livia, at the center of the hill, the sprawling Domus Flavia is the former site of a gigantic octagonal fountain that occupied almost the entire courtyard. Romans have traditionally associated octagons with power; you will see many octagonal rooms in places of social and political importance, such as the Vatican and at the bases of important statues. The building was divided into three halls and was used by the emperor for a variety of administrative functions. It was also the site of a huge throne room where Domitian could preside over public audiences. He clearly had a thing for fountains because the ruins of a smaller, elliptical one remain intact next to the sunken **triclinium,** a dining room where imperial banquets were held between a set of twin oval fishponds. On the other side of the *triclinium,* a walkway offers sweeping views of the grassy **Circus Maximus** (p. 153) and, farther to the left, the **Baths of Caracalla** (p. 153).

DOMUS AUGUSTANA. Next door, to the left, stands Domus Augustana, which served as the first emperor's court. It was constructed on the Palatine's most sacred site, where, according to legend, Romulus founded the city. The exterior walls that remain are so high that archaeologists are still unsure how Romans managed to place a roof over them. The structure, based on a Hellenistic palace, was built on the side of the hill, with three floors descending below the level of the main hall, including a sunken courtyard with a fishpond. The emperor's quarters were in the maze of staircases and corridors behind the courtyard leading toward the side of the hill. Farther down the hill were the **paedagogium**, the servants' quarters, and the **Domus Praeconum.** The palace's east wing contains the curious **Stadium Palatinum,** a sunken oval space used as a riding school.

HIPPODROME. Perhaps the most visible ruins on the Palatine are in the east wing of the palace, where the Stadium Palatinum, or Hippodrome, stands. Set below the level of the Domus Augustana, this curious stadium has at its southern end a sunken oval space, once surrounded by a colonnade, now decorated by the Archaeological Superintendency with fragments of porticoes, statues, and fountains. Although it is fairly certain that this was not a racetrack for hippopotami ("hippodrome" comes from the Greek *"hippos"* for horse and *"dromos"* for track), its exact nature remains uncertain. There are two prominent theories: first, that it was a private arena, where the imperial family members would get their kicks watching the lesser classes fight for their lives; and second, that it was a private garden. It likely served a dual purpose. From the northern end of the stadium, a winding path leads around to the **Domus Severiana,** a later addition to the imperial complex with a central heating system.

PALATINE ANTIQUARIUM. Built on the ruins of Domitian's imperial palace, this museum traces the Palatine's development over the last 50,000 years. Since the museum was built around the palace's foundation, brick remnants of Domus Flavia and other imperial structures protrude between ground floor exhibits. Ground floor rooms showcase recently discovered evidence of human presence during the Middle Paleolithic Era (100,000-35,000 BC) as well as remains of the Romans' earliest dwellings. Rooms on the upper floor trace the Palatine's imperial past and feature many frescoes and sculptures—both originals and Roman copies of Greek masterpieces. *(Between the Domus Augustana and the Domus Flavia. ☎06 67 85 496; www.archeorm.arti.beniculturali.it. Open daily 8:30am-1 hr. before sunset. Visiting slots every 20min.; only 30 people per floor per slot. Free with entry to the Palatine Hill.)*

COLOSSEUM

☎06 70 05 469. ⓂB-Colosseo or bus 75 from Termini. Open daily 8:30am-7:15pm. Last entry 6:15pm. ▨**Tour with archaeologists** in Italian Sa-Su, English and Spanish daily every 30 min.-1 hr. 9:45am-5:15pm. Tours €4. Audio tour in Arabic, Chinese, English, French, German, Italian, Russian, and Spanish €4.50. Video tour €5.50. Combined tickets with Palatine Hill and Roman Forum €12, EU citizens 18-24 €7.50, EU citizens over 65 or under 18 free. Cash only.

WHOSE LINE IS IT ANYWAY? To avoid waiting up to 2 hours for tickets to the Colosseum, purchase from the less-crowded *biglietteria* on V. di San Gregorio, behind the Arch of Constantine.

The Colosseum—a hollowed-out ghost of travertine marble that dwarfs every other antiquity in Rome by reputation, if not by sheer size—stands as the enduring symbol of the Eternal City. Recent renovations have cleaned the exterior and reconstructed several missing sections (in brick instead of marble, unfortunately) to give a better sense of what the ancient amphitheater looked like at its prime, although the interior is still barren. The gaping holes in the walls are the only signs left indicating where the brilliant marble ornamentation used to lie. Romans repeatedly stripped monuments of their marble to reuse in new monuments, a process called spoilage. You can see signs of spoilage throughout the ancient city's ruins; look for the holes where iron hooks were ripped out of the wall. The city of Rome does its part to make the Colosseum come alive by hiring poor souls to dress up as gladiators and centurions outside, as well as the occasional historically inaccurate and provocatively-dressed gladiatrixes. They're amusing enough to look at, but what they want is to have their picture taken with you for a cool €5. Enter on the lowest level of seating (the arena floor is off-limits) and take the stairs to the upper level.

The term "Colosseum" is actually a nickname for the **Amphitheatrum Flavium,** which Vespasian began building in AD 72 to block out the private lake that Nero had installed. The nickname derives from the gilded bronze statue of Nero as sun-god that used to grace the area next to the amphitheater (see **Domus Aurea,** p. 147), known as *The Colossus,* which was itself based on the Colossus of Rhodes. The Colosseum we know today was built by Titus in AD 80 with spoils from the emperors' campaigns in Judaea. Its longer axis measures 360 feet.

Titus allegedly threw a monster bash for the Colosseum's inauguration: a 100-day fête that saw 5000 wild beasts perish in the bloody arena (from the Latin for sand, *harena,* which was put on the floor to absorb blood). Though the maximum capacity is still debatable, it is guessed that the Colosseum was capable of hosting crowds of at least 50,000. Three concentric corridors allowed for the flow of people in and out—the first was the entrance, the second contained stairs for the audience to reach the seats, and the third held exit stairs. This system allowed the massive amphitheater to be filled in about 10 minutes. Though there was an imperial entrance, the emperor usually considered it too dangerous to be used. Instead, an underground passage connected to his palace, and he entered via a secret

THE LOCAL STORY

ROME IS FALLING (APART)

Over the years, sites like Ostia, Nero's Golden Palace, and the Palatine Hill, which together bring the country revenues heftier than a hunk of marble, have slowly degraded. The culprits: water damage, lack of funding, and natural decay. Now, Italian officials fear the worst for Roman landmarks. Millennia of decay have suddenly become an emergency.

Like any state emergency, the decomposition of Rome's ruins call for a small government committee with special disaster-worthy powers. In March 2009, Guido Bertolaso joined the ranks of an elite group (think Caesar, Vespasian, St. Leo) who have been charged throughout history with preventing the fall of Rome. As the new special commissioner for Italian treasures in Rome and Ostia, Bertolaso will, hopefully, carpe the diem and halt the destruction. His position, among other things, will allow him to circumvent the notorious Italian bureaucracy to give Rome's past a viable future.

The task may seem epic, but Bertolaso has dealt with more dire emergencies. Two years ago, when a waste-collection crisis filled the streets of Naples with piles of trash, he was able to clean the mess. His solution—a trash train from Naples to Germany, where the garbage was incinerated. Here's to hoping he doesn't employ the same remedy for the Colosseum.

staircase. Because the Colosseum events took place for the "public good," tickets to see the slaughter were always free.

Gladiatorial games were suspended in 438 by a Christian-dominated empery and Senate, and animal hunts soon bit the dust as well. The Colosseum was used briefly as a fortress in the Middle Ages and as a quarry in the Renaissance, when popes, beginning with Urban VIII, pillaged marble for use in their own grandiose enterprises, including **St. Peter's Basilica** (p. 163) and **Palazzo Barberini** (p. 196). The former pagan symbol became the site of Christian liturgical rites in the 17th and 18th centuries, and a chapel and rows of crosses were eventually built on the north end of the hollowed-out amphitheater. The crosses were removed in the 19th century when excavations began on the Colosseum, leaving the structure, with the exception of the ongoing exterior renovations, as it is today.

The outside of the arena, with the layers of Doric, Ionic, and Corinthian columns, was considered the ideal orchestration of classical architectural orders, from the most staid to the most ornamental. On the outer side opposite the entrance, look for five marble posts on the edge of the pavement. These posts are remnants of anchors for a giant *velarium*, the retractable shade that once covered the amphitheater. During each game, 1000 naval troops operated the *velarium*. Inside, a section of seating has been reconstructed using original Roman marble to represent what the stands used to look like. Spectators sat according to a hierarchy of class and gender, with senators, knights, and Vestal Virgins closest to the arena and women of lower classes on the highest tier. A large net covered the lower levels, and archers were positioned in the square recesses surrounding the arena to protect the upper echelons from the carnage below.

Note the large cross across from the side entrance. It symbolizes the Colosseum's escape from total destruction at the hands of pillagers by a lucky mistake. The Pope, in order to commemorate the martyrdom of the thousands of Christians supposedly killed in the amphitheater, declared the monument a sacred place and forbade any more demolition. Since that time, it has been discovered that no Christians had ever been killed in the Colosseum. These days, in fact, the Pope holds occasional masses there. Additionally, in the summer of 2000, the Colosseum was used as a stage for several Italian TV variety show extravaganzas as well as Greek drama and classical music performances. Organizers bragged that it was the first time in 15 centuries that it had been used as an entertainment venue, though the maximum audience of 700 for these events paled in comparison to the arena's former glory.

ARCH OF CONSTANTINE

Between the Colosseum and the Palatine Hill, marking the tail end of the Via Sacra, is the Arch of Constantine, one of the latest and best-preserved imperial monuments in the area. The Senate dedicated the arch in AD 315 to commemorate Constantine's victory over his rival Maxentius at the Battle of the Milvian Bridge in 312. The arch's friezes show how heartfelt that dedication actually was: one side's images depict life in Constantine's camps and war, while the other side depicts life after Constantine's victory and the virtues of peace and humanity. There are a few rough 4th-century friezes that demonstrate just how much Roman sculptural art declined from the onset of the millennium, but otherwise the triple arch is cobbled together almost entirely from fragments pilfered from earlier Roman monuments. The four sad-looking men near the top, for example, are Dacian prisoners taken from one of Trajan's memorials; the medallions once belonged to a monument for Hadrian and include depictions of his lover, Antinous; the rest of the scatterings celebrate the military prowess of Marcus Aurelius.

ROMAN FORUM

Main entrance on V. dei Fori Imperiali, at Largo Corrado Ricci, halfway between P. Venezia and the Colosseum. Other entrances are opposite the Colosseum, at the start of Via Sacra, and at the Clivus Capitolinus, near P. del Campidoglio. The Forum can also be accessed via the Palatine Hill. ⓂB-Colosseo or bus to P. Venezia. Access to the Forum is unpredictable, as areas are sometimes fenced off for excavation or restoration. Open daily from last Su of Mar. to Aug. 8:30am-6:15pm; Sept. 8:30am-6pm; from Oct. 1 to last Sa of Oct. 8:30am-5:30pm; from last Su of Oct. to Dec. 8:30am-3:30pm; from Jan. 2 to Feb. 15 8:30am-4pm; from Feb. 16 to Mar. 15 8:30am-4pm; from Mar. 16 to last Sa of Mar. 8:30am-4:30pm. Audio tour in Arabic, Chinese, English, French, German, Italian, Japanese, Russian, and Spanish €4. Combined audio tour with the Palatine Hill €6. Cash only.

The Forum—once a marshland prone to flooding and thus eschewed by Rome's Iron Age inhabitants—spreads from the Colosseum west toward the Capitoline Hill. Today, many of the Forum's structures have been reduced to piles of jagged rocks, and the locations of many sites are uncertain.

In the seventh and eighth centuries BC, Etruscans and Greeks used Tiber Island as a crossing point for trade and the Forum as a market. Rome itself was founded as a market town for sober farmers who came to trade and perform religious rites. The **Curia,** the meeting place of the Senate; the **Comitium Well,** or assembly place; and the **Rostra,** the speaker's platform, were built here to serve the young government of the Republic established in 510 BC, after the disgrace of the last of Rome's kings. Across Via Sacra, Rome's oldest street, temples to Saturn, Castor, and Pollux were dedicated in honor of the revolution. The conquest of Greece in the second century BC brought new architectural forms to the city. The lofty **Basilica Aemilia** was used as a center for business and judicial work before Christians transformed it and many of the existing structures in the Forum into churches.

The Forum was never reserved for any single activity. Senators debated the fates of far-flung nations over the din of haggling traders. The **Vestal Virgins** kept the city's eternal flame burning in their house on a street full of prostitutes. Elsewhere, priests offered sacrifices in the temples, generals led triumphal processions up to the Capitoline, and pickpockets relieved tourists of their possessions. Some things never change.

The Forum witnessed political turbulence in the Republic in the first century BC. Cicero's orations against the antics of corrupt young aristocrats echoed off the temple walls and Julius Caesar's dead body was cremated, amid rioting crowds, in the small temple that bears his name. Augustus, Caesar's great-nephew and adopted son, exploited the Forum to support his new government, closing off the old town square with a temple to the newly deified Caesar and building a triumphal arch honoring himself. His successors followed suit, clotting the old markets with ever grander tokens of their majesty (often looted from the monuments of their predecessors). The construction of the imperial palace on the Palatine in the first century AD and new fora on higher ground to the north cleared out the old neighborhoods around the square. This caused the Forum, despite its gleaming white monuments, to become a deserted ceremonial space in the second century. Close to a hundred years later, emperor Constantine's Christian city closed the pagan temples. By the fifth century, the looting of the Forum by barbarians attested to Rome's dramatic decline.

In the Middle Ages, many buildings were converted to churches and alms houses; the Forum gradually became *Campo Vaccino,* a cow pasture, with only the tallest columns peeking through the towering grass. The last bits of

The Roman Forum (Western Section)

Arch of Augustus, 20
Arch of Tiberius, 8
Base of Decennials, 9
Comitium, 12
Domitian's Hall, 22
Equus Constantine, 18
Equus Domitiani, 17
Fountain of the Juturna, 24
Golden Milestone, 7
Horrea Agrippiana, 21
Lacus Curtius, 16
Lapis Niger, 13
Mamertine Prison, 4
Oratory of the Forty
  Martyrs, 25
Portico of Dei Consentes, 1
Puteal Libonis, 24
Republican Rostra, 14
Rostra of Augustus, 10
S. Lorenzo in Miranda, 27
S. Maria Antiqua, 23
SS. Giuseppe e Falegnami, 3
Secretarium Senatus, SS
  Luca e Martina, 11
Shrine of Venus Cloacina, 19
Temple of Antoninus and
  Faustina, 28
Temple of Concord, 2
Temple of Janus, 15
Temple of Vesta, 26
Umbilicus Romae, 5
Vulcana, 6

ENTRANCE

Regia

House of the Vestals

Via Nova

See Eastern Section

Basilica Aemilia

Temple of the Deified Julius

Temple of Castor and Pollux

Via Sacra

Via Sacra

Vicus Tuscus

Curia

Market Square

Column of Phocas

Memorial Columns

Via Sacra

Basilica Julia

Via del Foro Romano

Forum of Caesar

Arch of Septimius Severus

Vicus Jugarius

Temple of Saturn

Tabularium

Temple of Vespasian

Clivus Capitolinus

50 yards

50 meters

SIGHTS

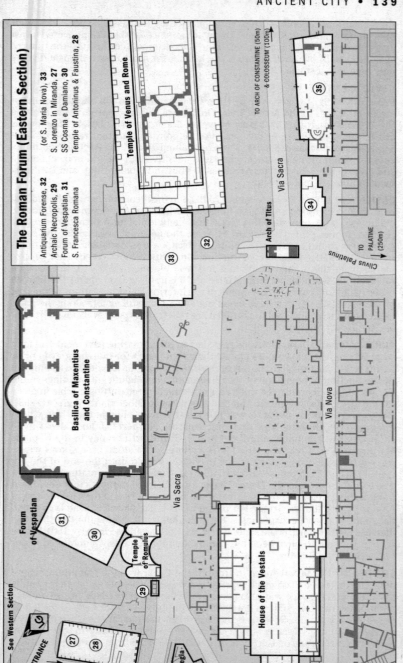

The Roman Forum (Eastern Section)

Antiquarium Forense, **32**
Archaic Necropolis, **29**
Forum of Vespatian, **31**
S. Francesca Romana

(or S. Maria Nova), **33**
S. Lorenzo in Miranda, **27**
SS Cosma e Damiano, **30**
Temple of Antoninus & Faustina, **28**

Temple of Venus and Rome

Basilica of Maxentius and Constantine

Forum of Vespatian

Temple of Romulus

House of the Vestals

Via Sacra

Via Nova

Arch of Titus

Via Sacra

TO ARCH OF CONSTANTINE (50m)
& COLOSSEUM (100m)

TO PALATINE (250m)

Clivus Palatinus

Regia

ENTRANCE

See Western Section

(27) (28) (29) (30) (31) (32) (33) (34) (35)

the Forum's accessible marble were quarried by Renaissance popes for their own monumental constructions. Excavations since 1803 have uncovered a vast array of remnants, but also rendered the site extremely confusing—the ruins of structures built over and on top of each other for more than a thousand years now compose a single view.

CIVIC CENTER

From the Arch of Constantine by the Colosseum, take Via Sacra, the oldest street in Rome, to the **Arch of Titus.** On the left as you approach the arch lie the **Thermae** (Baths), the **Temple of Jupiter Stator,** and the **Temple of Antoninus and Faustina.** On the right is a series of 10 columns, all that remain of Hadrian's **Temple of Venus and Rome.** The Capitoline Hill and the Arch of Septimius Severus stand in the distance. Via Sacra cuts through the old market square and civic center; the **Basilica Aemilia** is to your immediate right, and the brick **Curia** building is just beyond.

BASILICA AEMILIA. Completed in 179 BC, the Basilica Aemilia was the judicial center of ancient Rome. It also housed the guild of the *argentarii* (money-changers), who operated the city's first cambiomat and provided *denarii* (Roman money) for traders and tourists, though doubtless not at the same great rates found today at Termini. The basilica was damaged several times by fires and subsequent reconstructions; in the pavement you can see bronze marks from the melted coins lost in these blazes. In AD 410, the basilica received its death blows from Alaric and his raiding Goths, and the broken bases of columns are all that remain of the interior. The foundations of the row of *tabernae* (shops) that once faced the Forum are still visible along the path. In the back right corner of the basilica are reliefs of *Rape of the Sabine Women* and the *Death of Tarpeia.*

CURIA. Mussolini's restorations revealed an inlaid marble pavement and long steps where Roman senators placed their own chairs for meetings; even prior to this work, the Curia (to the left of the Basilica Aemilia as you face it) enjoyed the distinction of being one of the oldest and most significant buildings in the Forum. Tullus Hostilius, the third king of Rome, started putting marble in place for the first Curia, but the current building dates to Diocletian's reign (AD 283). Contrary to popular belief, it was not in the square outside the Curia where the group of (literally) back-stabbing senators murdered Julius Caesar in 44 BC. Caesar was actually murdered in the Theater of Pompey in the Campus Martius. In 630, it was converted into a church. The stone base shows where Augustus's legendary golden statue of Victory rested until the end of the 4th century, when Christian senators irked by paganism had the statue destroyed. The Curia also houses the **Plutei of Trajan,** two sculpted parapets that decorated the Rostrum, depicting the burning of the tax registers and the distribution of food to poor children. To the left of the Curia is the **Church of Santi Luca e Martina,** once the **Secretarium Senatus.** Farther up the hill, below the **Church of San Giuseppe dei Falegnami,** is the second century BC **Mamertine Prison** (p. 150), where St. Peter is said to have been imprisoned and miraculously summoned water to baptize his cellmates.

COMITIUM. The broad space in front of the Curia was the Comitium, where male citizens came to vote and representatives of the people gathered for public discussion. This space was also home to the famed **Twelve Tables,** bronze tablets upon which the first codified laws of the Republic were inscribed. To the left of the Arch of Septimius Severus is the large brick **Rostrum,** or speaker's platform, erected by Julius Caesar in 44 BC (just before his death). The term *rostra* refers to the metal ramrods on the bows of warships. *Rostra* from warships captured at Antium in 342 BC decorated the platform. The literal *rostrum* is gone, but regularly spaced holes in its platform remain. Senators and consuls orated to the Roman plebes from here, and any citizen could mount to voice his opinion (theoretically, at least). After his assassination, Cicero's hands and head (with a needle stuck through his tongue) were displayed here as a warning to those who practiced unbridled free speech. Augustus's rebellious daughter, Julia, is said to have showed her objections to her father's legislation promoting family values by engaging in amorous activities with Augustus's enemies on the spot where the laws had been announced.

ARCH OF SEPTIMIUS SEVERUS. The hefty Arch of Septimius Severus stands between the Comitium and the slopes of the Capitoline Hill, directly ahead on Via Sacra. Raised in AD 203 to celebrate the emperor's victories in the Middle East, the arch is covered with reliefs that depict the imperial family. After Caracalla, Severus's restless son and successor grabbed the throne by killing his brother, Geta, and scraping his name and portrait off of the arch. Directly behind the arch the grey tufa walls of the **Tabularium** line the rear of the Forum. Once a repository for the Senate's archives, this structure now serves as the basement of the Renaissance **Palazzo dei Senatori**. It forms the base of the **Campidoglio**.

MARKET SQUARE. The original market square (in front of the Curia) was occupied by a number of shrines and sacred precincts. Immediately down the stairs from the Curia lies the **Lapis Niger** (Black Stone), surrounded by a circle of bricks. Republican Romans believed this is where the legendary founder of the city, Romulus, was murdered. Modern scholars now think the Lapis Niger was actually an early shrine to Vulcan. The shrine was considered passé even during the Republic, when its statuary and columns were covered by gray pavement. Below the Lapis Niger rest the underground ruins of a sixth-century BC altar, along with a pyramidal pillar where the oldest known Latin inscription in Rome warns the public against defiling the shrine. In front of the Rostrum, halfway between the Curia and the Basilica Julia, the **Three Sacred Trees** of Rome—olive, fig, and grape—have been replanted by the Italian state (never mind that grapes grow on vines).

The "newest" part of the Forum is the **Column of Phocas,** erected in 608 to celebrate the visiting Byzantine emperor, Phocas—a sacrilege that would have probably made early Republican Romans roll over in their graves if most of them hadn't been cremated. The **Lacus Curtius** to its left is marked by concentric marble semicircles in the ground and a small frieze of a man on horseback; it commemorates the heroism of the legendary Roman warrior Marcus Curtius, who threw himself into a deep chasm in 362 BC to save the city from collapse. The marketplace may also have been home to three important markers: the Umbilicus Urbis, the Golden Milestone, and the Vulcanal. The exact locations of these, which not only marked the center of the city, but also that of the entire Roman world, still remains a matter of speculation.

LOWER FORUM

To the south of the Arch of Septimius Severus lie the Basilica Julia and the three extant temples of the lower Forum: the Temple of Saturn, the Temple of Castor and Pollux, and the Temple of the Deified Julius. The remnants of these ancient monuments are across the Market Square from the Curia and the Basilica Aemilia.

TEMPLE OF SATURN. Eight columns mark the Temple of Saturn, one of the first buildings constructed in Rome. The Romans believed that Saturn had taught them the art of agriculture and filled his statue inside the temple with fresh olive oil. The temple was the site of **Saturnalia,** the Roman winter bash that signified the end of the year. During this raucous party, class and social distinctions were blurred as masters served slaves.

Behind the temple are (left to right): twelve columns of the **Portico of the Dei Consentes** dedicated to the twelve most important Roman gods; the three Corinthian columns of the **Temple of Vespasian,** completed by his son Domitian; and the foundations of the **Temple of Concord,** which was built to celebrate the peace between patricians and plebeians in 367 BC.

BASILICA JULIA. Around the corner to the left of the Temple of Saturn, rows of deserted column bases are the sole remnants of the Basilica Julia. Begun by Julius Caesar in 54 BC, completed by Augustus, and restored by Diocletian, it followed the same plan as the Basilica Aemilia (p. 140) on a larger scale. The central hall, flanked by three rows of columns on each side, was used as a courtroom. Look for grids and circles in the steps where anxious Romans, waiting to go before the judge, played an ancient version of Snakes and Ladders. If you've had your fill of culture, the end of the basilica opposite the Temple of Castor and Pollux is part of the **Cloaca Maxima,** the huge sewer which drained from the Forum directly into the Tiber. Resist the temptation: this is *not* a public toilet.

TEMPLE OF CASTOR AND POLLUX. At the end of the Basilica Julia, three white marble columns mark the massive podium of the Temple of Castor and Pollux, dedicated in 484 BC to celebrate the Roman rebellion against their tyrannical, less-than-superb Etruscan king, Tarquinius Superbus. The Romans attributed their victory over the Latins at Lake Regillus in 499 BC to the help of the twin gods, Castor and Pollux, who outflanked the mortal Etruscans. Legend has it that immediately after the battle, the twins appeared in the Forum to water their horses at the nearby **Lacus Juturnae** (Basin of Juturna). Now marked by a reconstructed marble *aedicula* to the left of the gods' temple, the site was once the location of the ancient city's water company. Behind the temple, the **Church of Santa Maria Antiqua** is the oldest in the forum, dating back to the sixth century. Unfortunately, it will be closed for renovations until 2011.

TEMPLE OF THE DEIFIED JULIUS. Across from the Temple of Castor and Pollux is the rectangular base of the Temple of the Deified Julius, which Augustus built in 29 BC to honor his murdered adoptive father and to proclaim himself the inheritor of Julius Caesar's divine spirit. The circular altar of rocks housed within the temple marks the spot where Caesar's body is believed to have been cremated in 44 BC, and where Marcus Aurelius gave his famous funeral speech. He was burned in a funeral pyre with a piece of wood, flowers, and a cage with an eagle over his body. As the fire was started, the eagle was released from the cage, a symbol of the soul of the dead emperor flying away toward the heavens. Every year on July 12, Caesar's alleged birthday, people bring flowers to the shrine.

UPPER FORUM

HOUSE OF THE VESTAL VIRGINS. The sprawling complex of rooms and courtyards uphill from the arch and behind the Temple of the Deified Julius was the House of Vestal Virgins. Here, in spacious seclusion in the shade of the Palatine, lived the six virgins who officiated over Vesta's rites. Among the most respected individuals in ancient Rome, the Vestal Virgins were female priests. Chosen from the most important families by the Pontifex Maximus, they had to be between the ages of six and ten and without physical imperfections. A virgin served 30 years, after which she could choose whether to continue in the priesthood or leave, but as the average lifespan was around 35 years, few made it to the end of their term. The Virgins were the only women who could walk unaccompanied in the Forum. They were able to pardon prisoners, travel in private chariots, and sit in special reserved seats at gladiatorial games and theatrical shows. They were responsible for the city's sacred eternal flame, keeping it continuously lit for over 1000 years (things started to go badly for the Romans when it went out in the fourth century). This esteem had its price; if a virgin strayed from celibacy, she was buried alive with a loaf of bread and a candle on the assumption that the sustenance would give her time to contemplate her sins during her prolonged death. Only a handful of women met this fate.

Off-and-on restoration means that visitors can only peer through the iron gates surrounding the House of the Vestal Virgins. Still, there is a view (head up to the Palatine for a really good one) of the central courtyard where statues of the priestesses who served between AD 291 and 364 reside, including one (eighth on the left as you enter the courtyard) thought to have been Claudia, the Vestal Virgin who, at the end of the fourth century, converted to that new-fangled religion from the south, Christianity.

TEMPLE OF VESTA. Adjacent to the House of Vestal Virgins, the Temple of Vesta, once circular, is now just a vaguely curved wall. It was originally built by the Etruscans, but was later rebuilt by Septimius Severus at the end of the second century AD. Within one of the temple's secret rooms, visited only by the Vestal Virgins, stood the **Palladium,** the small statue of Minerva that Aeneas was said to have brought from Troy to Italy.

Behind the temple, between the House of Vestal Virgins and the Temple of Antoninus and Faustina, lies the triangular **Regia,** the office of the Pontifex Maximus, Rome's high priest and titular ancestor of the pope. Long before the first Pontifex *(Numa Pompilius)* took it over, as early as the sixth century BC, the Regia was the site of sacrifices to the gods of agriculture (as well as Mars, Jupiter, Juno, and Janus). One of the rites performed was the October harvest ritual, in which the tail and genitalia of a slain horse were brought to the Regia in an offering to the god of vegetation. Sadly, this ceremony has been discontinued.

TEMPLE OF ANTONINUS AND FAUSTINA. Back on Via Sacra is the Temple of Antoninus and Faustina (opposite the Temple of Vesta, to the immediate right as you face the entrance ramp), whose strong foundation, columns, and rigid lattice ceiling have preserved it unusually well over the ages. In the seventh and eighth centuries, the **Church of San Lorenzo in Miranda** was built in the interior of the abandoned temple. The temple's columns and frieze were incorporated into the Christian structure. This is not to say that the Christian rulers didn't try to destroy the pagan temple: the deep grooves at the top of the columns show where cables were tied in attempts to demolish this steadfast symbol of pagan worship. The church is an example of the medieval approach to the pagan ruins—either tear down the temples or convert them into churches. The original building was constructed by Emperor Antoninus and dedicated to his wife, Faustina: his name was added after his death in AD 161. In the shadow of the temple (to the right as you face it) is the **Archaic Necropolis,** with Iron Age graves dating back to between the 10th and eighth centuries BC, which lend credence to Rome's legendary founding date of 753 BC. The bodies from the ancient graveyard were found in hollow tree trunks. The remains are visible in the Antiquarium (see **Velia,** p. 144).

TEMPLE OF ROMULUS. Farther up V. Sacra stands the round Temple of Romulus, which retains its original bronze doors, with a working lock, from the fourth century AD. The name of the structure, however, is misleading for two reasons. First, the "Romulus" in question here was probably the son of the fourth-century emperor, Maxentius, not the legendary founder of Rome. Second, the temple probably wasn't a temple at all, but rather an office of the urban magistrate during the Empire. The temple now houses the **Church of Santi Cosma e Damiano** (p. 145). Across Via Sacra from the structure, remains of fortifications from between 730 and 540 BC have been discovered. Behind the temple, recently excavated ruins of Vespasian's **Forum Pacis** (Forum of Peace) are visible along V. dei Fori Imperiali, beginning just past the main entrance. *(Closed to the public.)*

VELIA

Take Via Sacra out of the Forum proper, toward the Arch of Titus.

BASILICA OF MAXENTIUS AND CONSTANTINE. The gargantuan Basilica of Maxentius and Constantine is on the left as you walk down Via Sacra. The three gaping arches that remain are only the side chapels for an enormous central hall, whose coffered ceiling covered the entire gravel court and three chapels on the other side. Emperor Maxentius began construction of the basilica in 306, but was overthrown by Constantine at the Battle of Milvian Bridge in 312 before its completion. Constantine oversaw completion of the basilica, but despite his conversion to Christianity, refrained from converting it into a church out of reverence for the pagan traditions of the Forum. He built the basilica of **San Giovanni in Laterano** instead, based on a similar architectural plan. Constantine's new religious piety failed to impact the size of his inflated ego. The middle apse of the basilica once contained a gigantic statue of him; the body was bronze, and the head, legs, and arms were marble. The remains that were found (on exhibit at the **Museo Capitolino**, p. 193) include a 6½ ft. long foot. The enormous statue met a less exalted end in the seventh century, when all the bronze in the basilica was melted down to cover the first basilica of St. Peter.

The Baroque facade of the **Church of Santa Francesca Romana** (or **Santa Maria Nova**) is built over Hadrian's Temple to Venus and Rome (Amor and Roma). It hides the entrance to the **Antiquarium Forense,** a small museum that houses artifacts from the Forum. Among the items on display are skeletons from the necropolis. *(The Antiquarium Forense is to the right of the front entrance to the Church of Santa Francesca Romana. Open daily 9:30am-noon and 4:30-7pm. Subject to unannounced closures. Free.)*

ARCH OF TITUS. On the summit of the Velian hill, where Via Sacra intersects with the road down from the Palatine, is the Arch of Titus, built in AD 81 by Domitian to celebrate his brother Titus's destruction of Jerusalem 10 years earlier. Though the paranoid Frangipane family turned it into a fortified tower in the Middle Ages, Pope Pius VII ordered it restored to its original state in 1821. On the interior of the arch is a famous frieze depicting Titus's victory and the treasure he took from the Great Temple. The right panel shows a triumphal Titus on a quadriga chariot, while his soldiers carry back the spoils of war on the left panel. Titus used these riches and the 50,000 slaves he brought back in order to construct the Colosseum. The arch is missing the two-sided arches typical of a triumphal arch (two lower arches flanking a taller middle arch) because they were damaged when it was removed from its original location.

FORI IMPERIALI

Bus 175 from Termini. ☎ 06 67 97 786. Open daily 9:30am-6:30pm. Free.

The sprawling Fori Imperiali stretch from the Basilica of Maxentius and Constantine to P. Venezia on either side of V. dei Fori Imperiali, a boulevard Mussolini paved to connect the old empire to his own in P. Venezia, destroying a third of the ruins in the process. The temples, basilicas, and public squares that make up the Imperial Fora were constructed between the first century BC and AD second century in response to increasing congestion in the old Forum. "Excavations will proceed indefinitely" means that the area is closed off, but you can still get free views peering over the railing from V. dei Fori Imperiali or V. Alessandrina. Excavation in the area began in the early 1930s. Currently, a path for visitors is being constructed from the Forum of Trajan through the Forum of Augustus and the Forum of Nerva, eventually connecting with the rest of the Roman Forum underneath V. dei Fori Imperiali. It is scheduled to be completed by early 2010 but, as with all excavations and construction in the area, is prone to continuous delays.

The visitor center on V. dei Fori Imperiali, across from the Basilica of Maxentius and Constantine, has a scale model reconstruction of the entire Forum area, maps, guidebooks, and a film about the history of the Ancient City playing on loop, with headphone stations translating it into several languages, including English.

FORUM OF CAESAR. Julius Caesar was the first Roman leader to expand the city center outside the Forum proper, constructing the Forum of Caesar in 46 BC. Caesar's motivations were political: the new forum and temple he built in honor of Venus, his supposed ancestress, seriously undercut the prestige of the Senate and its older precinct around the Curia. The remains of the **Temple of Venus Genetrix** are marked by three columns. Additions from the reign of Trajan include the brick **Basilica Argentaria,** an ancient bank, and the heated public bathroom—the semi-circular room with holes along the walls. Nearby, a replica of a bronze statue of Caesar originally from the Forum has been placed on the sidewalk of V. dei Fori Imperiali, perfect for Kodak moments. *(On the left-hand side of V. dei Fori Imperiali, just past the Forum as you walk toward P. Venezia.)*

FORUM OF AUGUSTUS. Completed in 2 BC, the Forum of Augustus was dedicated to Mars Ultor (Mars the Avenger). It commemorates Augustus's victory over the murderer's of his adoptive father Julius Caesar, Brutus and Cassius, at the Battle of Philippi in 42 BC. Three columns remain of the **Temple of Mars Ultor,** which centered upon a statue of Mars (oddly enough, it bore a striking resemblance to a certain avenging Emperor) and lined with statues of Roman history's most important figures. A copy of the Mars statue can be seen at the **Capitoline Museums** (p. 193). The hefty wall behind the temple, built to protect the precious new monument from the seedy Subura slums that spread up the hill behind it, doesn't run exactly straight. As the legend goes, when the land was being prepared for construction, even Augustus couldn't convince one stubborn homeowner to give up his domicile, so the great wall was built at an angle around it. The aptly named **Forum Transitorium** (also called the **Forum of Nerva**) was a narrow, rectangular space connecting Augustus's forum with the old Roman Forum and the forum of Vespasian (near present-day V. Cavour). Most of it now lies under the street, but new excavations have begun to uncover more. Although Domitian began it, Emperor Nerva inaugurated the Forum in AD 97, displaying the wit that Roman emperors were known for: he dedicated the temple to Minerva, the deity whose name was closest to his own.

CHIESA DI SANTI COSMA E DAMIANO. The only remnant of **Vespasian's Forum** was built in 527 out of a library in Vespasian's complex. The interior displays a set of sixth-century mosaics, including a multicolor Christ with his robes blowing in the wind. A recently installed viewing window allows for a look into the adjacent Temple of Romulus the Divine. In the northwest corner of the church courtyard is a large Neapolitan nativity scene, featuring more than 130 human figures. *(Near the entrance to the Roman Forum at the intersection of V. Fori Imperiali and V. Cavour.)*

MARKETS OF TRAJAN. Across V. dei Fori Imperiali from the Vittorio Emanuele II monument stand the brick Markets of Trajan. The three-floor, semicircular complex, built during the early second century BC, is perhaps the first example of a Roman shopping mall. It was designed to buttress sections of the Quirinal Hill, which was excavated to make room for the Forum of Trajan. The market had space for 150 shops, selling everything from imported fabrics to Eastern spices. Recent scholarship has confirmed that the long and somewhat bizarre Roman fascination with pubs began here, with the taverns that lined the street outside the market. As you enter the markets, you will find yourself flanked by three levels of vaulted chambers within the Great Hall, which was most likely designed for official functions. Between this hall and the rest of the markets runs via Biberatica, named for the beverages sold in shops on either side of it. The **Torre delle Milizie,** dating from the 12th century, rises from atop the central semicircular complex. This tower was originally part of a palace, which was later fortified, most notably by Pope Boniface VIII.

FORUM OF TRAJAN. Marked by an imposing column, the Forum of Trajan, the largest, newest, and most impressive of the imperial *fora,* is hard to miss. Built between AD 107 and 113, the forum was a celebration of Trajan's campaigns in Dacia, mostly present-day Romania. Its creation rendered the older Roman Forum a tourist attraction. The complex served practical functions, housing two important libraries of Latin and Greek documents, in addition to a colossal equestrian statue of Trajan and a triumphal arch. In the back of the forum, the enormous **Basilica Ulpia** once stood in judicial might. The largest basilica ever built in Rome (17m by 60m), the Ulpia today is just two rows of truncated columns and fragments of the friezes.

TRAJAN'S COLUMN. At one end of the decimated forum stands the almost perfectly preserved spiral of Trajan's Column, one of the greatest surviving specimens of Roman relief sculpture ever found. At 40m, it is exactly the same height as the hill leveled in order to build Trajan's Forum. The continuous frieze that wraps around the column narrates the Emperor's campaigns. From the bottom, you can survey Roman legionnaires preparing supplies, building a stockaded camp, and loading boats to cross the Danube. Twenty-five hundred figures in all have been making their way up the column since 113. The statue of their Emperor that crowned the structure in ancient days was destroyed in the Middle Ages and replaced by the figure of St. Peter in 1588. The column survived the sixth and seventh centuries only because Pope Gregory I was so moved by some of the reliefs that he prayed for Trajan's acceptance into heaven. The pope then claimed that God had come to him in a vision, ensuring Trajan's safe passage but refusing to admit any other pagans. The small holes in the column are actually windows that illuminate an internal staircase. In the column's base is a door that leads to the tomb of Trajan and his wife, where Trajan's ashes rested in a golden urn until it was stolen in the Middle Ages.

OPPIAN HILL

From P. Venezia, follow V. dei Fori Imperiale past the Colosseum; the park is on the left. Open daily 6:30am-9pm. Free.

Take a break from the relentless sun and venture into the shade of Oppian Hill, where chirping birds and homeless men while away the hours. The park houses part of Nero's "Golden House," a 35 hectare palace, which covered much of Ancient Rome but is now entirely closed for restoration—again.

DOMUS AUREA. The extant ruins at the Domus Aurea were only a small part of Emperor Nero's residence, which once took up one-third of Rome. "Golden House" is something of a misnomer, as this edifice was a series of banquet halls and galleries; Nero's private rooms were likely on the Palatine.

Having determined, like so many before him, that he was a god, Nero had the architects Severus and Celer design a palace to suit his divinity. "Using art and squandering the wealth of the Emperor," writes Tacitus, they created "eccentricities which went against the laws of nature." Between the Oppian and Palatine palaces was an enclosed lake, where the Colosseum now stands, and the Caelian Hill became private gardens. The Forum was reduced to a vestibule of the palace; Nero crowned it with a colossal statue of himself as the sun. Standing 35m tall, it was the largest bronze statue ever made and was justly called the Colossus. Nero also pillaged all of Greece to find works of art worthy of his abode, including the famous *Laocoön*, now held in the Vatican's collections.

The party didn't last long, however. Nero was forced to commit suicide only five years after building his gargantuan pleasure garden, and his memory was condemned by the Senate. Following suit, the Flavian emperors who succeeded Nero replaced all traces of the palace with monuments built for the public good. The Flavian Baths were built on top of the Caelian Hill, the lake was drained, and the Colosseum was erected. Trajan filled the Domus Aurea with dirt (so that it would make a stronger foundation) and built his baths on top of it in AD 115, and Hadrian covered the western end with his Temple of Venus and Rome in 135. The Domus Aurea itself was rediscovered in the 14th century.

CHIESA DI SAN PIETRO IN VINCOLI. This fourth-century church is named for the sacred *vincoli* (chains) that supposedly bound St. Peter in prison on the Capitoline. The two chains were separated for more than a century, one in Rome and one in Constantinople, but were reunited in the fifth century and currently reside below the altar. Most tourists head right for Michelangelo's ◾**statue of Moses,** which is tucked in the back right corner. According to Exodus, when Moses descended from Sinai with the Ten Commandments, "rays" (similar to "horns" in Hebrew) shone from his brow; hence the two horns on his head, which are actually beams of light indicating wisdom. The adoring females at his side, Leah and Rachel, here represent active and contemplative lives, respectively. This Moses was meant to serve as the centerpiece for the unfinished Tomb of Pope Julius II, but a series of budget cuts and delays put a stop to the project. Julius had planned a gargantuan sepulcher for himself, with roughly 40 statues, but, alas, he died before the monument was completed. Needless to say, his successors were less interested in immortalizing his death, and Julius ended up in an unmarked grave in the Vatican. (Ⓜ*B-Cavour. Walk along V. Cavour toward the Forum and take the seemingly endless stairs on the left to P. San Pietro in Vincoli. Open daily 8am-12:30pm and 3-6pm. Fully covered shoulders and legs required.*)

CAPITOLINE HILL

The Capitoline was the smallest of ancient Rome's seven hills, but also one of the most sacred. The highlight of the modern hill is the spectacular **Piazza del Campidoglio,** designed by Michelangelo in 1536 in honor of the visit of Emperor Charles V and in celebration of the hill's ancient glory. The hill was

TIME: 3-4hr. walk; longer if you visit the museums along the way.

DISTANCE: About 8km.

SEASON: A sunny day is preferable; bring lots of water.

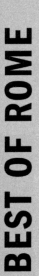

1. COLOSSEUM. The bad news: millions of Christians, contrary to a number of Hollywood movies, did not meet their unfortunate ends within these partially deteriorated walls. The good news: at least 5000 wild animals did, during the stadium's inaugural festivities in AD 80. Titus's grand addition to the principle of bread and circuses may look like a heap of sun-bleached rock today—thanks in no small part to Julius II's not-so-clandestine pillaging during the Renaissance—but in its youth, it was an engineering marvel, containing, among other things, a system of awnings that protected the bloodthirsty populace from the inconveniences of sun and rain. Allow an extra 20min. if you plan to make the climb to the upper tiers of the structure, or stride confidently across the new wooden walkway—just don't look down (p. 134).

2. SANTA MARIA IN ARACOELI. The archetypal Roman Church. In the first century, the Romans worshipped the spirit of money in the guise of Jupiter Moneta. Later, piety replaced productivity, and the mint originally located here became a meeting place for the Franciscans, who were generally uninterested in making money. In the meantime, the Sibyl once quartered within the walls of the old temple informed Augustus that although he did enjoy divine status, one greater than even he would come to rule Rome. In response, the emperor erected the Ara Coeli, or the altar to heaven (p. 150).

3. IL GESU. Historically, the Jesuits were an order known throughout Europe for their commitment to evangelism and their love of extravagant luxury items. The Gesù is the living incarnation of both strains, built in 1584 but left undecorated for more than 100 years (the prescient founders of the Order apparently realized that only Baroque could provide the gilded opulence that such a project required). The Chapel of St. Ignatius and its crowning piece of artistic achievement, the altar topped with an enormous globe of lapis lazuli, are rendered almost unholy by their grandeur, but the real triumph of the church is Baciccia's Triumph of the Holy Name of Jesus, in which sinners, cast from the communion of souls, appear to be hurtling from heaven toward the observers on the ground (p. 155).

4. TEATRO DI MARCELLO. Arranging a walk past the Marcello on a summer evening is a rewarding enterprise: some of Rome's best classical musicians often use the crumbling structure as a venue for concerts in nice weather. Without venturing too far into the stark, dusty collection of ruins, you can visit the oldest building in Rome permanently designated as a theater (p. 151).

5. ISOLA TIBERINA. A stroll around this island, enclosed by the Romans with travertine marble so that it would resemble a ship, is a good way to cross the Tiber on the way to Trastevere. The first structure on the island was a temple to Aesclepius, son of Apollo and god of medicine. During the plague of 293 BC, a statue of him was brought from Greece to the island, which has been dedicated to healing ever since. The Fatebenefratelli (literally "do good brothers") Hospital and San Bartolomeo, Holy Roman Emperor Otto III's church of choice, are both located on the grounds (p. 165).

6. CASTEL SANT'ANGELO. The popes often used this former site of Hadrian's mausoleum as an escape from the pressures, problems, and riots that often plagued St. Peter's. The wealth of the Vatican was often stored here when the Holy Roman Emperors decided that a little trip to the south was the perfect way to fill their coffers. The lower building served as quarters for some of Rome's more rowdy residents, including the boastful autobiographer and sometime artist Benvenuto Cellini, heretical monk Giordano Bruno, and Beatrice Cenci, accused of incest

BEST OF ROME

and patricide and memorialized by Shelley's *The Cenci*. The papal apartments are worth a look, especially the Camera d'Amore e Psiche (p. 165).

7. PIAZZA SAN PIETRO. Far too often, tourists eager to rub flesh with millions of other pensive pilgrims in the Sistine Chapel rush past Bernini's masterpiece without a second look. The artist is undoubtedly taking the proverbial route of disgruntled dead people and turning over in his grave; his work was meant to awe the Protestant heretics who came to Rome in order to talk politics with the pope. A set of four colonnades crowned by 140 distinct saints was part of the visual effect planned by Bernini, in addition to the sensation of leaving the narrow streets of the medieval quarter for the comparative openness of the square. Mussolini ruined the characteristic Baroque metaphor (darkness into light) by constructing the V. di Conciliazione, but the square, and the obelisk placed in the middle by Sixtus V, are nonetheless impressive to even the biggest heretic in the crowd (p. 168).

the home of a gilded temple to Jupiter (dedicated in 509 BC) and contained the state mint and the senatorial archives. The northern peak of the hill was home to Juno's sacred geese, which saved the city from ambush by the Gauls in 390 BC by honking loudly and waking the populace. *Let's Go* does not recommend geese as an alarm system. In keeping with the hill's ancient significance, Michelangelo set up the statues of the twin warriors **Castor and Pollux** that flank the wide and gently sloping staircase, as well as the two reclining river gods and the statue of the goddess **Roma**. To the right and left of P. del Campidoglio stand **Palazzo dei Conservatori** and **Palazzo Nuovo,** home to the **Capitoline Museums** (p. 193). At the far end, opposite the stairs, is the turreted **Palazzo dei Senatori** (Rome's city hall).

PIAZZA DI CAMPIDOGLIO. In the center of the *piazza* stands the famous equestrian statue of **Marcus Aurelius**, brought here from the Lateran Palace. The gilded bronze was one of a handful of ancient bronzes to escape medieval meltdown, only because it was thought to be a portrait of Constantine, the first Christian emperor. Unfortunately, both man and steed succumbed to the assault of modern pollution and were removed for restoration in 1981, leaving behind only their pedestal. The emperor now resides in climate-controlled comfort in the courtyard of the Palazzo Nuovo, and the statue you see now is a weatherproof copy. Across the way, in the courtyard of the Palazzo dei Conservatori, lie the gargantuan head, arm, kneecap, and foot of the statue of Constantine that once graced the Basilica of Maxentius. On the open side of the *piazza*, rejoin *La Cordonata* to make the descent to P. Venezia. The staircase was designed so that Charles V, apparently penitent over his sack of the city a decade before, could ride his horse up the hill to meet Paul III during his triumphal visit. On the right-hand side of *La Cordonata* stands a dark statue of a hooded man, **Cola di Rienzo,** the leader of a popular revolt in 1347 that attempted to reestablish a Roman Republic. The statue marks the spot where the disgruntled populace tore him limb from limb shortly after electing him as first consul. *(Take bus to P. Venezia, face the Vittorio Emanuele II monument, and walk around to the right to P. d'Aracoeli. Take the stairs up the hill.)*

MAMERTINE PRISON. The gloomy, slightly claustrophobic Mamertine Prison, consecrated as the **Church of San Pietro in Carcere,** once held St. Peter, who supposedly caused water to flood into his cell and used it to baptize his captors. Although a stairway now leads down to the dank, lower chamber, a small hole used to be the only entrance to the dungeon. The Romans used the lightless lower chamber as a holding cell for prisoners awaiting execution. Inmates were tortured and occasionally strangled to death in the dark by order of the government. Among the more well-known residents were Jugurtha, King of Numidia; Vercingetorix, chieftain of the Gauls; and the accomplices of the dictator Catiline. *(Walk downhill from Piazza del Campidoglio, past the left side of the Palazzo dei Senatori, toward the Forum. ☎ 06 67 92 902. Open daily in summer 9am-7pm; in winter 9am-12:30pm and 2-5pm. Donations requested.)*

CHIESA DI SANTA MARIA IN ARACOELI. The seventh-century Church of Santa Maria in Aracoeli lies on the site of the Temple to Juno Moneta. "Aracoeli" comes from a medieval legend, says that which the Emperor Augustus had a vision of the Virgin Mary, causing him to raise an altar to Heaven *(Ara Coeli)* on the spot she indicated; this explains the rather unusual fresco of Augustus and the Tiburtine Sibyl in the company of saints and angels. The stunning **Bufalini Chapel** (on the right as you face the altar) is home to Pinturicchio's Renaissance frescoes of St. Bernardino of Siena. The third chapel on the left houses a beautiful fresco of St. Antonio of Padova, the only one left of a late 15th-century series by Benozzo Gozzoli. **Cappella del San Bambino** to the left of the altar is home to the *Santo Bambino*, a cherubic statue that receives letters from sick children. *(Climb 124 pilgrims' steps up from the left side of La Cordonata, or the shorter stairs from Palazzo Nuovo. Santa Maria open daily in summer 9am-12:30pm and 3-6:30pm, in winter 9:30am-12:30pm and 2:30-5:30pm. Donations requested.)*

THE VELABRUM

The best way to access its sights is to walk down V. Teatro di Marcello, to the right of the Vittorio Emanuele II monument, from P. Venezia.

The Velabrum is a low plain west of the Forum and south of the Jewish Ghetto in the shadow of the Capitoline and Palatine hills. This Tiber floodplain was a sacred area for the Romans, and for that reason there are a number of ancient ruins there. Mighty Hercules kept his cattle here; according to legend, it was here where Aeneas first set foot on what was to become Rome, and here where baby Romulus and Remus were discovered by the she-wolf that nursed them. During the days of the Republic, the area's proximity to a port on the Tiber made it an ideal spot for the city's cattle and vegetable markets. Civic-minded merchants spotted the riverbanks with temples, arches, and a grandiose theater—all dedicated to the gods of trade and commerce. Even after the empire's fall, the area remained a busy market center.

THEATER OF MARCELLUS. The Teatro di Marcello is the round building reminiscent of the Colosseum two blocks down from the Piazza Venezia on the right side of V. Teatro di Marcello. You cannot enter the theater, but excellent views are available from the outside. Caesar began construction on the theater and after his sudden demise, Augustus finished the job in 13 BC. It bears the name of Augustus's nephew, a potential successor of whom he was particularly fond, and the cause of whose early and sudden death remains a mystery. Some speculate family drama as the culprit: he may have been poisoned by Augustus's wife, Livia, who intended her own son from a previous marriage, Tiberius, to be the next emperor. Architecturally speaking, the arches and pilasters on the exterior of the theater served as a model for the Colosseum. It represents the classic arrangement of orders, which grow more complex from the ground up: stocky Doric pilasters support the bottom floor, Ionic capitals hold up the middle, and elaborate Corinthian columns once crowned the top tier. Vitruvius and other ancient architects considered this arrangement the most perfect exterior decoration, inspiring Michelangelo, Bramante, and other Renaissance architects to copy the pattern. A succession of medieval families used its seats and stage as the foundation for fortified castles, so the exterior is all that remains. The park around the theater is open for classical concerts on summer nights.

PORTICO D'OTTAVIA. At the bend of V. dei Portico d'Ottavia in the Jewish Ghetto, a shattered pediment and five marble columns in the shadow of the Theater of Marcellus are all that remain of the once magnificent Portico d'Ottavia, one of Augustus's grandest contributions to Rome's architecture. Built by Quintus Metellus in 149 BC, it was revamped and imperially restyled by Augustus, who dedicated it to his sister Octavia in 23 BC. The portico was a rectangular enclosure sheltering temples to Jupiter and Juno, some libraries, and public rooms adjunct to the Theater of Marcellus. The Romans stuck many of their imported Greek masterpieces here, including the famous Medici *Venus* now residing in Florence's Uffizi. She was rediscovered under the crumbling detritus and refuse that had accumulated on the site thanks to the ravages of a nearby fish market.

TEMPLE OF APOLLO SOSIANUS. Through the fence to the right of the portico are the polished white columns of the Temple of Apollo Sosianus. While the temple dates as far back as 433 BC, it was rebuilt by Gaius Sosius, who attached his own name to it. The three Corinthian columns support a well-preserved frieze of bulls' skulls and floral garlands. The temple's ornate original fifth-century Greek pediment is visible in the Museo Centrale Termoelettrica Montemartini (p. 210).

SAN NICOLA IN CARCERE. This dark, solemn 12th-century church rests on the foundations of three Republican temples, which were built and dedicated to the gods Juno, Janus, and Spes (Hope) during the hairy times of the First Punic War. The ancient buildings were converted into a prison during the Middle Ages—hence the name *carcere*, meaning "prison." The only captives in the deserted interior today are well-labeled paintings and restored engravings, including part of the church's original dedication from May 12, 1128. On the right side of the church lies the best-preserved temple, its Ionic columns scattered in the grass and embedded in the church's wall. The left wall preserves the Doric columns of another temple. The third temple is buried beneath the church and its remains can be accessed through a staircase near the narthex. Ask about accessing the buried temple in the office to your left as you enter the church. *(Adjacent to Teatro di Marcello at V. dei Teatro di Marcello and V. dei Foro Olitorio. ☎ 39 32 89 02 69 24; www.romeunderground.com. Open Sept.-July M-Sa 4-7pm.)*

BOCCA DELLA VERITÀ. The Church of Santa Maria in Cosmedin, originally constructed in the sixth century to serve the local Greek colony, is not the reason that most tourists make the trek from the Theater of Marcellus. In the eternal quest to get up close and personal with the parts of the Roman landscape that have been featured in Hollywood movies, most people visit for the famous Bocca della Verità in the portico. Originally a drain cover carved as a river god's face, the circular relief was credited with supernatural powers in the Middle Ages, when it was claimed that the hoary face liked to chomp off the fingers of anyone who dared the gods by speaking an untruth while his hand was in its mouth. To keep the superstition alive, the caretaker-priest used to stick a scorpion in the back of the mouth to sting the fingers of suspected fibbers. The Bocca made a cameo in *Roman Holiday*; during the filming, Gregory Peck stuck his hand in the mouth and jokingly hid his hand in his sleeve when he yanked it out, causing Audrey Hepburn to yelp in shock. The scene wasn't scripted, but it worked so well that it was kept in the movie. Inside, perhaps St. Valentine's skull and bones will ignite your romantic side; nothing says *amore* like centuries-old human remains. *(2 blocks south of the Theater of Marcellus along V. Luigi Petroselli. ☎ 06 67 81 419. Portico and church open daily 9:30am-5:50pm. Byzantine mass Su 10:30am.)*

FORO BOARIO. P. della Bocca della Verità is also the home of the ancient Foro Boario (cattle market). Its two ancient temples are among the best-preserved in Rome. The rectangular **Temple of Portunus,** once known as the Temple of Fortuna Virilis, reveals both Greek and Etruscan influence. The present construction dates from the late second century BC, although there was likely a temple on the site for years. The circular temple next door, thought to be the **Temple of Hercules Victor,** was believed to be dedicated to Vesta because of its similarities to the Temple of Vesta in the Forum (p. 143).

CHIESA DI SAN GIORGIO IN VELABRO. Behind the hefty **Arch of Janus** (built in the fourth century AD as a covered market for cattle traders) once stood the little Church of San Giorgio in Velabro. A marvelous edifice, it boasted a ninth-century porch and pillars, a simple early Romanesque interior, and a brick and stone arch *campanile* (bell tower). The oldest written records suggest that the main portion of the church's modern day structure was constructed in the late seventh century under the auspices of Pope Leo II (682-3). The bell tower was first added in the 12th century and then rebuilt in 1837 after the original was struck by lightning. A terrorist car bombing in 1993 reduced the church's famed portico to a single arch and part of a stone beam. It has since been entirely rebuilt. Inside, the apse bay contains a fresco of Christ blessing the world. To the left of the church, the **Arch of the Argentarii** was erected in the AD third century by the *argentarii* (money changers) and cattle merchants who used the *piazza* as a market in honor of Emperor Septimus Severus. It is decorated with detailed reliefs illustrating the legends of treasures hidden in the Velabrum's underground chambers and tunnels. *(1 block from Foro Boario on V. dei Velabro in the direction of the Capitoline Hill. ☎ 06 697 97 536; sangiorgioinvelabro.org. Open daily 10am-12:30pm and 4-6:30pm.)*

CHURCH OF CONSOLATION. Here in P. della Consolazione, prisoners in ancient times were given a prayer, a pat on the back, and a "good luck out there," before they were summarily executed. The church itself was once home to an order of monks (equipped humanely with smelling salts and liquor flasks) who were dedicated to giving succor to the condemned and accompanying them on their last mortal journey.

OTHER SIGHTS

CIRCUS MAXIMUS. Cradled in the valley between the Palatine and Aventine hills, the Circus Maximus is today only a grassy shadow of its former glory as Rome's largest stadium. This rather plain hollow of a park was the sight of all the uproar depicted by Charlton Heston in *Ben Hur*. After its construction around 600 BC, more than 300,000 Romans gathered here to watch the careening of chariots around the quarter-mile track. Obelisks in the arena's center served as distance markers, and the turning points of the track were perilously sharp to ensure enough thrills 'n' spills to keep the crowds happy. The excitement of the chariot races was interspersed with a variety of other competitions ranging from bareback horse-racing to more esoteric events like tent-pegging. Emperor Augustus watched from special terraces built onto the Palatine palaces. Today the ruins are all but gone, and the Circus is mainly a park and concert venue. Crowds still fill it today for summer concerts and triumphant celebrations, such as the one after Italy's 2006 World Cup victory. *(Ⓜ B-Circo Massimo, bus #118, or walk down V. di San Gregorio from the Colosseum. ☎ 06 39 96 77 00. Open 24hr.)*

BATHS OF CARACALLA. The Baths of Caracalla were constructed in AD 212 and fully operational until the sixth century, when the invading Goths severed the supply of water from the aqueducts. The largest baths in Rome at the time they were built, they are also the best preserved. The baths were erected under the watchful guidance of Caracalla, the same emperor who killed his brother Geta, stole the throne from his father Severus, and then scratched his brother's image off the arch of Janus and the arch of Septimus Severus.

Though Caracalla's conduct toward his immediate family was perhaps less than benevolent, he nevertheless did the entire Roman population a grand favor by building this monumental complex. The monstrous baths were capable of handling approximately 2000 Romans at any given time; men bathed in the mornings, women in the afternoons, and slaves in the evenings. The colorful mosaic floors are extremely intricate in design and remarkably well-preserved, especially in the *apodyteria* (dressing rooms). The original tiling alone warrants a trip to the gigantic *thermae*, but it is the size of the proto-health club that continues to amaze the plebes. The complex had a central hall opening onto a round, warm swimming pool on one side and a cold pool on the other. Romans would follow a particular regimen for cleaning, beginning with the warm bath, followed by a procession from hot *(caldarium)* to colder rooms (the lukewarm *tepidarium* and the cold *frigidarium*), finishing with a dip in the *natatio*, which was a cold, open-air pool.

Remains of a rectangular brick wall mark the boundary of the ancient gym where Romans played sports, sipped juices, and had their body hair plucked by special servants. Rome's opera company used to stage Verdi's *Aïda* here, complete with horses and elephants, until it was discovered that, due to either the weight of the animals or the sopranos' voices, the performances caused structural damage. There are still opera performances in the gardens on summer nights from the first week of June until the last week of August. *(From the eastern end of Circus Maximus, walk up the pleasant, tree-lined V. dei Terme di Caracalla. Open Apr.-Oct. M 9am-1pm, Tu-Su 9am-7:15pm; Nov.-Mar. M 9am-2pm, Tu-Su 9am-3:30pm. Last entry 1hr. before closing. €6, EU residents ages 18-24 €3, EU residents over 65 and under 18 free. Tickets valid for one entry into the Baths, the Tomba di Cecilia Metella, and the Villa dei Quintili over a 7-day period. Audio tour €4, available in Chinese, English, French, German, Italian, Japanese, Russian, and Spanish.)*

 WHEN NATURE CALLS. It's difficult to find public restrooms without having to spend a little money. Duck into a department store, such as La Rinascente or COIN, or a large bookstore, such as Feltrinelli, to use a free restroom.

CENTRO STORICO

VIA DEL CORSO AND PIAZZA VENEZIA

Once Rome's premier race course, V. del Corso now hosts many parades, including **Carnevale** (see **Holidays and Festivals**, p. 76). Running between P. del Popolo and P. Venezia, it boasts a range of restaurants, hotels, gelaterias, and affordable boutiques (see **Shopping**, p. 213).

VITTORIO EMANUELE II MONUMENT. Running south from P. del Popolo, V. del Corso ends at P. Venezia, home to this massive white marble monument, lovingly referred to as "the wedding cake" or "Mussolini's typewriter." Such monikers are apt, given that the building stands next to the Capitoline Hill like a word processor covered with a doily. The monument was designed in 1884 to commemorate Italian unification, but it took ages to construct. It was inaugurated in 1911, dedicated in 1921, and finished by Mussolini only in 1927—52 years after Rome became the capital of the Italian state. At the top of the outside staircase is the **Altare della Patria,** which has two eternal flames guarded night and day by the Italian Navy in remembrance of the Unknown Soldier. Walk upstairs to the **Museo Centrale del Risorgimento** for a comprehensive exhibit on Italian unification. *(Open daily 9:30am-6:30pm. Free.)*

PALAZZO VENEZIA. Once used by Mussolini as both an office and a soapbox, this *palazzo* is one of Rome's earliest Renaissance structures. Today it's home to a library and the **Museo Nazionale de Palazzo di Venezia.** A recent exhibition was dedicated to the work of Leonardo da Vinci. *(V. del Plebiscito 118. Open Tu-Su 9am-7pm. Ticket office open Tu-Su 9am-6pm. Special exhibition €9; under 18, over 65, students with ID, groups of over 15 people €7; children under 6 free.)*

SIGHTS

PALAZZO DORIA PAMPHILIJ. This Baroque edifice was once home to one of Rome's most preeminent families. The building was constructed between 1659 and 1675 by Antonio del Grande for the former cardinal Camillo Pamphilij (nephew of Pope Innocent X) and his wife Olimpia Aldobrandini. (Hey, at least *he* gave up his Church position before he married her.) In addition to the Palazzo's art museum, which contains some great Renaissance works, visitors must see the **Gallery of Mirrors,** featuring Murano crystal lamps and modeled on its cousin at Versailles. Although the exterior of the building is a bit grimy from air pollution, its ornate facade is still spectacular. The Palazzo also boasts a beautiful courtyard garden. *(V. del Corso 304. From P. Venezia, walk up the Corso. Open daily 10am-5pm. Box office open daily 10am-4pm. €9; over 65, university students under 30 with ID, and groups of 10 or more €6. Audio guide included except for large groups.)*

PIAZZA COLONNA. It's hard to miss: an ornately carved column in the center of the square towers over all of the visitors craning their necks. This is the **Column of Marcus Aurelius;** Pope Sixtus V dedicated it to the Apostle Paul and had it capped with a statue of the saint looking down on the *piazza.* (The popes had a thing for rededicating pagan structures.) Elsewhere on the square, you'll spot **Palazzo Wedekind,** home to the newspaper *Il Tempo.* It was built in 1838 with columns from the Etruscan city of Veio. *(Keep walking up the Corso and you'll eventually see the square on your right.)*

CHIESA DEL GESU. The impressive and sumptuous Il Gesù is the principal Jesuit church in Rome and one of the richest in the city. Its construction was decreed in 1540 by St. Ignatius Loyola, founder of the Jesuit order. Jacopo Barozzi began constructing Il Gesù in 1568; it was completed in 1577 by Giacomo della Porta, who drew from some of Michelangelo's designs for St. Peter's, including his paired pilasters. Architecturally, Il Gesù became the standard for Counter-Reformation churches. It was designed with a wide single nave in a Latin rather than a Greek cross, so that worshippers attending the church would focus their attention on the altar. The interior is lavishly ornate; the Jesuits' motto is *"Ad maiorem dei gloriam"* ("to the greater glory of God") and impressively rich churches were believed to glorify God and inspire faith and respect. On the ceiling of the nave, Il Baciccia's celebrated fresco, *Triumph of the Name of Jesus*, uses innovative perspective, painted panels, and stucco figures to draw the painting into the same space as the viewers. Baciccia also decorated the brilliant dome. Look left of the dome for the enormous **Cappella di Sant'Ignazio di Loyola,** dedicated to the founder of the order lying under the altar of bronze, marble, and lapis lazuli. Across the apse is another altar, this one displaying the hand of St. Francis Xavier, Ignatius' friend and another famous Jesuit who led missions to India and Japan. *(With your back to the Vittorio Emanuele II monument, turn left on V. C. Battisti, which becomes V. del Plebiscito and intersects P. del Gesù.)*

BASILICA DE SANT'IGNAZIO DE LOYOLA. A few blocks north of the Gesù, this Jesuit church was modeled after it on roughly the same scale. The ceiling is decorated with Andrea Pozzo's incredible *trompe l'oeil* fresco, *The Triumph of St. Ignatius.* Pozzo designed the ceiling so that its figures appear to exist in the same space as the church's architecture and used foreshortening to make it appear as though several more stories continued above before breaking into heaven. The fascinating fresco represents the spread of Christianity to Europe, America, Asia, and Africa. In this context, it includes some depictions of black figures ascending to heaven, an artistic move that would have been quite unusual during the Renaissance. Be sure to see Legros's reliefs at the altar to St. Louis Gonzaga, a Roman noble who gave up his wealth to join the Jesuits (the chapel to your right at the crossing). More eye-popping fake perspective is to be found in the ceiling above the altar, painted to look like a dome after a group of neighboring nuns stopped the construction of the real one, fearing that it would cut off the light to their garden. *(V. de San Ignazio. Open daily 7:30am-12:30pm and 3-7:15pm. Free.)*

CHIESA DEI SS APOSTOLI. The large basilica does feature some impressive paintings, but the real draw here is the indoor *piazza* and two lovely open-air courtyards. You'll have the area almost to yourself—it's perfect for a quiet afternoon stroll. The corridors sometimes play host to small art exhibitions and other events. Also on display is a large marble relief commemorating Michelangelo. The Basilica hosted the artist's corpse in February of 1564 while it was in transit to Santa Croce in Firenze. *(55/57 P. dei SS Apostoli. Open daily 7am-noon and 4-7pm. Free.)*

PANTHEON AND ENVIRONS

PANTHEON. The granite columns, bronze doors, and soaring dome of the Pantheon's still, cool interior have changed little over the two millennia that the building has existed. Architects still puzzle over the engineering; its dome, a perfect half-sphere constructed from poured concrete without the support of vaults, arches, or ribs, is the largest of its kind. It was built under Hadrian from AD 118 to 125 over the site of an earlier Pantheon destroyed in AD 80. In AD 608 the Pantheon was consecrated as the **Chiesa di Santa Maria ad Martyres.** Several noteworthy figures are buried within: Renaissance painter Raphael; King Vittorio Emanuele II, the first king of united Italy; his son, Umberto I, second king of Italy; and finally, Umberto's wife, Queen Margherita, after whom the *pizza margherita* was named in the 19th century. *(Open M-Sa 8:30am-7:30pm, Su 9am-6pm, holidays 9am-1pm. Closed Jan. 1, May 1, Dec. 25. Free. 20min. audio tour €3.)*

PIAZZA DELLA ROTONDA. In front of the Pantheon, an **Egyptian obelisk** dominates the ever-crowded P. della Rotonda. Like the column in **Piazza Colonna** this once pagan monument was altered when Clement XI stuck a cross on top. Around the Pantheon's left side and down the street, another similarly modified obelisk, supported by Bernini's curious **elephant statue,** marks the center of tiny P. Minerva. The monument was established in 1667 in honor of Pope Alexander VI. The gist of the inscription is that it takes a strong mind (the elephant) to support wisdom (the obelisk). Behind the obelisk is Rome's only Gothic church.

CHIESA DI SANTA MARIA SOPRA MINERVA. Built on the site of an ancient Roman temple, this hidden gem shelters Renaissance masterpieces like Michelangelo's *Christ Bearing the Cross*, Antoniazzo Romano's *Annunciation*, and a statue of St. Sebastian recently attributed to Michelangelo. Check out the ceiling frescoes that, unusually, depict the night sky rather than the day. The **Cappella Carafa** in the southern transept boasts a brilliant series of Fra Filippo Lippi's frescoes on the life of St. Thomas Aquinas. A decapitated St. Catherine of Siena is reportedly buried under the altar; her head rests in Siena's duomo. St. Victoria's skull is on view, propped up creepily in its glass case on a little dummy in repose. *(Open daily 7am-1pm and 3-7pm.)*

CHIESA DI SAN LUIGI DEI FRANCESI. France's national church in Rome is home to three of Caravaggio's most famous paintings: *The Calling of St. Matthew, St. Matthew and the Angel,* and *The Crucifixion.* Between 1597 and 1602, the flamboyant artist decorated the last chapel on the north side, dedicated to the evangelist St. Matthew. All of the paintings showcase Caravaggio's dramatic use of light to highlight the theological and emotional import of his subject. The attention he paid to natural grimy details was so intense that the picture of *St. Matthew and the Angel* was toned down because the patrons of the chapel found the first one inappropriate. Warning: spotlights for the paintings are coin-operated, so someone will have to pony up—wait it out and it won't be you. *(P. San Luigi dei Francesi 5. 1 block down V. di Salvatore from C. del Rinascimento, opposite P. Navona. Open daily 10am-12:30pm and 4-7pm.)*

WATER, WATER, EVERYWHERE Remember that Rome's water is *potabile* (drinkable), and many fountains or spigots run throughout the city. Take a drink, or fill up your water bottle from these free sources of cold, refreshing *acqua naturale*.

PIAZZA NAVONA AND ENVIRONS

⬛CHIESA DI SANT'IVO. On nearby C. del Rinascimento, Chiesa di Sant'Ivo's corkscrew cupola hover over the Palazzo della Sapienza, originally home to the University of Rome before it was enlarged under Mussolini. *(Open M-Sa 9am-6pm. Service Su 9am-noon.)*

PIAZZA NAVONA. Originally a stadium built by Domitian in AD 86, P. Navona is now filled with puppeteers, mimes, and artists selling caricatures and paintings of Tuscany. Bernini's **Fontana dei Quattro Fiumi** (Fountain of the Four Rivers) commands the *piazza*. Each river god represents a continent: the Ganges for Asia, the Danube for Europe, the Nile for Africa, and Rio de la Plata for the Americas. Once again, the fountain is topped by an Egyptian obelisk, this one bearing the mark of Pope Innocent X. Giacomo della Porta's 16th-century **Fontana del Moro** and the **Fontana di Nettuno** stand at opposite ends of the *piazza*.

CHIESA DI SANT'AGNESE IN AGONE. This cavernous church holds the tiny skull of its namesake saint. Legend has it that Agnes was condemned to death for refusing to marry the son of a Roman prefect. To circumvent the law against executing virgins, she was dragged naked to a brothel, but her hair miraculously grew to cover her body. Then, when they tried to burn her alive, she would not light, so one indefatigable Roman soldier swiftly chopped off her head. Find this relic in a simple little chapel to the back-left side of the church. Also be sure to take a look at the sculptures that hang in each nave in place of the typical frescoes—the figures seem to emerge from the walls. *(West side of P. Navona, opposite Fontana dei Quattro Fiumi. Open daily 9:30am-12:30pm and 4-7pm.)*

CHIESA DI SANTA MARIA DELLA PACE. This church houses Raphael's *Sibyls* in its **Chigi Chapel** and **cloisters** by Bramante. Originally built in 1482, its facade got a facelift from the imaginative Baroque architect da Cortona in 1656, giving it a charming semi-circular porch and making it so popular among Rome's upper crust that the *piazza* was jammed with the carriages of devout patricians. It was only in the 19th century that the *piazza* was expanded, a development so impressive that a Latin inscription was put up declaring that no stone in the *piazza* could ever be moved. *(Open M, W, and Sa 9am-noon. Closed on religious holidays.)*

CHIESA NUOVA. Originally founded in the 12th century as Santa Maria in Vallicella, Chiesa Nuova became the home base for Philip Neri's congregation of Counter-Reformation Oratorians. Neri rebuilt Santa Maria in Vallicella in 1575 and renamed it the "New Church." This compassionate man was one of the great church reformers in the Counter Reformation, a champion of equality who organized pious associations that united believers across social lines. He often tested the piety of his aristocratic followers by tasking them with ridicu-

ON THE MENU

WHEN IN ROME... EAT KOSHER?

Pizza, prosciutto, pasta... matzah? You might be surprised to discover that traditional Roman cuisine has a healthy kick of kosher.

Jews have lived in and around Rome for almost 2000 years, making Rome the site of the longest-standing community of Jews in the Western World. But in 1555, the anti-Semitic Pope Paul IV confined all Roman Jews within the four walls of a ghetto in the midst of the Jewish quarter. For the next 300 years, Jews were cut off from outside Italian influences—and ingredients.

Yet Italians they remained, and maintaining a thriving culinary culture was a top priority. With little access to ingredients outside of the ghetto, Roman Jews made do with what they had, with mouthwatering results.

Enter the friggitori, street vendors who fried up anything and everything they could. Suppli, deep-fried battered mozzarella balls encased in risotto, is a quick bite you can still savor along the streets of the Roman Jewish quarter today.

To end your fried feast on a sweet note, grab a plate of pizzarelle con miele, a fried piece of matzah covered in pine nuts, raisins, and warm honey. Mazel tov! To fried food!

lous labors of faith: some were made to wear foxtails through the streets; others did construction work on the church.

As Chiesa Nuova was rising, the future St. Philip had a vision of the Virgin rescuing parishioners by supporting a collapsing section of the old church; inspection of the beams proved that they were indeed about to fall. Pietro da Cortona represented this mini-miracle in a 1644 **fresco** on the church's ceiling. He also painted the decorations of the dome and the apse over the altar. The **altar** itself is decorated with three excellent early paintings by Peter Paul Rubens. The **chapel** on the left holds the remains of St. Philip Neri and a mosaic version of Guido Reni's painting of the saint. Head through the door to the left of the altar to enter the **sacristy**. It was designed by Borromini and contains a statue by Algardi of (you guessed it) Philip Neri. Ask if the rooms of the saint are open—there you'll find more paintings by Reni, Cortona, and Guercino. (*In P. Chiesa Nuova on C. Vittorio Emanuele II, to the west of Chiesa Santa Andrea della Valle. Open M-F 7:30am-noon and 4:30-7:30pm, Sa-Su 8am-1pm and 4:30pm-8pm.*)

CHIESA SANT'ANDREA DELLA VALLE. Begun in 1591 by Grimaldi and completed by Baroque bigwig Carlo Maderno, this church sports a 1665 facade by Rainaldi, who junked the frou-frou favored by his contemporaries and displayed rows of columns and pediments in place of swirls and curls. The rather more conventional interior, where Puccini's opera *Tosca* begins, is modeled on Il Gesù (p. 155) and dominated by an array of excellent Baroque paintings. Lanfranco frescoed the dome with its depiction of layers of angels, while Domenichino painted the pendentives and the scenes of the life of the saint in the curved area above the altar (check out the beautiful landscapes). The most striking paintings are Mattia Preti's scenes of the martyrdom of St. Andrew behind the altar. (*1 block west of Largo Argentina, on C. Vittorio Emanuele II. Open M-Sa 7am-12:30pm and 4-7:45pm.*)

PALAZZO SPADA. Built in 1544 for Cardinal Girolamo Capodiferro, this Baroque palace houses the picture collection of the **Galleria Spada** (p. 196). The *palazzo* is a treasure in itself, recently restored to its original beige whiteness. Outside, eight ancient Roman kings, generals, and emperors stand proudly under Latin inscriptions describing their achievements. Inside, 18 even less modest Roman gods stand, buck naked, around the court—even the prudish Vesta. Cardinal Bernardino Spada, who acquired the palace in the 17th century, commissioned the elaborate decorations to compensate for the relatively puny size of his palace. To make the *palazzo* seem even bigger, he went beyond naked gods and had Borromini design a trompe-l'œil colonnade beyond the library on the right side of the courtyard. The colonnade seems to stretch back through a spacious garden, framing a life-size classical statue. In reality, Borromini manipulated perspective by shrinking the columns and pavement dramatically. The colonnade is only a few meters long, the statue stands a meter tall, and the garden is no more than a narrow alley. *(P. de Capo 13. Open Tu-F 9am-7pm, Sa-Su 9am-1pm.)*

VIA GIULIA. As part of his campaign in the early 1500s to clean up Rome after the Babylonian captivity (when the popes moved to Avignon and the city fell into serious disrepair), Pope Julius II commissioned Bramante to construct a straight road leading to the Vatican. **Via Giulia** (ah, modesty) runs parallel to the Tiber northwest from Ponte Sisto to P. d'Oro. This relatively wide road was a contrast to the narrow and winding medieval streets of the day. Throughout the 16th century, the charming road was home of a fashionable neighborhood, and later architects built its expensive residences in accordance with Bramante's restrained, classical vision. In the 17th century, Pope Innocent X built a prison here to slum down the area and make his own P. Navona more important. It didn't work: the tiny neighborhood still attracted other popes, nobles, and artists—including Raphael, who lived at #85. Perhaps the most striking of the area's sights is the ivy-draped **bridge** that spans V. Giulia from the back of the Palazzo Farnese to the Tiber embankment. Michelangelo designed the bridge, which was originally intended to be the first leg of a much longer one that would cross the Tiber. Alessandro Farnese wanted to connect his *palazzo* with the Villa Farnesina on the other side by a private walkway, but funds dried up before its completion. Off the southeast corner of Farnese's *palazzo* is the **Fontana del Mascherone**.

LARGO DI TORRE ARGENTINA. This busy square is named for the **Torre Argentina** that dominates its southeast corner. The sunken area in the center of the *Largo* (square) is a complex of four Republican temples unearthed in 1926 during Mussolini's project to demolish the medieval city. The site is now a cat shelter, and dozens of felines patrol its grounds, providing photo opportunities for cat calendar photographers everywhere. The shelter welcomes donations and volunteers to help take care of the cats. The *piazza* also serves as a handy point of orientation, as it lies along C. V. Emanuele between the P. Navona area and the area surrounding C. dei Fiori and the Jewish Ghetto. *(At the intersection of C. V. Emanuele II and V. di Torre Argentina. Shelter ☎06 45 42 52 40; www.romancats.com. For more info on the shelter, see Beyond Tourism, p. 79)*

JEWISH GHETTO

Bus #64. The Jewish Ghetto is across V. Arenula from Campo dei Fiori. Alternatively, walk down V. Arenula from C. V. Emanuele and make a left at the river; the Ghetto will be on your left. The neighborhood's main attractions and eateries are located on and around V. del Portico d'Ottavia.

Rome's Jewish community is the oldest in Western Europe—Israelites came in 161 BC as ambassadors of Judas Maccabee, asking for Imperial help against invaders. After nearly 1500 years of relatively peaceful cohabitation, Pope Paul IV decided that the Jews of Rome should be confined to their own neighborhood and so he erected the walled ghetto in a neighborhood prone to flooding. He restricted its inhabitants to careers in money-lending and used-clothes peddling, and required them to swear oaths of submission to the pope in annual ceremonies by the Arch of Titus, a monument celebrating the Roman conquest of Jerusalem. The ghetto was torn down after Italy's unification, and more than 2000 of Rome's Jews were deported to concentration camps during the Nazi occupation. Today, the Ghetto is still the center of Rome's Jewish population of 15,000.

PIAZZA MATTEI. This square, home of Taddeo Landini's 16th-century **Fontana delle Tartarughe,** marks the Ghetto's center. Nearby in the Portico d'Ottavia, the eighth-century **Chiesa di Sant'Angelo in Pescheria** is named for the fish market that once flourished there. Jews were once forced to attend mass here, an act of evangelism that they quietly resisted by stuffing their ears with wax. *(V. dei Funari. Heading toward the Theater of Marcellus on V. del Teatro Marcello, go right on V. Montavara, which becomes V. dei Funari after P. Campitelli. The church is under restoration indefinitely.)*

SINAGOGA ASHKENAZITA. Built between 1901 and 1904, this temple symbolizes the unity of the Jewish people in Rome and proclaims its unique role in a city of Catholic iconography. Ashkenazita incorporates Persian and Babylonian techniques, attempting to differentiate its architectural style from that of Christian churches. A gray metal dome tops the edifice. Take note of the stained glass high up on the right hand side of the synagogue, commemorating a terrorist bombing in 1982, which killed a small child. The broken glass was replaced by clear glass in honor of the victim. In response to the attacks, guards now search all visitors, and *carabinieri* (Italian police officers) patrol the vicinity. In 1986, Pope John Paul II made the first-ever papal visit to a Jewish synagogue here and declared that Jews are the oldest brothers of Christians. The synagogue houses the **Jewish Museum,** a collection of ancient Torahs and Holocaust artifacts that document the community's history. Orthodox services, open to all, are segregated by gender and conducted entirely in Hebrew. *(☎06 68 40 06 61. At the corner of Lungotevere dei Cenci and V. Catalana. Open for services only. Museum open June-Sept. M-Th and Su 10am-7pm, F 9am-4pm; Oct.-May M-Th and Su 10am-10pm, F 10am-4pm. Last entry 45min. before closing. Closed Jewish holidays from 1pm the day before and Catholic holidays, after 1pm. €7.50, groups €6.50, students €3, under 10 free. Reservations required. Cash only.)*

PIAZZA DI SPAGNA

⬛FONTANA DI TREVI. Nicolo Salvi's Fontana di Trevi has for centuries been a mecca for romantic pilgrims to the Eternal City. There's good reason: this towering masterpiece is one of Rome's finest works of art, architecture, and design—all wrapped up in an alabaster marble package. The Fontana's name refers to its location at the intersection of three streets *(tre vie)*, perpetually crowded with visitors wanting to catch a glimpse of the fountain and tenacious vendors taking advantage of them. Neptune, in the center, stands in front of the goddesses of abundance and good health, while the two horsemen in the water represent the mercurial sea, covered by both rough waves and placid ripples. Pope Clement XII commissioned Salvi to design the work in the heat of a Baroque-era building craze. Although you should hold back to avoid a steep fine, actress Anita Ekberg couldn't resist taking a dip in the fountain's cool waters in Fellini's famous scene of *La Dolce Vita.* Legend has it that a traveler who throws a coin into the fountain is ensured a speedy return to Rome, and one who tosses two will fall in love there. Three coins ensure that wedding bells soon will ring. For a less crowded view, head to the fountain in the late evening. The water flows all night, even after most tourists have gone to bed. On a less poetic note, the crypt of the **Chiesa dei Santi Vincenzo e Anastasio,** opposite the fountain, preserves the hearts and lungs of popes from 1590 to 1903.

Fortunately or unfortunately—depending on your preference—the crypt is not open for public viewing.

SPANISH STEPS. Designed by an Italian, paid for by the French, named for the Spaniards, occupied by the British, and lately colonized by a brigade of tourists so diverse it could form its own United Nations, the **Scalinata di Spagna** is, to say the least, multicultural. Piazza di Spagna is also home to designer boutiques like Gucci, Prada, and Valentino, and thousands of visitors and Romans alike flock here daily to shop, people-watch, and socialize. The Scalinata dates back to 1723, when work began on the contest-winning design of the now-forgotten Roman architect Francesco de Sanctis. The Vatican had pushed for the Steps as a way to connect the new church, **Trinità dei Monti,** to the piazza below. Both France and the Holy See had a hand in financing and directing the project; however, tensions mounted between the two powers when it emerged that the plans included a massive equestrian statue of Louis XIV. The fountain that lies in front of the steps is known as the **Fontana della Barcaccia.** It was built in 1626, long before the Steps were even considered, by the sculptor Bernini the Elder. The steps were later beloved by British writers, particularly by the Romantics. John Keats died in 1821 in the pink-orange house by the Steps; it's now the charming **Keats-Shelley Memorial Museum,** displaying several documents of the Romantic poet and his contemporaries, including Lord Byron, Percy Bysshe Shelley, and Mary Shelley. (☎06 67 84 235; www.keats-shelley-house.org. Open M-F 9am-1pm and 3-6pm, Sa 11am-2pm and 3-6pm. €3.50.)

TRINITA DEI MONTI. After committing two of the seven deadly sins (greed and gluttony) at your choice of establishments on V. Condotti, ascend the stairs of heaven to the Church of Santa Trinità dei Monti. (Confessionals on the right.) The Neoclassical church was designed by Carlo Maderno and provides a worthy incentive to climb the Spanish Steps—plus you'll get a sweeping view of the city. Known as the Church of the Kings of France, Santa Trinità was built in 1502 under the auspices of French King Charles VIII. Shortly thereafter the church was unceremoniously pillaged during the infamous 1527 sack of the city by Spanish King Charles V. Work was completed on the new building in 1570, and it was consecrated in 1595. This time, the church lasted over 200 years until it was sacked anew in 1798 by the armies of Revolutionary France. After the fall of Napoleon, however, the church was restored; today, the only original part is the transept, above the largest altar.

The third chapel on the right and the second chapel on the left contain works by Michelangelo's star pupil, Daniele da Volterra. Poussin once rated the painter's *Deposition from the Cross* as one of the three greatest paintings ever. Restored twice and having twice and traveled to the Medici Villa and back, it's a bit worse for the wear. The fourth chapel on the left in the north transept was frescoed in the 16th century by the Zuccari brothers. The obelisk in the center of the church's *piazza* was brought to Rome in the second century; its hieroglyphics were plagiarized from the obelisk in P. del Popolo. (At the top of the Spanish Steps.)

PIAZZA DEL POPOLO. Once a favorite venue for the execution of heretics, this is now the "people's square." In the center is the 3200-year-old **Obelisk of Pharaoh Ramses II,** which Augustus brought from Egypt in 10 AD. Climb the hill on the east side of the *piazza* for a spectacular view. **Santa Maria del Popolo** holds Renaissance and Baroque masterpieces. Two exquisite Caravaggios— *The Conversion of St. Paul* and *Crucifixion of St. Peter*—are in the **Cappella Cerasi,** next to the altar. Raphael's **Cappella Chigi** was designed for the Sienese banker Agostino Chigi, reputedly the richest man of his time. Niches on either side of the altar feature sculptures by Bernini and Lorenzetto. With so much artwork, an exquisite portrait of the late Pope John Paul II appears orphaned, leaning against a chapel wall. At the southern end of the *piazza* are Carlo Rinaldi's 17th-century twin churches, **Santa Maria di Montesano** and **Santa Maria dei Miracoli.** (☎ *06 36 10 836. Open M-Sa 7am-noon and 4-7pm, Su and holidays 8am-1:30pm and 4:30-7:30pm.)*

MAUSOLEUM OF AUGUSTUS/ARA PACIS. These twin sights present a bizarre view to first-time visitors. As you walk down V. de Ripetta from P. del Popolo, you'll see a massive, decrepit brick structure rising out of the ground on your left and a sleek, white, modern building hovering on the right. It wasn't always this way—the Ara Pacis used to be displayed in a simple glass case in the same spot. The architect Richard Meier's new home for the monument is hulking and white and cube-ish; Romans either love it or despise it.

The circular brick mound of the Mausoleum of Augustus once housed the funerary urns of the Imperial family. The oversized tomb (about 87m in diameter) may have been inspired by Alexander the Great's mausoleum, which Augustus visited while in Egypt. Cyprus trees once lined the tomb's circumference, and are back today. A colossal statue of the emperor may have stood at the building's peak. Two obelisks, now relocated to other *piazze*, once guarded the entrance. And the mausoleum isn't just for dead people, either. At various times, it was converted to a Colonna family fortress, a wooden amphitheater where Goethe watched some bearbaiting in 1787, and even a concert hall. Mussolini finally restored it in 1936 and surrounded it with Fascist buildings, trying as always to imitate his hero, Augustus.

Meier's baby stands opposite the Mausoleum. It sometimes hosts art exhibitions, but the real attraction here is the Ara Pacis. Millennia after its design, it serves as a monument to both the grandiosity of Augustan propaganda and the ingenuity of modern-day archaeology. The marble altar, completed in 9 BC, was designed to celebrate Augustus's success in achieving peace after years of civil unrest and war in Gaul and Spain. The reliefs on its front and back include depictions of allegorical figures from Rome's most sacred myths: a Roman Lupercalia, Aeneas sacrificing a white sow, Tellus the earth goddess, and the goddess Roma. The side panels show the procession in which the altar was consecrated, with realistic portraits of Augustus, his family, and various statesmen and priests, all striding off to sacrifice cattle on the new altar dedicated to peace.

The Meier building, which was completed in 2006, is not quite as ingenious. Architecture critics panned the structure, calling it context-less—it in no way refers to its Roman setting. Still, it was a breakthrough of sorts; the museum was the first major civic building constructed in historic Rome in over half a century. (Ⓜ*A-Flaminio. Mausoleum ☎ 06 06 08; www.arapacis.it. Mausoleum open Sa-Su 10am-1pm. €2, under 18 and over 65 free. Museo Ara Pacis open Tu-Su 9:30am-7pm; last entry 6pm. €6.50, EU citizens 18-25 €4.50, EU citizens under 18 or over 65 free.)*

VATICAN CITY

The official Comune di Roma tourism kiosk has helpful English-speaking staff who will provide free maps, brochures, hours, location, and ticket info for any of the sites related to the Vatican or Rome. (Castel Sant'Angelo, P. Pia. ☎ 06 58 33 34 57. Open daily 8:30am-7pm. 10 other locations in the city around the major tourist sites.)

The administrative and spiritual center of the Roman Catholic Church, once the mightiest power in Europe, occupies 108 independent acres within Rome. The Lateran Treaty of 1929 allows the Pope to maintain legislative, judicial, and executive powers over this tiny theocracy, but requires the Church to remain neutral in national politics and municipal affairs. The Vatican has historically and symbolically preserved its independence by minting coins (Italian *lire* and euro with the Pope's face), running a separate press and postal system, maintaining an army of Swiss Guards, and preserving some of the world's finest art in the **Musei Vaticani.** Devout pilgrims, atheists, and everyone in between are awed by the stunning grace and beauty of its two famous churches—the Sistine Chapel and St. Peter's Basilica. (☎06 69 81 662.Ⓜ A-Ottaviano; bus #40, 64, 271, or 492 from Termini or Largo Argentina; or tram #19 from P. Risorgimento, 62 from P. Barberini, or 23 from Testaccio.)

BASILICA DI SAN PIETRO (SAINT PETER'S BASILICA)

The multilingual staff of the Pilgrim Tourist Information Center, located on the left between the rounded colonnade and the basilica, provides Vatican postage, brochures, and currency exchange. A first-aid station and free bathrooms are next to the tourist office. Open daily Apr.-Sept. 7am-7pm; Oct.-Mar. 7am-6pm. Mass M-Sa 8:30, 9, 10, 11am, noon, 5pm; Su and holidays 9, 10:30, 11:30am, 12:15, 1, 4, 5, 5:30pm. Vespers 5pm. Modest attire strictly enforced: no shorts, short skirts, or exposed shoulders allowed. Guided tours Tu and Th 9:45am and W 3pm; meet at Info Center. Free.

PIAZZA AND FACADE. Bernini's famous colonnade around **Piazza San Pietro,** lined with the statues of 140 saints perched around the perimeter, was designed to provide a long, impressive vista to pilgrims after their tiring journey through the tiny, winding streets of Borgo and the *centro storico.* The open circle created by the two sides of the colonnade leading away from San Pietro is said to represent the welcoming arms of the Church, embracing its followers as they enter the *piazza.* Mussolini's broad V. della Conciliazione, built in the 30s to connect the Vatican to the rest of the city, opened a broader view of the church than Bernini ever intended. A visitor who stands on the round disks will see the quadruple rows of colonnades merge into one perfectly aligned row. Statues of Christ, John the Baptist, and all the apostles except Peter are on top of the basilica. In warm months, the Pope holds papal audiences on a platform in the *piazza* on Wednesday mornings. *(To attend an audience, contact the Prefettura della Casa Pontificia ☎ 06 69 88 46 31 or stop by the Bronze Door, located on the right after you pass through security. Ascend the steps and ask the Swiss Guard for a ticket.)*

 COLOR-CODED. The Virgin Mary can usually be recognized in art by her red dress and bright blue mantle. Blue became her trademark color because the pigment was made from *lapis lazuli,* the most expensive of all paints.

INTERIOR. The iconic basilica rests on the reputed site of St. Peter's tomb. In Holy Years, the Pope opens the **Porta Sancta** (Holy Door)—the last door on the right side of the entrance porch—by knocking in the bricks with a silver hammer. The interior of St. Peter's Cathedral measures 187m by 137m along the transepts. Metal lines on the marble floor mark the lengths of other major world churches. To the right of the entrance, Michelangelo's glowing *Pietà* has been encased in bullet-proof glass since 1972, when an axe-wielding fanatic attacked it, smashing Christ's nose and breaking Mary's hand. (Call the plastic surgeon!)

Bernini's **baldacchino** (canopy) rises on spiraling columns over the marble altar, reserved for the Pope's use. The Baroque structure, cast in bronze pillaged from the Pantheon, was unveiled on June 28, 1633, by Pope Urban VIII, a member of the wealthy Barberini family. Bees, the family symbol, buzz whimsically around the canopy, and vines climb toward Michelangelo's cavernous

cupola. Seventy oil lamps glow in front of the *baldacchino* and illuminate Maderno's sunken *Confessio*, a 17th-century chapel. Two staircases directly beneath the papal altar descend to St. Peter's tomb. The staircases are closed to the public, but the underground grottoes offer a better view of the tomb, as well as the tombs of countless other popes, including John Paul II. *(Open daily Apr.-Sept. 7am-6pm; Oct.-Mar. 7am-5pm. Free.)*

High above the *baldacchino* and the altar rises **Michelangelo's dome,** designed in a style similar to that of the Pantheon (p. 156). Out of reverence for that ancient architectural wonder, Michelangelo is said to have made his *cupola* a meter shorter in diameter than the Pantheon's; the difference is not noticeable, however, as the dome towers 120m high and 42.3m across. When Michelangelo died in 1564, only the drum of the dome had been completed. Work remained at a standstill until 1588, when 800 laborers were hired to complete it. Toiling round the clock, they finished the dome on May 21, 1590.

AROUND THE BASILICA

To the left of the basilica is a courtyard protected by Swiss Guards. The Ufficio Scavi, administrative center for the Pre-Constantinian Necropolis, is here. Ask the Swiss Guards for permission to enter. To the right of the basilica, at the end of the colonnade, the Prefettura della Casa Pontifica gives free tickets to papal audiences in the morning on Wednesdays.

CUPOLA. The cupola entrance is near the Porta Sancta. Ascend 551 stairs to the top or take an elevator to the walkway around the dome's interior. Beware: even using the elevator, you'll still have to climb 320 steps to see the top ledge's panorama. *(Open daily Apr.-Sept. 8am-5pm; Oct.-Mar. 8am-4pm. By stairs €4, by elevator €7.)*

TREASURY OF SAINT PETER. The Treasury contains gifts bestowed upon St. Peter's tomb. At the entrance, look for a list of all the popes. Highlights include the dalmatic of Charlemagne (the Holy Roman Emperor's intricately designed robe), a Bernini angel, and the magnificent bronze tomb of Sixtus IV. *(Inside the basilica on the left. Open daily Apr.-Sept. 9am-6:15pm; Oct.-Mar. 9am-5:15pm. Last entry 30min. before close. Closed when the Pope is celebrating mass in the basilica and on Christmas and Easter. Wheelchair-accessible. Photographs forbidden. €6, under 13 €4.)*

TOMB OF SAINT PETER AND PRE-CONSTANTINIAN NECROPOLIS. After converting to Christianity, Constantine built his first basilica directly over St. Peter's tomb. In order to build on that exact spot, the emperor had to level a hill and destroy a necropolis that once stood on the site. The basilica's history was mere legend until 1939, when workers came across ancient ruins underneath. Unsure of finding anything, the Church secretly set about looking for St. Peter's tomb. More than 20 years later, the tomb was identified under a small temple beneath the altars of Constantine's basilica. The saint's bones, however, were not found. A hollow wall nearby held what the church later claimed to be the holy remains. Some believe that the bones were displaced from the tomb during the Saracens' sack of Rome in 849 AD. Multilingual tour guides will take you around the streets of the necropolis, which hold several well-preserved pagan and Christian mausolea, funerary inscriptions, mosaics, and sarcophagi. *(Entrance to the necropolis is on the left side of P. San Pietro, beyond the info office. ☎ 06 69 88 53 18; scavi@fsp.va. Office open M-Sa 9am-5pm. To request a tour, arrange in person or write to: The Delegate of the Fabbrica di San Pietro, Excavations Office, 00120 Vatican City. Give a preferred range of times and languages. Phone calls only accepted for confirmations. Reserve as far ahead as possible. Instructions available on website. €10.)*

OTHER SIGHTS

CASTEL SANT'ANGELO. Built by Hadrian (AD 76-138) as a mausoleum for his family and himself, this gigantic brick-and-stone mass overlooking the Tiber has served as a fortress, prison, and palace. When a plague struck in AD 590, Pope Gregory the Great saw an angel sheathing his sword at the top of the complex. The plague abated soon thereafter, and the building was rededicated to the angel. Military aficionados will relish in the armory, located on one of the top floors. Be sure to check out the terrace cafe on the third floor—it's covered in flowering vines and has a beautiful panoramic view of Rome and Vatican City. Outside, the marble **Ponte Sant'Angelo,** lined with statues by Bernini, marks the beginning of the traditional pilgrimage route from St. Peter's to **San Giovanni** in **Laterano** (p. 177). *(☎06 68 19 111, reservations 39 96 76 00. Bus #40, 62, 64, 271, 280 to Ponte V. Emanuele or P. Pia. Dungeon. Along the Tiber River on the Vatican side when going from St. Peter's toward the Tiber River. From the centro storico, cross Ponte Sant'Angelo. Open in summer Tu-Su 9am-7pm; in winter daily 9am-7pm. Last entry 1hr. before close. Tours Su 12:30pm in Italian, 11:30am in English. €8, EU students 18-25 €5.50, EU citizens under 18 or over 65 free. Audio tour €4.)*

TRASTEVERE

ISOLA TIBERINA

According to legend, the Tiber Island shares its birthday with the Roman Republic. After the Etruscan tyrant Tarquin raped the virtuous Lucretia (see **Life and Times,** p. 48), her outraged family killed him and threw his corpse in the river; so much muck and silt collected around his corpse that an island eventually formed, proving once and for all that he was a real dirtbag. These violent origins may have deterred Republican Romans from settling the island—its first living inhabitants were slaves abandoned after they'd become too weak to work.

On the island, the slaves prayed to Asclepius, the Greek god of healing. Rumor has it that in 293 BC, the god appeared to Romans as a snake and slithered onto the island. They took it as a sign that Asclepius wanted his temple there and, with their typical architectural aplomb, encased the island in marble. They built its walls in the shape of a boat to commemorate the god's arrival. Traces of the original travertine decoration are still visible on the southeast side of the island—look for the serpent carved in relief near the "prow."

The Romans also built a large temple to Asclepius, with porticos where the sick could wait for the god to visit them in their dreams and prescribe a cure— the likely origin of the modern experience of going to a doctor's office, except Aesclepius probably set out newer magazines. Nearby, archaeologists have found pits full of *ex voto* statuettes of arms, legs, and other body parts offered in thanks. Leprosy always inspires people to give generously of themselves.

FATEBENEFRATELLI HOSPITAL. The demise of Asclepius's worshippers in the AD fourth century was not enough to undo the island's long associations with healing. In 1548, a group of charitable Fatebenefratelli monks erected a hospital on the site of the temple, which still occupies the northwestern half of the island. In over 450 years of proud service, not a single person has ever pronounced the name correctly. Expectant Roman mothers consider the hospital the most fashionable place in the city to give birth: it looks like a tropical villa on the outside and like a church, replete with open-air *piazze*, on the inside. To those whose fashion sense leans more toward the ironic, the catacombs (p. 187) are a better choice. It was at the Fatebenefratelli Hospital that English

King Henry I's courtier, Rahere, reputedly fought off malaria. He was so thankful to the Romans who had helped him that he promised to show his gratitude by building a church and a hospital—back in England. What a guy. True to his word, he built the structures, which still stand in London's Smithfield district.

BRIDGES. The footbridge leading from the east bank of the river (on the Centro Storico side) is the **Ponte Fabricio**—commonly known as the **Bridge of Four Heads** for its two busts of Janus, the two-headed god of beginnings and endings). It is the oldest in the city, built by Lucius Fabricius in 62 BC. From the *lungotevere*, you can see the inscription Lucius carved into the bridge to record his public service. To the south of the bridge, the beleaguered **Ponte Rotto**, one of Rome's less fortunate ancient constructions, is also visible. Built in the second century BC, the poor bridge underwent medieval repair after medieval repair, each time succumbing to the Tiber's relentless floods, which really went medieval on it. From the time of its last collapse in 1598, it had been slowly disintegrating, until it was accidentally blown up during the construction of the current metal bridge just downstream, the **Ponte Palatino.** Now all that remains is a single marble arch planted squatly but proudly midstream. On the other side of the island, the **Ponte Cestio**, originally built by Lucius Cestius in 46 BC and rebuilt in 1892, takes you across to Trastevere. The little bridge offers a stellar view of the Gianicolo and the Church of Santa Maria in Cosmedin. Stairs lead to the bank, where lovers, graffiti artists, and other social derelicts enjoy the many charms of secluded anonymity.

CHIESA DI SAN BARTOLOMEO. This 10th-century church has been flooded and rebuilt many times. It is now something of an architectural chimera, with a Baroque facade, a Romanesque bell tower, 14 ancient columns, and avant-garde 20th-century stained glass windows. (*P. San Bartolomeo all'Isola 22.* ☎ *06 68 77 973. Open M-F 9:30am-1pm and 3:30-7pm, Sa 9:30am-1pm and 3:30-5:30pm, Su 9:30am-1pm and 7-8pm.*)

CENTRAL TRASTEVERE

Off Ponte Garibaldi stands the statue of poet Giuseppe Gioachino Belli in his own *piazza*, which borders P. Sonnino, Trastevere's transportation hub, and marks the beginning of Vle. di Trastevere. A right onto V. di Lungaretta takes you to P. di Santa Maria in Trastevere.

PIAZZA SIDNEY SONNINO. The 13th-century **Torre degli Anguillara** stands to the left, over a *palazzo* that used to sport the same name. The building now stands in honor of Dante Alighieri with the name **Casa di Dante**, as the various members of the Anguillara family were notoriously priests, magistrates, warlords, criminals, and swindlers—the full package.

CHIESA DI SAN CRISOGONO. This basilica is etched with the name of Cardinal Borghese. Founded in the fifth century, the church has been rebuilt many times; twenty feet beneath the most recent structure lie the visitable remains of the original. To visit the ruins, walk into the room left of the altar, and the sacristan will lead you down the wrought-iron staircase. Traces of original wall paintings and some well-preserved sarcophagi and inscriptions are visible. On the left side of the church, you can view a memorial and listen to an explanation of the life and times of Beata Anna Maria Taigi, a life-like (creepy) model of which rests in peace in a glass display. The housewife and saint did good deeds while tending to seven sons and her husband, "a difficult, rough character." Husbands—especially difficult, rough ones—beware: this display tends to incite violence from commiserating wives. (*Across the street from the Casa di Dante, at P. Sonnino 44.* ☎ *06 58 18 225. Open M-F 9am-noon and 2-7pm. Ruins and crypt €3.*)

CHIESA DI SAN FRANCESCO A RIPA. Head down V. di Trastevere and turn left on V. di San Francesco a Ripa to visit one of the first Franciscan churches in Rome. The church showcases Bernini's *Beata Lodovica Albertoni* in a chapel on its left side. She lies in a state of surprising euphoria for a dead woman, flanked by cherubim busts and suspended as if floating in thin air. *(Open M-F 7am-noon and 4-7pm, Sa-Su 7am-1pm and 4-7:30pm.)*

BASILICA DI SANTA CECILIA. During the third century, Cecilia converted to Christianity and managed to convert her husband, Valerian, and brother-in-law. The men were later beheaded for their refusal to worship Roman gods, while she escaped their fate and inherited their considerable fortunes. She became one of the richest women in Rome and incited such resentment that the prefect of Rome ordered her death in 230. She was locked in her own steam room to die, but through some miracle survived. Deciding that death by spa wasn't harsh enough, her relations tried to behead her, but despite three tries, the executioners botched the job and she survived, slowly bleeding to death. Tirelessly optimistic, the hemorrhaging evangelist converted over 400 people in the three days before she finally succumbed to her fate. She bequeathed her palace to build this beautiful church. Cecilia is known as the patron saint of music because she was found singing after her three-day stint in the steam room. On November 22, St. Cecilia's day of martyrdom, every year churches hold a musical service.

Pope Urban I consecrated the church in her palace in the fifth century, but Pascal I rebuilt it in 821 when, according to one Vatican account, he dreamed that St. Cecilia revealed her true burial grounds in the catacombs of St. Callisto. He had her body exhumed and moved to the new church. Stefano Maderno's statue of Santa Cecilia lies under the high altar, showing what she looked like when exhumed from her tomb in 1599 in Maderno's presence—pretty good for a 1300-year-old corpse.

Sadly, Rococo restorers wreaked havoc on the medieval frescoes by Pietro Cavallini that once covered the church. However, fragments of his magnificent 1293 *Last Judgment* remain in the gated cloister on the right. Beneath the church lie the ruins of Roman buildings and an ancient church. The entrance is on the left as you enter the church, marked "*cripta e scavi."* Cardinal Rampolla, the man responsible for the excavations, is memorialized in the last chapel outside the church. *(From P. Sidney Sonnino, walk away from the river and go left on V. G. C. Santini, which runs into V. di Genovesi. From V. Genovesi, turn right on V. Santa Cecilia. Open daily 9:30am-12:30pm and 4-6:30pm. Crypt entrance through bookshop, to the left as you enter the church. See Cavallini's frescoes M-F 10:15am-noon, Sa-Su 11:15am-12:15pm; entry from the monastic choir, to the left, outside the basilica entrance. Church free; donation requested. Crypt €2.50. Frescoes €2.50.)*

CHIESA DI SANTA MARIA IN TRASTEVERE. The church has the distinction of being the first in Rome dedicated to the Virgin Mary. Though this structure dates from the 12th century, an earlier basilica was built on the site in the third century under Pope Calixtus. The mosaics of the Virgin and the 10 saintly women lining the exterior give way to a sea of gold and marble inside. The 12th-century mosaics in the apse and the chancel arch depict Jesus, Mary, and a bevy of saints and popes in rich Byzantine detail. What appears to be a trash heap around the statue of the friar and the infant at the entrance is actually a pile of prayers written on anything from Metro tickets to napkins. *(From P. Sidney Sonnino, head west on V. di Lungaretta. Open M-F 9am-5:30pm, Sa 5:30-8pm, Su 8:30am-10:30am and noon-5:30pm.)*

PIAZZA TRILUSSA. Next to Ponte Sisto is a large, travertine fountain that forms the focal point of Piazza Trilussa. Commissioned by Pope Paolo V in 1613, it features as its central decoration the Borghese coat of arms. Today, the *piazza* is a central meeting area for revelry-seekers, some of whom can be found on Saturday and Sunday mornings, passed out on the bottle-littered steps leading up to the fountain. Vco. del Moro, a small alley connected to the main square, is one of Trastevere's primary nightlife destinations. In summer, many bars set up outposts along the Tiber, just below the *piazza*. The nightly partying has become so rowdy in recent years that residents sometimes hang white sheets out their windows, in quiet solidarity and protest of the fun going on below. Like the numerous Italian and foreign hooligans who frequent P. Trilussa, you too can grab a beer and a megaphone and join in the counter-protest—just know that the white sheets show no mercy.

GIANICOLO HILL

◼BOTANICAL GARDENS. At the base of the hill, enter a botanical break in the cityscape. Filled with well-labeled specimens of trees and flowers, the gardens remain green and luxuriant even when the rest of Rome is dull and brown. The remarkable assemblage of flora stretches from valleys of ferns through groves of bamboo to a hilltop Japanese garden. Of interest are the garden of roses cultivated during the Baroque period in Rome, containing the two founding bushes from which all the world's roses are supposedly descended, and the stellar **Garden for the Blind,** a star-shaped garden of various plants labeled in Braille. (*At the end of V. Corsini, off V.d. Scala (V. della Lungara), at Largo Cristina di Svezia, 23A. ☎06 49 91 71 44, ext. 7135. Grounds open M-Sa from Oct. 19 to Mar. 29 9am-6:30pm; from Mar. 30 to Oct. 18 9am-5:30pm. Greenhouses open M-Sa 9am-12:30pm. Guided tours Tu-W 10:30am, Sa 10:30am and noon. Comes with leaflet and audio tour in Italian, English, or French. Call for reservations and more info. €4, ages 6-11 and over 60 €2, under 5 free.*)

◼PIAZZA GIUSEPPE GARIBALDI. Continuing the nationalistic theme, this *piazza* is the site of a patriotic statue complex crowned by a bronze statue of the revolutionary leader himself on horseback. It marks one of the last places that Garibaldi's ragtag Italian troops tried to hold off the numerically superior French forces. Even if you fail to experience a surge of Italian nationalism after all that build-up, you're likely to appreciate the sweeping panoramas of the Vatican from one side and the entirety of Rome from the other side of the gorgeous *piazza*. The Republic may have fallen, but freedom-loving Italians everywhere will never forget the Garibaldi. (*Walk down Passeggiata del Giancolo from Porta di San Pancrazio, along the walls.*)

PIAZZA SAN PIETRO IN MONTORIO. Up the hill, the **Chiesa di San Pietro in Montorio** stands on what is believed to be the site of St. Peter's upside-down crucifixion. The church's biggest draw is the masterly *Flagellazione di Gesù*, painted on slate by Sebastiano del Piombo from designs by Michelangelo. The church also contains the tombs of Irish noblemen, exiles persecuted by English Protestants. Next door, in a small courtyard behind locked gates, is Bramante's tiny ◼**Tempietto** (1499-1502). A combination of ancient and Renaissance architecture, the Tempietto was constructed to commemorate the site of St. Peter's martyrdom and provided the inspiration for the dome of St. Peter's in Vatican City. (*Reach the summit on bus #41 from the Vatican, 115 from Trastevere, 870 from P. Fiorentini, where C. V. Emanuele meets the Tiber, or walk up the medieval V. Garibaldi from V. della Scala in Trastevere for 10min. Church at V. Garibaldi 33. ☎06 58 13 940; www.sanpietroinmontorio.it. Open M-F 8:30am-noon and 3-4pm, Sa-Su 8:30am-noon.*)

SIGHTS UP TO THE SUMMIT. Visible from Chiesa di San Pietro in Montorio, just up the hill, is **Mausoleo Ossario Garibaldino,** a starkly fascist monument erected in 1941 to enclose the remains of Goffredo Mameli, the composer of the Italian national anthem. A little ways farther on V. Garibaldi is the ⬛**Acqua Paola.** On this site, the accurately named *Il Fontanone* (The Big Fountain) marks the end of an aqueduct built in 1612, which honors Pope Paul V. Take a break from fighting gravity and enjoy the splendor of the Roman vista expanding into the distance. At the end of V. Garibaldi, where it leads into V. di Porta San Pancrazio, stands the road's portly namesake. Originally built under Pope Urbanus VIII, the **Porta San Pancrazio** was the main gate in the walls built around the Gianicolo to protect Rome against attacks coming from the sea. Alas, it was completely destroyed during the French siege of 1849, despite Garibaldi's month-long stand, making way for the current structure to be erected in 1854.

OTHER SIGHTS

VILLA DORIA PAMPHILJ. Just behind the Porta San Pancrazio, the entry road to this villa was shared with Villa Corsini in 1849. When the French seized control of Corsini, a strategically important site, Garibaldi's troops sustained massive losses in several unsuccessful attempts to retake it, setting up the commander's imminent, final defeat. Today, the villa's grounds serve as Rome's largest landscaped public park. Each summer from June to August, it plays host to numerous outdoor theater, dance, and music performances. *(Entrance at V. di Porta San Pancrazio 10. Park open daily Apr.-Aug. 7am-9pm, Mar. and Sept. 7am-8pm, Oct.-Feb. 7am-6pm. Visit www.estateromana.comune.roma.it for a performance schedule.)*

VILLA SCIARRA. Built on the original site of the Caesar Gardens, the 6-hectare villa changed hands many times before being purchased in the early 20th century by the American diplomat George Wurth. After he converted it into a beautiful terrace garden, it fell into the control of Mussolini in 1930 and became a public park. Fountains, pools, and statues stand in the midst of tropical plants and manicured hedges, providing a serene setting in which Italians sit and read or walk their dogs—and pigs, which some enterprising swine enthusiasts strut around on leashes. *(From V. Garibaldi, turn onto V. Nicola Fabrizi and walk to the end. The entrance is directly across the street, at V. Calandrelli 23.)*

VILLA BORGHESE

VILLA BORGHESE

Get off at Ⓜ A-Spagna and follow the signs. Or, from the Ⓜ A-Flaminio stop, take V. Washington under the archway. From P. del Popolo, climb the stairs to the right of Santa Maria del Popolo, cross the street, and climb the small path. ☎ 06 32 16 564. Free.

Imagine NYC's Central Park, but a little less central, a little more Mediterranean, and of course, with a little more marble sculpture and Roman grace. To celebrate becoming a cardinal, Scipione Borghese financed construction of the Villa Borghese, a stunning park northeast of the *centro storico,* replete with hidden fountains and meandering paths. Today, the park is a favorite with young families, strolling lovers, art fans, and anybody else who feels like checking out the often lush greenery and historic sights.

The Villa Borghese is roughly triangular in shape. The eastern point of the triangle is anchored by the **Galleria Borghese** (p. 203), perhaps the finest museum in all of Rome. The museum is ticketed, and reservations are strictly required, but the lovely gardens behind the museum are open to all and perfect for a leisurely walk. The western point harbors the **Museo Nazionale Etrusco di Villa Giulia**

(p. 207) and begins to shade back into residential areas. To the south, curious visitors will see the **Galoppatoio,** a large track used for horse-racing. **Viale del Muro Torto,** a main artery, runs through this area as well.

GIARDINO BIOLOGICO. The "Bioparco," as it is affectionately known, is to the north of Villa Borghese. A favorite of families with young children, it is particularly notable for its massive **Reptile House,** which shelters an extensive collection of the cold-blooded creatures. *(Entrance at Lungarno V. Gassman, along Vle. del Giardino Zoologico. Open Apr.-Sept. 9:30am-7pm; Oct. 9:30am-6pm; Nov.-Mar. 9:30am-5pm. €10, under 12 and over 60 €8, children under 1m free.)*

PINCIO. This small garden square has a lot to see. The Vle. del Orologio (*orologio* means clock) is named for the **Idrocronometro,** a real working clock powered and set by the motion of water through a series of fountains. Incredibly enough, it was designed in 1867—although the date does explain its rather incongruous American Log Cabin aesthetic. A **carousel** in the vicinity is a hit with the kiddies, as is the **San Carlino,** a puppet theater. A caveat: all this fun is located up a substantial hill, and the Metro won't carry you up there. Whether you climb gradually from the area around V. Veneto or quickly scale the cliff by P. del Popolo, be prepared to huff and puff. A great view is your reward. *(Near the park entrance off P. del Popolo. Idrocronometro free.)*

THE GLOBE THEATER. This circular, wooden structure is an exact replica of the 16th-century Elizabethan theater. Shakespearean plays are performed in Italian on the outdoor stage. *(On Vle. Aqua Felix. Reservations ☎ 06 82 05 91 27; www.globetheatreroma.com. Box office open M-F 2-7pm, Sa-Su noon-7pm. Open July-Sept. Tickets €5.50-17.50.)*

OTHER SIGHTS

PIAZZA BARBERINI. Though the busy traffic circle at V. del Tritone feels more like a modern thoroughfare than a Baroque square, P. Barberini features a Bernini fountain, the **Fontana Tritone.** Maderno, Bernini, and Borromini collaborated on the **Palazzo Barberini,** home to the Galleria Nazionale d'Arte Antica. The severe **Chiesa della Immacolata Concezione** houses the morbidly fascinating 🆂**Capuchin Crypt,** decorated with hundreds of human skulls and bones in themed rooms. If you're not too creeped out to function, stroll up the lovely **Via Veneto** and watch the well-to-do quaff €15 cocktails and lose themselves in the pleasures of the flesh at the **Westin Excelsior** and the **Cafe de Paris.** Ooh, a celebrity! *(Church at V. V. Veneto 27. www.cappucciniviaveneto.it. Open M-W and F-Su 9am-noon and 3--6pm. Church free; cash donation requested.)*

PONTE MILVIO. This bridge across the Tiber, to the north of Villa Borghese, has seen a lot of action it its day. It was one of the first bridges in Rome—built in 206 BC, and rebuilt in 115 BC in its current form. In AD 312, Emperor Constantine I won a surprising victory here over his enemy and co-Emperor Maxentius at the Battle of Milvian Bridge; it was the beginning of the end for Rome's ruling Tetrarchy and the commencement of Constantine's successful bid to become sole emperor. Lately, however, the action has been of a different sort. Couples began attaching padlocks to a lamppost on the bridge after the author Federico Moccia invented the ritual for his book *I Want You.* By April of 2007, the lamppost had partially collapsed, and lovers could no longer symbolically declare their passion—that is, until authorities installed steel posts in summer 2007. Those travelers with minimal interest in either romance or ancient history can revel in the rather nice view.

TERMINI AND ENVIRONS

BASILICA DI SANTA MARIA MAGGIORE. Take a moment and prepare yourself; you are about to enter one of the world's oldest and best-preserved basilicas, home to an original cycle of early Christian mosaics that have looked down upon worshippers for some 16 centuries. The Basilica of Santa Maria Maggiore, which crowns the summit of the **Esquiline Hill,** combines ancient mosaics with the splendor of Renaissance and Baroque additions. Fourth among the seven "Patriarchal" basilicas traditionally visited on the pilgrimage to Rome, it is also one of the five churches in Rome granted extraterritoriality, making it officially part of Vatican City.

According to tradition, the Virgin Mary appeared before Pope Liberius in August of AD 358 and requested that he build a church in her honor at the place that would be covered in snow the next morning. The next day, the Pope discovered that snow had miraculously fallen on the highest point of the hill. He promptly set out to design and build the church, first named Santa Maria della Neve (St. Mary of the Snow). Priests recreate the miracle by sprinkling white rose petals from the top of the church every fifth of August.

It appears that the basilica was actually built 80 years later by Pope Sixtus III, who noticed that Roman women were still visiting a temple dedicated to the mother goddess Juno Lucina, located on the hill next to Liberius's smaller church. Sixtus enthusiastically tore both down to construct the new basilica, not only substituting a Christian sect for a pagan one, but also celebrating the recent Council of Ephesus, which declared Mary to be imbued with a divinity that raised her above general humankind. Most of the mosaics inside are designed to commemorate her new status.

Maria Maggiore has a deceptive exterior: while the shell that Ferdinando Fuga built for it in 1750 is Baroque, inside is one of the best-preserved Classical basilicas in Rome. Ancient columns divide the rectangular church into a central nave with two side aisles surmounted by celestial windows. The triumphal arch over the high altar swims in mosaics honoring the Holy Virgin Mary; the image (on the right) of Mary spinning a basket of purple wool to make a veil dates to the fifth century. Although difficult to see without the aid of binoculars, the mosaics on the left side of the church contain scenes from the lives of Abraham, Jacob, and Isaac, and, on the right, of Moses and Joshua. The coffered ceiling above it all is believed to have been gilded with the first gold sent from America by Christopher Columbus.

In the subterranean confessions before the altar, a marble Pope Pius IX kneels in front of a relic of the baby Jesus' crib. Though now sheathed in globs of silver, the crib is revealed each Christmas morning. A dazzling *baldacchino* (canopy) looms over the altar, which enshrines the famous image of the Madonna. To the right of the altar, a marble slab marks the **tomb of Gian Lorenzo Bernini.** A visit to the *loggia* (the open-air corridor on the facade) grants access to the once-private chambers of Pope Paul V and Bernini's spiral staircase. Its glorious 14th-century mosaics recount the story of the August snowfall that showed the Pope where to build the basilica. Don't miss the **baptistery,** featuring a magnificent statue of St. John the Baptist covered with animal skins and holding a clam shell. Since 2001, Santa Maria Maggiore has hosted a **museum** containing art and papal artifacts significant to the history of the basilica; enter through the souvenir shop. *(From Termini, exit right onto V. Giolitti, and walk down V. Cavour. At P. dell' Esquilino, walk around to southeastern side of the basilica to enter. Reservations:* ☎ *06 69 88 68 02. Open daily 7am-7pm. Museum and loggia open daily 9am-6pm. Daily tours of the archaeological area. Modest dress required. Museum €4, reduced €2. Loggia €5, reduced €3.)*

PIAZZA DEL QUIRINALE. This *piazza*, at the southwest end of V. del Quirinale, occupies the summit of the tallest of Rome's original seven hills. From the belvedere, the view takes in a sea of Roman domes, with St. Peter's in the distance. In the middle of the *piazza*, the heroic statues of **Castor and Pollux**—mythical warrior twins whom the ancient Romans embraced as their protectors—flank an obelisk from the Mausoleum of Augustus. The fountain over which they preside was once a cattle trough in the Roman Forum. *(M A-Barberini. Walk 2 blocks south along V. delle Quattro Fontane, turn right on XX Settembre; the piazza is a few blocks straight ahead.)*

CHIESA DI SANTA MARIA DEGLI ANGELI. It was a long time coming, but the Christians avenged their persecution and exploitation under Diocletian with this church. Centuries after Diocletian's death (and his baths' demise), a Sicilian priest had a vision of a swarm of angels rising from the baths; he subsequently pestered Pius IV to build a church on the dilapidated site. In 1561, Pope Pius IV ordered an 86-year-old Michelangelo to convert the ruins into a church. This would be his last architectural work. Imitating the architecture of the baths, Michelangelo used the remains of the *calidarium* (hot baths) as the church facade. On the bronze door to the left, a startling cross cuts deeply into Christ's body, symbolizing his resurrection. This is how it appears today, although much of his interior plan was changed after the Pope and Michelangelo died three years later. Despite the departure from Michelangelo's plan and the many years of design revisions, the cavernous interior preserves a sense of the ancient baths. The church was constructed in the ancient *tepidarium* (lukewarm baths); Michelangelo scavenged material from the baths to construct the red porphyry columns that line the church interior. A sundial, located in the floor leading from the east transept to the altar, provided the standard time for Roman clocks for hundreds of years. The sacristy leads to ruins of the *frigidarium* (cold tables) as well as a small exhibit on the construction of the church. *(P. della Repubblica. ☎06 48 80 812; www.santamariadegliangeliroma.it. Open M-Sa 7am-6:30pm, Su and holidays 7am-7:30pm. Modest dress required. Daily demonstrations of the sundial at 12:50pm; nice weather only. Reserve a spot via email at least 1 week in advance for a free tour with an archaeologist in English, French, or Italian: gvaleri@fastwebnet.it.)*

CHIESA DI SANTA PRASSEDE. Built in 822, the Church of Santa Prassede houses a stunning set of Christian **mosaics.** Prassede and Pudenziana, the daughters of the powerful senator Pudens, reputedly buried the corpses of 3,000 persecuted Christians and were converted to Christianity themselves by St. Peter around AD 50. The Vatican doubted this story enough, however, to remove the girls from the register of saints in 1969. In the apse is the New Jerusalem, a triumphal lamb, and the two sister saints being presented to Christ, with Peter and Paul encouraging them. From the right aisle step into the **Chapel of Saint Zeno,** a small room of mosaics that shimmers like a ninth-century tween's glitter makeup, lit by a machine outside the door (€0.50 per 5min; the best half-euro you'll ever spend). The chapel is populated by various saints, while four angels hold up a Byzantine Christ floating in a sea of gold. Note the Empress Theodora above the doorway leading into the gift shop, who has a square halo, indicating that she was still alive when the mosaics were made (i.e., before her death in the early ninth century). Another reading, understandably less popular with the Vatican, is that this represents a female bishop. The chapel holds part of a column of rare oriental jasper retrieved from Jerusalem in 1228 during the sixth Crusade, reputedly the column to which Christ was strapped and flogged before his crucifixion. *(From the front of Santa Maria Maggiore, walk up V. Merulana, taking the 1st right onto tiny V. San Giovanni Gualberto; the church is at the dead-end. Open daily 7am-noon and 4-6:30pm. Free.)*

CHIESA DI SANT'ANDREA AL QUIRINALE. Another stunning church courtesy of Bernini. In fact, this oval church was reputedly Bernini's favorite, and its small scale gives it an intimacy that is lost in larger basilicas. Sant'Andrea nicely exemplifies Bernini's ability to combine sculpture with architecture to create a dynamic space and his skilled use of light and colored stone in a coherent project. Statues of angels and cherubs clamber over the dome of the church and play with architectural garlands, while Sant'Andrea looks upward to the symbol of the Holy Spirit. Look for the statues of men with nets, representing St. Andrea's fellow fishermen. Left of the altar are the rooms of St. Stanislaus, a Jesuit saint, immortalized in a detailed sculpture. *(P. Quirinale. Take V. Quirinale; the church is on the right, past V. Ferrara. Open daily 8am-noon and 4-7pm.)*

CHIESA DI SANTA MARIA DELLA VITTORIA. This church, home to an icon of Mary that accompanied the Catholics to victory in a 1620 battle near Prague, houses one of Bernini's most stunning ensembles, dedicated to Spanish mystic St. Teresa of Avila. Bernini's fantastically controversial ◪**Ecstasy of Saint Theresa of Ávila** continues to amaze and bemuse visitors in the **Cornaro Chapel** (the last one on the left). At the time of its creation, people were outraged by the depiction of the saint in a pose resembling sexual climax; today, many viewers don't notice the innuendo until told of the controversy. The statue illustrates St. Theresa's heart being pierced by an arrow wielded by an angel, filling her with ardent love for God. The scene was subsequently expanded to resemble a theater, with statuesque members of the Cornaro family looking on. Saintly and family values just aren't what they used to be. *(On the south side of P. San Bernardo, away from P. Repubblica. Open M-F 8:30am-noon and 3:30-6pm, Sa and Su 3:30-6pm.)*

CHIESA DI SAN CARLINO. This ingenious church by Francesco Borromini, officially **San Carlo alle Quattro Fontane,** provides a sharp contrast to neighboring Sant'Andrea al Quirinale and highlights the architect's unique vision. Borromini avoided the kind of multi-colored extravaganzas that Bernini perfected. The interior of the church is undecorated, but is organized in a complex mathematical system incorporating the church's undulating curves and pairs of columns. The dome further illustrates his mathematical approach to architecture, with interlocking geometric forms receding to give an illusion of depth. The church has the distinction of being both Borromini's first and last work: though he designed the simple interior early on in his career, he finished the more ornate facade just before his suicide. Borromini also designed the cloister next door, which holds the crypt where it is said that he hoped—in vain—to be buried. Also be sure to check out Bernini's ◪**Four Fountains,** which are built into the corners of the intersection of V. delle Quattro Fontane and V. del Quirinale. Be careful when viewing the fountain; sidewalks are nonexistent. *(Near the corner of V. Quirinale (V. XX Settembre) and V. Quattro Fontane. Open M-F 10am-1pm and 3-6pm, Sa 10am-1pm, Su noon-1pm. If the interior is closed, ring at the convent next door.)*

SANTA BIBIANA. A hidden gem tucked away next to Termini, a water tower, and the grime of Esquilino, Santa Bibiana is Bernini's first church. Its interior hides several impressive works of art that make it worth the visit despite the sketchiness of the area and its ubiquitous graffiti. Bernini carved a statue of the saint for the altarpiece, while the great Baroque painter Pietro da Cortona painted a series of frescoes of her life and martyrdom for refusing to sacrifice to pagan gods. The sacristan will turn on the lights for you upon request. *(Follow V. Giolitti which runs alongside Stazione Termini to the intersection with V. Cairoli, near the end of the station. Church is alongside the station wall. Open daily 7:30am-9:30am and 5:30-7:45pm.)*

BASILICA OF SAN LORENZO FUORI LE MURA. This basilica, dedicated to Rome's *numero tre* saint after Peter and Paul, long remained one of the seven pillar-churches of a pilgrimage to Rome—that is, before a wayward American bomb missed its Stazione Tiburtina target and severely damaged the church and its priceless artwork on July 19th, 1943 (an event commemorated with due bitterness 60 years later, in July 2003). Restoration projects were speedily completed by 1949, and the church—in fact comprised of two basilicas, one from the sixth and one from the 13th century, joined together—still houses a sixth-century mosaic of Christ seated on a globe mounted on the triumphal arch. The church's 12th-century cloister fared better in the bombing, and leads to the catacombs where San Lorenzo was supposedly buried after being burned alive in 258. Fragments of the original reliefs and engravings are set into the walls, and a portion of the infamous bomb's casing is given its own pedestal. *(Bus #492 from Termini to P. Verano, or tram #19 from Porta Maggiore. Open daily 8am-noon and 4-6:30pm.)*

CHIESA DI SANTA PUDENZIANA. Legend has it that this small church was built by Pope Pius I in AD 145 on the property of the late senator Pudens, in gratitude to his daughters. The difference between old and new (meaning only a couple of centuries old) is especially clear. The original windows, though walled up, are still visible, as are the remnants of the original buildings and frescoes from the 11th century in the corridor behind the altar. The mosaic of Christ teaching the Apostles in the apsidal vault, dating from the late fourth century, is the oldest known mosaic in a Roman place of worship. *(From behind Santa Maria Maggiore, walk down V. Agostino Depretis and turn left onto V. Urbana; the church is on the right. Open M-Sa 8:30am-noon and 3-6pm, Su 9am-noon and 3-6pm.)*

PALAZZO DEL QUIRINALE. You best stay in line here: outside stand two guards with machine guns at the ready, waiting for you to try something. Since 1947, the President of the Republic has officially resided in this imposing *palazzo*, following in the tradition of the popes and Italian kings before him. The *palazzo* is a Baroque collaboration by Bernini, Carlo Maderno, and Domenico Fontana. Maderno designed the front, while Bernini set himself to the *manica lunga* (long sleeve) on V. del Quirinale. Look through the portals on the *piazza* for a glimpse of the white-uniformed, silver-helmeted Republican Guards (each of whom must be at least 6 ft. tall to get his job) and the *palazzo*'s lush gardens. The neighboring white stone **Palazzo della Consulta** houses the constitutional court. Though the President has reserved most of the *palazzo* for himself, the humble public may enter the former papal stables that now house revolving exhibitions. *(Not open to the public.)*

VIA XX SETTEMBRE. The beginning of V. XX Settembre showcases one of Pope Sixtus V's more gracious additions to the city. In an effort to ease traffic and better define the city's regions, the 16th-century pontiff straightened many of Rome's major streets and erected obelisks at important junctions. From the crossroads with V. delle Quattro Fontane (yes, from the middle of the road, so be careful), you can survey the obelisks at P. Quirinale, at the top of the Spanish Steps, and at Santa Maria Maggiore. V. Quirinale becomes V. XX Settembre at V. Quattro Fontane, heading east, and after a few blocks opens into the Baroque **Piazza San Bernardo,** site of Fontana's colossal **Fontana dell'Acqua Felice,** built in 1587 where Pope Sixtus V's aqueduct entered the city. Prospero Antichi's beefy and ill-proportioned statue of Moses was inspired by Michelangelo's, but is supposedly glowering at having been carved by such an inept sculptor.

CHIESA DI SANTA SUSANNA. The Church of Santa Susanna, the American parish in Rome, is run by an exceptionally friendly community of Cistercian nuns. Note the church's distinctive Counter-Reformation facade by Carlo Maderno. Inside, Baldassarre Croce's Mannerist frescoes of the life of the biblical Susanna cover the walls, and Giovanni Antonio Paracea's four large statues of the prophets stand on pillars dating from the ninth century. St. Susanna, niece of Pope Caius, converted to Christianity as a youth and "sacrificed herself to God, making an offering to him of her virginity." When she refused Emperor Diocletian's orders to marry his son and worship an idol of Jupiter, he had her beheaded in his home. Talk about hospitality. *(On the north side of P. San Bernardo. Open M-Sa 9am-noon and 4-7pm, Su 9am-1pm. English masses Su 9 and 10:30am. Vigil Sa 6pm.)*

BATHS OF DIOCLETIAN. The tattered brick remains of the Baths of Diocletian loom over news kiosks and vendors camped out around Termini. The towering thermal baths are well preserved inside a hall to the left when entering the courtyard. The baths were a colossal construction project, undertaken by Diocletian's brother Maximianus, employing 40,000 Christian slaves from AD 298-306. The baths, which could serve up to 3000 people, once contained gymnasiums, art galleries, gardens, libraries, concert halls, sports facilities, and—for those who felt too clean after a day in the baths—brothels. Going to the heated, marble public toilet was a social event in itself, as it could accommodate 30 people at a time. Romans would wrap one end of sticks with cloths or sponges for use in, erm, cleansing. This practice can be tried at home, but remember the classic (perhaps ancient Roman) adage and take care not to be one of the unlucky few who "gets the wrong end of the stick." The *frigidarium* (cold bath) alone measured 2500 sq. m, the size of a small lake. The baths were modeled on Trajan's thermal baths, the first to abandon a strict north-south axis to make better use of solar energy; the *calidarium*, or hot bath, faced southwest, thus facing the sun during the warmest parts of the day, and the *frigidarium* faced northeast. The complex fell into ruin in AD 538 when the aqueducts supplying water for the baths were destroyed, perhaps out of jealousy, by Witigis and his unbathed Ostrogoths. Damn barbarians. *(P. dei Cinquecento, across the street from Termini. Enter on V. Volturno. ☎06 47 82 61 52. Open Tu-Sa 9am-7:45pm. Free. Museum at opposite end of baths' entrance courtyard. See p. XX for details.)*

ROTONDA AND BATHS EXHIBIT. The AD fourth-century rotunda displays statues from the baths, and the entrance holds gorgeous, stained-glass windows. It is home to two of the most important ▨**Hellenistic sculptures** in existence. One is a first-century depiction of an aging boxer, looking up tiredly, complete with cauliflower ear, and signed by Apollonius. The other is a general leaning on a lance, in imitation of Lysippos's famous statue of Alexander the Great; his nudity exhibits his semi-divine nature, if not proportions. Glass sections of the floor provide a peek at the foundations of the baths. *(V. Romita 8. Baths and rotunda on right after exiting Santa Maria degli Angeli, between V. Cernaia and V. Parigi. Open Tu-F 9am-2pm, Sa-Su 9am-1pm. Free.)*

PIAZZA VITTORIO EMANUELE II. This large *piazza* used to be famous for its free-for-all outdoor market with piles of fresh fish, fresh fruit, clothes, shoes, and luggage. The market has since moved to the covered Mercato Esquilino (on the intersection of V. Guglielmo Pepe and V. Giovanni Giolitti, on the southeast side of Termini; open M-F mornings). The market may have moved, but the area still brims with a multicultural mix of shops and restaurants. Its serene, scenic park houses the curious remains of a fourth-century fountain, a bunch of stray cats, and bad games of pick-up basketball. The **Porta Magica,** a few steps away, reveals an alchemist's ancient instructions for turning lead into gold. Nearby, and with considerably more success, contemporary alchemists are hard at work producing fake Prada bags. *(Ⓜ A-Vittorio Emanuele. Down V. Carlo Alberto from the front steps of Santa Maria Maggiore.)*

CAMPO VERANO AND JEWISH CEMETERY. More beautiful than bone-chilling, Campo Verano, Rome's largest public cemetery, features a maze of underground tombs topped with elaborate marble huts and decked with fresh-cut flowers, statuary, and numerous portraits of the dead incorporated into tombstones. On November 1 and 2, All Saints' and All Souls' Days, Romans make pilgrimages to the tombs of their relatives, placing chrysanthemums on the stones. The Jewish Cemetery is next door on the far side of Campo Verano. (*Bus #492 from Termini to P. Verano. To the right of Basilica San Lorenzo Fuori le Mura, down V. Tiburtina, in San Lorenzo. A bus runs through the cemetery Sa and holidays. Open daily June-July 7am-6pm; Aug.-Sept. 7:30am-6pm; Oct.-Dec. 7:30am-5pm; Jan.-Mar. 7:30am-5pm; Apr.-May 7:30am-6pm.*)

THE AUDITORIUM OF MAECENAS. This underground Roman ruin was once romantically thought to have been the site for Horace and Virgil's poetic recitations in the first century BC to their patron, Maecenas—hence the name. Today, the general consensus is that it formed part of his luxurious summer dining complex. The remains of frescoes, especially those depicting an outside garden viewed through false windows, are still visible behind the stairs. (*In Largo Leopardi, down V. Merulana from Santa M. Maggiore, or V. Leopardi from P. V. Emanuele II. Open Tu-Sa 9am-1:30pm, Su 9am-1pm; Apr. 1-Sept. 30 Tu, Th, Sa 4-7pm. €3.*)

VIA NOMENTANA

Beginning at Michelangelo's **Porta Pia**, this breezy road lined with pleasant villas, embassies, and parks runs northeast, out of the city. Hop on bus #36 in front of Termini or head back to V. XX Settembre and catch bus #60; both traverse the boulevard.

VILLA TORLONIA. About a kilometer from the Porta Pia is Benito Mussolini's former estate, which he "leased" from the Torlonia family for the princely annual sum of one lira—for comparison's sake, a small gelato used to cost about 2000 lira at the time of the currency's retirement. The house was long abandoned after WWII, though over the last few years the park has undergone an extensive redevelopment program. Walk in through the foreboding gates to see over 50 species of birds, 100 types of trees and shrubs, and one type of Italian (the common lounging-around variety). It is also now home to the **Musei di Villa Torlonia,** three collections showcasing important Italian works and various leftovers from the villa's occupancy by both the Torlonia and Mussolini families. The **Casina delle Civette** displays numerous framed art deco designs for stained glass, with a recurring owl theme. The real attraction is the house's various architectural oddities, like the "thinking room" upstairs, which undoubtedly aided Mussolini in forming his brilliant foreign and domestic policy. The **Casino dei Principi** houses Benito's bed and other memorabilia, as well as an important collection of 18th-century Neoclassical sculpture by Antonio Canova and Bartolomeo Cavaceppi. It is also home to the villa's temporary exhibitions. The **Casino Nobile** contains a display following the history of the complex from its founding through modernity, in addition to a floor dedicated to paintings by Roman masters from the 1920s through the 1960s. Grab your books and kiss your mother goodbye, because you're going to Roman School. (*V. Nomentana 70. ☎06 82 05 91 27; www.museivillatorlonia.it. Villa grounds open daily June-Aug. 7am-8:30pm, Sept. and Apr.-May 7am-7:30pm, from Oct. 1 to the last Sa in Oct. and from Mar. 1 to the last Sa in Mar. 7am-6pm, from the last Su in Oct. to Feb. 7:30am-5pm. Museums open Tu-Su from the last Su in Mar. to Sept. 9am-7pm, from Oct. 1 to the last Sa in Oct. and from Mar. 1 to the last Sa in Mar. 9am-5:30pm, from the last Su in Oct. to Feb. 9am-4:30pm. Casino dei Principi only open during exhibitions. Casina delle Civette €3, reduced €1.50. Casino Nobile €4.50, reduced €2.50. Combo ticket €6.50, reduced €3. Reduced prices available for EU citizens aged 18-25; under 18 and over*)

65 free. Max. 30-person guided tour in several languages €90; ☎06 06 08 or villeparchistorici@ comune.roma.it for reservations. Audio guide in English, French, and Italian €3.50.)

BASILICA & CATACOMBS OF SANT'AGNESE FUORI LE MURA. This church's seventh-century apse shows off an extraordinary Byzantine-style mosaic of the young saint with a pair of popes. Under the basilica winds a network of Rome's best-preserved and least-crowded catacombs (AD 100-500). Although the catacombs were ransacked—along with the rest of Rome—in the fifth century, you can still get up close and personal with some skeletons. The tour guide explains the early Christian method of marking the tombs of the dead and the use of private family chapels. One of the 7000 graves contains the body of St. Agnes, a 12 year old martyred by Diocletian for refusing to marry. Her remains reside in the church in P. Navona (p. 157), the location of her beheading. As with other catacombs, these are not recommended for people who have difficulty walking, are claustrophobic, or might otherwise lose their heads. *(V. Nomentana 349, 2km from Porta Pia, on the left side of the street. ☎06 86 20 54 56; www.santagnese.org. Open M-Sa 9am-noon and 4-6pm, Su 4-6pm. Closed religious holidays. Last tour of catacombs 30min. before closing. Modest dress required. Catacombs €6, ages 7-15 €3.)*

MAUSOLEUM OF COSTANZA. Decorated with stunning fourth-century mosaics, showing animals, and wine-making predating most Christian imagery, this early round church originally served as the mausoleum of Constantine's modestly-named eldest daughter, Constantina. Constantina was cured of leprosy while sleeping on St. Agnes's tomb, leading her to convert to Christianity and build her own tomb, which was later transformed into a baptistry and then this church. To visit the underground mausoleum, ask the custodian of the catacombs in the Basilica of Sant'Agnese Fuori le Mura. Right next to the church are the ruins of the fourth-century basilica of St. Agnes. *(V. Nomentana 349. ☎06 86 20 54 56 or 86 10 840. Open M-Sa 9am-noon and 4-6pm, Su 4-6pm. Closed religious holidays. €0.50 to illuminate the mosaics.)*

SAN GIOVANNI AND THE CAELIAN HILL

◪ARCIBASILICA OF SAN GIOVANNI IN LATERANO. Founded by Constantine in 314, the immense Church of San Giovanni in Laterano is the city's oldest Christian basilica, and the cathedral of the diocese of Rome. Although the pope doesn't hang his *zucchetto* (traditional skullcap) here, it is technically part of the Vatican City and shares its extraterritoriality. A terrorist bomb heavily damaged the basilica in 1993 (a simultaneous blast devastated the Church of San Giorgio in Velabro, p. 152): the north facade received the most damage but has since been restored. The church (and the adjoining Lateran palace) were home to the papal court before the Avignon papacy in the 14th century. Some of the grandeur of the old days returns on **Corpus Christi**, the ninth Sunday after Easter, when a triumphant procession leads the pontiff back to the Vatican after mass. It includes the College of Cardinals, the Swiss Guard, and hundreds of Italian Girl Scouts (the mortgage on the Sistine Chapel is refinanced every year to pay for their cookies). The doors of the main entrance, facing the P. San Giovanni, were moved here from the Curia, the Roman senate house in the Forum. Inside, Borromini's remodeling in the 17th century obscures the original plan of the basilica, creating a dramatic series of niches for 12 imposing statues of the Apostles. Note the immense **statue of Constantine** and the **fresco by Giotto.**

The stately Gothic *baldacchino* (canopy) over the altar houses two golden reliquaries containing **the heads of Saints Peter and Paul,** and an altar from which only the Pope can celebrate mass. A door to the left of the altar leads to the

13th-century cloister, home to the church's collection of sacred relics and *regalia* (along with the small museum of gold and precious vestments). The twisted double columns and inlaid pavement are typical of the Cosmati family, who designed much of the stone inlaid with marble chips that decorates medieval Roman churches. (Ⓜ*A-San Giovanni or bus #16 from Termini.* ☎ *06 69 88 64 33. Call ahead to reserve spots on tours of the Lateran complex and excavations under the basilica. Cathedral open daily 7am-6:30pm. Sacristy open daily 8am-noon, 4-6pm. Cloister open daily 9am-6pm. Museum open daily 9am-6pm. Cloister €2, students €1. Museum €1. Audio tour available in Italian, English, French, Spanish, and German €5, students €4; includes entrance into cloister. Last audio tour at 4:45pm. Cash only. Just west of the church on the southwest end of P. di San Giovanni in Laterano lies the baptistry. Open daily 7am-12:30pm and 4-7:30pm. Modest dress required. Free.*)

BAPTISTERY OF SAINT JOHN. Originally built by Constantine, the octagonal baptistery of Saint John served as the model for its more famous cousin in Florence. According to tradition, all Christians were once baptized here. Today, however, services are reserved only for Rome's upper echelon.

◪CHIESA DI SAN CLEMENTE. The upper church, reached through a 12th-century courtyard to the east (where, in summer, the **New Opera Festival of Rome,** p. 76, performs abridged productions), holds medieval mosaics of the Crucifixion, saints, and apostles. A series of frescoes dating from the 1420s by Masolino— possibly executed with help from his more famous pupil Masaccio—graces the **Chapel of Santa Caterina** at the back of the church. Hooligan pilgrims scrawled their names on the fresco of St. Christopher that decorates the left wall. The sixth-century marble choir enclosure displays a Romanesque paschal candlestick that belonged to the lower church. It's in the lower cluster of buildings and foundations, however, where San Clemente's uniqueness truly shows. The early plan of the fourth-century lower church has been obscured by piers and walls built to support the upper church. With a little imagination, you can trace the lines of the original nave, aisles, and apse, which retain rare 11th-century frescoes. On this level are a few curiosities, including the tomb of **Saint Cyril** (responsible for the Cyrillic alphabet) and a series of frescoes depicting Roman generals. Also on display, on the left wall immediately after the staircase, are a number of ancient Roman inscriptions reused by early Christians. Descend a third, fourth-century flight of stairs to view even earlier buildings, including a large late second-century shrine to Mithras with a ritual room, dining room, and Mithraic schoolroom. **Mithraism,** the last pagan state religion in Rome, was introduced by soldiers returning from Asia Minor in 67 BC, but it had disappeared by the end of the fourth century (see **Life and Times,** p. 59). More passages lead through the **insulae,** a series of brick and stone rooms where Nero is said to have played his lyre while Rome burned in AD 64. (Ⓜ*B-Colosseo. Bus #85, 87, 810. Tram #3. Turn left down V. Labicana, away from the Forum; then turn right into P. San Clemente. From* Ⓜ*A-Manzoni, walk west on V. A. Manzoni; turn left into P. San Clemente.* ☎ *06 77 40 021. San Clemente open M-F 8am-6:30pm, Sa-Su and holidays 9-11am and 3-6:30pm. Lower basilica and mithraeum open M-Sa 9am-12:30pm and 3-6pm; Su and holidays noon-6pm. Last entry 20min. before closing. €5, students under 26 €3.50. Cash only.*)

SCALA SANTA. The Scala Santa holds what are believed to be the 28 marble steps (now covered in walnut wood for protection) that were part of Pontius Pilate's house in Jerusalem, which Jesus ascended several times on the day of his crucifixion. Medieval pilgrims knocked several years off their time in Purgatory by similarly making their way up the steps—though on their knees and reciting proscribed prayers along the way. The tradition stood unquestioned until an unruly German named Martin Luther, in the middle of his way up, decided that the act was one of futility and false piety. He went on to stir up some minor trouble back home—which, of course, is not referenced in the official rendition of the steps' history, found at the top of the staircase. Today the stairs remain a place of pilgrimage, creaking with the traffic of earnest Catholics struggling up this metaphorical stairway to heaven.

If the thought of climbing these steps on your fragile kneecaps fills you with a distaste for the Church, use the secular stairs on either side to reach the chapel of the **Sancta Sanctorium**. Among other relics, it houses the **Acheiropoieton** ("picture painted without hands"), a depiction of Christ said to be the work of St. Luke with the assistance of an angel. The image was carried in processions to stop the plague. It has thus far proven ineffective against swine flu. (ⓜA-San Giovanni or bus #16 from Termini. Across from the main entrance of the church, on the east side of P. di San Giovanni in Laterano. ☎06 77 26 641. Open Apr.-Sept. M-Sa 6:15am-noon and 3-6:15pm, Su 3:30-6:45pm; Oct.-Mar. M-Sa 6:15am-noon and 3-6:15pm, Su 6:15am-noon and 3:30-6:45pm. Donation requested.)

CHIESA DEI SANTI QUATTRO CORONATI. Named for four sculptors who were martyred by Diocletian for refusing to carve (or worship) statues of the Roman god Asclepius, this church, though small and inconspicuous, has played a prominent role in Roman ecclesiastical history. Due to its proximity to the Lateran Palace (the early seat of the papacy), the church housed high-ranking Catholic officials for many years. Located on Caelian Hill, the Church was in a good position to defend the Lateran area, which is why the massive western walls were raised in the 13th century. Consequently, the church became a refuge for Popes under siege, as well as visiting royalty like Charles of Anjou, earning it the moniker, "The Royal Hospice of Rome." The little **chapel** to the right, off the entrance courtyard, next to the Monache Agostiniare sign, contains a vibrantly colored fresco cycle of the life of Constantine, painted in 1248.

Ring the bell of the convent; one of the cloistered nuns will come to the grate, ask for an offering, and let you in. Inside the small Church itself, note the 12th-century upper story: a *matroneum*, or gallery, for female participants. Left off the aisle, the 13th-century **cloister** ranks as one of the most beautiful in the city. Unlike the artistically striking cloisters at San Paolo Fuori le Mura and San Giovanni in Laterano, the cloister here strikes the senses with its elegant simplicity and peacefulness. Ring bell to enter. (V. dei Santissimi Quattro Coronati, 20. From San Clemente, bear south down the V. dei Querceti and head up the V. dei Santi Quattro; the church is on the right at the top of the steep hill. Basilica open M-Sa 6:15am-8pm, Su 6:45am-12:30pm and 3-7:30pm. Chapel of San Stefano open M-Sa 9:30am-noon and 4:30-6pm; Su 9-10:40am and 4-5:45pm. Cloister open M-F 10am-11:45am and 4-5:45pm; Sa and Su 9:30-10:30am, noon-12:30pm, and 4-5:45pm.)

CHIESA DEI SANTI GIOVANNI E PAOLO. The Church of San Giovanni e Paolo lies directly opposite its medieval *campanile*, curiously adorned with brightly-colored Islamic ceramic plates; the chandelier-filled basilica dates back to the 12th century. The real attraction here, though, is the set of rich Roman houses, complete with even richer decoration, which formed the foundations for an earlier church on the site probably in the fifth century. Only reopened to the public in 2002 the site contains brilliantly preserved wall paintings from the second and third centuries with excellent explanatory panels in both Italian and English. To the left of the entrance is a metal bridge, from which you can view ancient Romans' domestic life. The bridge crosses what used to be a street, with amazingly well-preserved facades. A small museum called the **Antiquarium** houses the artifacts found during the excavations, including remnants of the marble and mosaic tile flooring. Opposite the church, the beautifully-kept gardens of the **Villa Celimontana** reward you for the detour with a secluded spot for a picnic. Just don't confuse it with the neighboring military complex or the inattentive guards may run after you, 9's busted out. *(Just southeast of the Colosseum, take V. Claudia and turn right onto V. di San Paolo della Croce. Case Romane entrance is just west of the church, down the Clivo di Scauro. Call for advance booking or guided tours ☎ 06 70 45 444; www.caseromane.it. Church open M-Sa 8:30am-noon and 3:30-6:30pm. Casa Romane open M and Th-Su 10am-1pm and 3-6pm. Villa Celimontana open daily dawn-dusk. Church free. Case Romane €6, reduced €4, under 12 free. Villa Celimontana free.)*

CHIESA DI SANTO STEFANO ROTONDO. Built in the late fifth century, the Church of Santo Stefano Rotondo is one of the oldest circular churches in existence. Long-needed restoration continues on the church; it certainly takes some imagination to picture the building in its original form. It was once structured in three concentric rings, but centuries of decay and remodeling reduced it to the two inner rings by 1450. *(V. San Stefano Rotondo, 7. From P. San Giovanni, take V. San Giovanni. The road forks twice; stay to the left and follow V. Santo Stefano Rotondo to the end. ☎ 06 39 96 77 00. Open Tu-Sa 9:30am-12:30pm and 3-6pm, Su 9:30am-12:30pm.)*

CHIESA DELLA SANTA CROCE IN GERUSALEMME. This unique church is home to a motherlode of major relics, housed in the appropriately named and Fascist-designed **Chapel of the Relics,** off of the left aisle, which contains fragments of the "true cross" found by St. Helena. It also houses a chunk of the cross of Dismas (the Good Thief), thorns from Christ's crown, a copy of the Shroud of Turin, and a nail used in the crucifixion. Perhaps the eeriest of the chapel's relics is the dismembered finger used by doubting Thomas to probe Christ's wounds; it was still attached at the time. Unfortunately, the relics are so poorly lit that they are barely visible, prompting the placard's detailed description of the nail as "pointed" and the cross as "wooden," lest you be left in the dark. The church is believed to have been built around 326, but was rebuilt twice: in 1144, when the *campanile* was added, and in 1744, when the facade got a facelift. At the end of the right aisle in the church's interior, the **Chapel of Saint Helena** contains 15th-century mosaics depicting Christ, Peter, Paul, and Helena (Constantine's mother). Also be sure to look down and check out the intricately tiled floors.

The latest addition to the basilica, from 1999, is a **museum** just before the altar on the right. On display are the brightly-painted 12th-century frescoes that once adorned the nave and which were discovered in 1913, as well as particularly grumpy-looking 14th-century statues of St. Peter and St. Paul. Also added in 1999 was the **Chapel of Antonietta Meo,** dedicated to a local child who wrote 162 letters to God, Jesus, the Holy Spirit, and the Virgin Mary prior to her death at age six from chronic illness. For her precocious piety, she is the youngest mystic remembered by the Church. *(P. San Paolo della Croce in Gerusalemme Ⓜ A-San Giovanni. From P. San Giovanni north of the stop, go east on Vle. Carlo Felice; the church is on the right. Or, from P. Vittorio Emanuele II, take V. Conte Verde. ☎ 06 70 14 769; www.basilicasantacroce. com. Church open daily 7am-12:45pm and 2-7pm. Adjacent Musei Storico dei Granatieri open M-F 9am-noon. Modest dress required. Church donation requested. Musei Storico free.)*

PORTA MAGGIORE. The area around the Porta Maggiore (also called the **Porta Prenestina**) might be one of the smoggiest, not to mention slowest, of Rome's traffic intersections, but spend a moment appreciating the large inscribed arch erected by Emperor Claudius in AD 52. The well-preserved arch, which supported one of Imperial Rome's major aqueducts, was later built into the Aurelian walls that surrounded the city. Just outside the wall are the curious remains of the **Tomb of the Baker;** the funerary monument, decorated with sculpted bakery ovens below and a frieze charting the processes of bread-making above, was erected in honor of Marcus Virgilius Eurysaces in 30 BC to celebrate the lowly cause of bakers everywhere. Once you've gotten an appreciation for bakers and arches, leave promptly to avoid succumbing to the monument's own fume-fatigued fate.

AVENTINE

Enjoy awe-inspiring and sparsely traversed vistas from this exclusive area of town just a short walk south of the ancient Circus Maximus. With steep, narrow, winding streets framed by towering, shady trees, the Aventine Hill is the place to head for a quiet afternoon reading that Dante (or R.L. Stein) you promised yourself you would read, or to check out some of Rome's swankiest cribs. This exclusive area is relatively free from fellow travelers—and consequently from bars, restaurants, and cafes. But what the Aventine lacks in tourist amenities it makes up for in churches. While **Santa Sabina** is the most famous, the churches of **Sant' Alessio e San Bonifacio, San Saba,** and **Santa Prisca** (which was built over a third-century *mithraeum*, like San Clemente) can all boast a similar first-millennium ancestry. A full tour will take at least an hour and a half; reward your labors by bringing your own picnic and stopping in the **Giardino degli Aranci.**

ROSETO COMUNALE. If Lewis Carroll ever put his hand to designing a garden, this would be it. With over 800 varieties of rose bushes—but, sadly, no playing cards, swinging paint cans, or Queens of Hearts painting the town red—the Roseto Comunale is the place to stroll, rest, and, yes, smell the roses. A number of benches also make this an ideal place to spend a quiet afternoon reading, sitting in the sun, **making out,** or watching the tourists pant their way up the Palatine Hill in the distance. Each May, the horticultural world descends upon the Roseto to compete for the **Premio Roma,** the prize given to the best new variety of rose. Twenty-one countries compete for the honor, and you will find the winners displayed in the lower section of the Roseto's 10 sq. km grounds.

The first Roseto in Rome was destroyed during WWII, but intrepid gardeners built this new version on the site of the old Jewish Cemetery, which was relocated to Campo Verano. When asked for the land by the city, the Jewish community leader agreed but requested that the old site be memorialized. As a result, steles of the Tablets of Moses flank the entrances, and the upper section is shaped like a menorah. *(The garden lies along V. di Valle Murcia, up from P. Ugo la Malfa, across the Circus Maximus from the Palatine Hill.* ☎ *06 574 68 10 for information. Open daily May-June 8am-7:30pm. Free.)*

GIARDINO DEGLI ARANCI. Time to stop and smell the citrus after the hike up the hill. The ripe fruit scattered all over the ground of this small park is only one of the attractions. Spectacular views of Rome are also yours to enjoy, including the tops of St. Peter's Basilica in the Vatican and the Vittorio Emanuele monument in P. Venezia. The park is well kept and quiet, its peace only disturbed by occasional parties of picnicking school children and businessmen. Luckily, even they turn off their *telefonini* to enjoy the sights. *(Also known as Parco Savello, in P. Pietro d'Illiria, right next to the Church of Santa Sabina. Open daily dawn-dusk.)*

CHIESA DI SANTA SABINA. The famous residents of the adjoining monastery, which was the first monastery of the Dominican order, have included St. Dominic, Pius V, and St. Thomas Aquinas, but the actual church was built much earlier, during the reign of Celestine I in the fifth century. The mosaics (check out both the floor and the ceiling) are colorful, and the wooden doors from 450 are a rare find; they depict a variety of different biblical scenes, including one of the earliest representations of Christ hanging between two thieves (note Christ's cross-less crucifixion in the top left panel). Pop €1 into the machines next to the chapels to illuminate them. The vestibule also leads to the recently opened monastic cloister, a 13th-century colonnade with a beautifully maintained garden. *(At the southern (uphill) end of Parco Savello, in P. Pietro d'Illiria, next to the Giardino degli Aranci. Entrance to the church through the vestibule. Open daily 6:30am-12:45pm and 3-7pm.)*

BASILICA DI SAN SABA. In the AD seventh century, Sabaite monks from the order of Mar Saba fled Palestine during the Muslim conquest of Persia. After attending the Lateran council in 645, they remained in a palace on the **Piccolo Aventino** that had been abandoned during the dramatic decrease in Rome's population, founding a monastery on the present-day location of the church. From 680 on, the monastery's abbots held diplomatic positions in relations between Rome and Byzantium and the monastery received copious papal donations. In 768, Antipope Constantine II was held prisoner in the monastery before his eventual execution at the hands of the Lombards. In the following centuries, the church housed many different spiritual orders, and underwent two major overhauls. It was rebuilt in the 10th century, prior to being granted to the Benedictines of Montecassino, and again in the 13th century by the Cluniac monks. The Cistercians took control of the site in the 15th century. It is now served by the Society of Jesus, and was established as a Cardinal deaconry in 1959 by Pope John XXIII.

Entering the church, see if you can get a glimpse of the original facade, which is all but hidden by the 15th century portico and arcade. Inside, Cosmatesque mosaic floors extend underneath large wooden beams that support the roof. The left aisle features a vibrant 13th-century fresco cycle by an anonymous painter. One panel pays curious homage to St. Nicholas, depicting young girls lying nude on a bed, committed to prostitution by their father. St. Nicholas throws a bag of gold coins through the window, saving the girls from the fate that would have awaited them had their poverty continued. Jolly old St. Nick's altruism is pure; the would-be sex workers don't even reward him with cookies and milk. Be sure also to view the seventh- or eighth-century frescoes in the corridor leading to the sacristy, which depict monks from the original Mar Saba order. *(Ⓜ B-Circo Massimo. Walk south on V. Aventino and turn left on V. di San Saba. The church is at the top of the hill. Open M-F 8am-noon and 4-7pm, Sa-Su 9:30am-noon and 4-7pm.)*

PIAZZA DEI CAVALIERI DI MALTA. Although it is rarely open to the public, this postcard-perfect *piazza* is home to the Knights of Malta, a charitable organization officially known as the Order of the Knights of St. John of Jerusalem. The order dates to the 12th century, when their military services were offered to assist pilgrimage to the Holy Land. On the right as you approach the *piazza* is a large, cream-colored arched gate; peer through its tiny, circular ▨keyhole for a hedge-framed view of the dome of St. Peter's Cathedral. *(At the end of V. Santa Sabina, past the Church dei Santi Bonifacio e Alessio. Entrance to grounds at P. Cavalierie, 4. ☎06 67 58 12 34 for information. Open Sept.-June Sa 10 and 11am; call ahead to confirm hours, as they are subject to change. €5 donation requested.)*

TESTACCIO AND OSTIENSE

South of the Aventine Hill, the working-class neighborhood of Testaccio is known for its cheap *trattorie* and raucous nightclubs. The area centers around the castle-like **Porta San Paolo,** a remnant of the Aurelian walls built in the AD third century to protect Rome from barbarians. Another attraction is the colossal **Piramide di Gaius Cestius,** the namesake of the Metrostop/train station. Piramide also shuttles droves of sun-loving Romans to the beach on the weekends, so don't be surprised if you're sitting next to bathing-suit-clad *signore* on